Winds of Grace
Ways of Faith

Expanding the Horizons of Christian Spirituality

William K. McElvaney

Westminster/John Knox Press   Louisville, Kentucky

Scripture quotations from the Revised Standard Version of the Bible are copyright 1946, 1952, © 1971, 1973 by the Division of Christian Education of the National Council of the Churches of Christ in the U.S.A. and are used by permission. In some instances adaptations have been made for the sake of inclusive language.

Scripture quotations marked NEB are taken from *The New English Bible,* © Oxford University Press and Cambridge University Press, 1989. Used by permission.

Book design by Publishers' WorkGroup

First edition

Published by Westminster/John Knox Press
Louisville, Kentucky

PRINTED IN THE UNITED STATES OF AMERICA

9 8 7 6 5 4 3 2 1

Library of Congress Cataloging-in-Publication Data

McElvaney, William K., 1928–
    Winds of grace, ways of faith : expanding the horizons of Christian spirituality / William K. McElvaney. — 1st ed.
        p.   cm.
    Includes bibliographical references.
    ISBN 0-664-25120-X

    1. Spiritual formation.   2. Christian life—1960–   I. Title.
BV4501.2.M235 1991
248—dc20   91-17577

Contents

Acknowledgments   7

Introduction   9

1. The Way of the Will: Preserving the Sacred Story   16

2. The Way of the Will:
   Exploring Sermon Mentality and Sacramentality   29

Contents

3. The Way of Wonder:
   Discovering Spiritual Classics in Creation and Culture   45

4. The Way of Witness:
   Renewing Faith Through Compassion and Justice   64

5. The Way of Welcome: Experiencing God in Others   82

6. The Way of the Whisper: Validating the Still, Small Voice   102

7. The Way of the Whirlwind:
   Birthing Hope and Love in the Storm   121

Notes   134

Acknowledgments

Most books are dedicated to a special person or a single group of persons. However, the terrain of this book covers a broad array of faith issues. As the chapters unfolded many persons to whom I am indebted surfaced in my imagination and memory. Thus, each chapter is dedicated to one or more persons appropriate to that chapter.

I am also indebted to the insights of several readers whose suggestions led to many improvements. Not every suggestion was acted upon, but many were, and all were carefully considered. The readers represent an ecumenical background, both Protestant and Roman Catholic, and include laity and clergy. My deep appreciation is offered to Rita Clarke, Ruben Habito, John Holbert (response to chapters 6 and 7), Joanna Shields, Marjorie Procter-Smith, Sister Patricia Ridgley (chapters 1–4), William I. Smith, Marilyn Spurrell-Atkins, and Tom Timmins.

The essential writing of the book was accomplished during a January–May 1990 sabbatical from teaching duties at Perkins School of Theology. I am grateful to Dean James E. Kirby, to my Perkins colleagues, and to Southern Methodist University for this opportunity. Special gratitude is offered to Ann Ralston for her unfailing assistance in preparation of the manuscript.

Much of the content of these chapters has been explored for several years in a variety of conferences and local churches. In particular I wish to thank the planners of and participants in the New Mexico Conference of Churches Annual Assembly; the Midland, Texas, Ecumenical School of Christian Living; The Iliff School of Theology Graduate Lectures and Summer School; a conference at Philander Smith College, Little Rock, Arkansas, entitled "Jesus and Justice: A Liberating Gospel for the Local Church"; and the Nebraska Fellowship of Learning and the Kansas area Seminar on Professional Ministry, United Methodist Church. I also am indebted to the probing questions and reflections of Perkins School of Theology students, especially in preaching and liturgy classes and in the Spiritual Formation groups in which I have been privileged to serve as guide and coordinator.

Introduction

"Give us this day our daily bread." These familiar words offer an important insight into faith itself.

Sometimes I think, "I have been around the church and its message for a long time now. I ought to have it down pat. Surely the Word has taken root after all this time. Surely I don't need to keep hearing and updating the Word in my life. Am I a slow learner, or what?"

In reality it's never that way, is it? Life is change. I may build on yesterday. There can be continuity. But today is not yesterday. Personal circumstances change. Perspectives change. I change. The world changes. Once again—always again—my faith, as trust and commitment, needs constant renewal just as bread needs to be daily fresh. Yesterday's bread will soon be stale.

Martin Luther was right. Faith is an acoustical affair. We need a fresh hearing. Luther's high doctrine of the preached Word in his historical setting led him to use an image of the ear as central for faith renewal. Today we can broaden that image to include the whole range of human receptivity. Thus, faith is not only an acoustical affair but also a matter of seeing and touching—indeed, an affair of all the senses, for God works in many ways.

Expanded Spiritual Formation

The chapter titles in this book are intended to suggest some of the rich and varied means by which God's grace and human response interact. These means are amply present in scripture, in the church's tradition, and in the experience of countless people of faith.

By faith renewal I mean that our identity in God is reaffirmed and that some combination of the promise and claim of the gospel—the good news in Jesus Christ—comes alive again in our lives. Sometimes this happens by the direct initiative and involvement of God toward us. Sometimes faith is deepened through our willingness to search and strive in ways that expose us to God's grace. At other times our own attitudes and actions, while not deliberately or intentionally seeking a renewal of faith, result in a stronger, deeper faith. And at other times the faithful actions of others bring us to a more profound experience of faith.

It is my contention that the conventional ways of interpreting faith renewal tend to be centered in what I call the way of the will.[1] As we shall see, this way is intentional and deliberate and includes a broad range of spiritual disciplines, both corporate and individual—for example, corporate worship and individual prayer and scripture reading are ways of the will. Even when the purpose is to receive God's grace or to place ourselves at the disposal of God's will, the basic approach remains intentional and deliberate. I have provided two chapters on the way of the will because it is the most comprehensive and varied of the many ways of faith renewal and because it is so basic to Christian practice and tradition in its corporate expression of worship.

It is also my contention that many people of faith orientation do not resonate with so-called classical forms of individual spiritual discipline included in the way of the will. These persons may find corporate worship meaningful but have never been able to sustain regular prayer or scripture reading as individuals. Too often the church has made it sound as though something is wrong with those who cannot or do not practice these religious disciplines regularly, and further, that these time-honored disciplines are virtually the only means of deepening one's faith, hope, and love.

While I strongly encourage personal habits of prayer and scripture reading, I also wish to explore other possibilities affirmed by scripture, tradition, and experience. If you have thought that there must be something wrong with you or your faith because you have not been able to sustain a regular prayer or scripture reading habit, hold on! There are additional ways to be God-connected, faith-oriented, and neighbor-related. I believe it is the responsibility of the church to be a community in which the winds of grace are welcomed and in which a variety of faith ways are invited, honored, and strengthened.

Overview of the Chapters

The winds of grace and ways of faith are explored as follows: Chapter 1 invites you to consider the way of the will in terms of corporate worship which remembers the sacred story and which lives out the liturgy as the work of the people. In chapter 2 we continue the way of the will by examining sermon mentality and sacramentality in comparison, contrast, and mutual connection. These two chapters, perhaps more than the others, will invite the reader to consider some historical developments in order to increase understanding and appreciation of corporate worship. The way of wonder, discussed in chapter 3, points to a sacramental relation to life through creation and culture rather than the seeking and striving of the way of the will. Chapter 4, "The Way of Witness," suggests that God becomes real when we do the work of God and that faith is often renewed through self-forgetful compassion for others. Chapter 5, "The Way of Welcome," focuses on giving and receiving in relationships, both with friends and with strangers, by which the love of God becomes incarnate and life-giving. Chapter 6, "The Way of the Whisper," inquires into the direct address of God to individuals through the still, small voice and how we might test the authenticity of that voice. Chapter 7, "The Way of the Whirlwind," reflects on the path of sorrow and adversity and the presence and purpose of God therein. Biblical and contemporary examples are used for each way. Comparisons and contrasts of the various ways are provided for clarification in several chapters.

It should be noted that the way of the will—the intentional, deliberate way of exposure to God's Word—is explored mainly in terms of corporate worship. Another dimension of the way of the will is equally integral to faith renewal though not given specific attention here: the study of scripture. We should resist the claims of some that the Holy Spirit is more present in prayer than in study and loving God with our minds. While Jesus taught the disciples to pray he also challenged them to reflect and inquire into the deep issues of life. Likewise, Judaism has insisted on meeting God in the study of Torah, as well as in keeping the commandments (*mitzvoth*), and in the devotion of prayer. Succinctly put, "God is present in the words of Torah. Enter into the words, speaking them with all your strength. Your soul will then meet God in the word. . . ."[2] John Wesley found the roots of spirituality in study and related use of the mind as well as in the piety of prayer and sanctified deeds. My decision to center on corporate worship rather than study of scripture as an expression of the way of the will does not reflect a lack of deep appreciation for the study of scripture and its profound and basic place in the history of Christian spirituality. Rather, I believe there are more adequate resources available to the reader which address the study of scripture.

As you will see, each chapter begins with the notion that the winds of grace are always blowing, in one fashion or another. In a time when some religious and secular writers alike speak of "the absence of God," a notion of grace availability may sound trite or irrelevantly quaint. My claim for grace is not a denial of doubt or ambiguity as part of a faith posture. It may aid some readers to think of "the winds of grace" as a metaphor for the possibility of a new future, a dimension of depth, the inbreaking of the sacred, or the meaningfulness of the given. I believe that the winds of grace are known by many names.

Suggestions for Reading the Book

This book is written with an ecumenical readership in mind. Although I have written primarily for laity, my experience as pastor and theological educator has influenced the material. Thus, I have written with clergy and seminarians in mind as well. Whether lay or clerical we always minister from the strength and viability of our own faith. Let me suggest several ways in which the book can be used. One approach is reading by an individual, whether lay or clerical, or by sharing with another person. Where possible, however, I invite you, the reader, to engage these chapters by sharing your own experience of faith's journey in a study or discussion group. A seven-week series (one chapter per week) may be most valuable.

My guess is that most of us have experienced several if not all of these means of grace and renewal. I doubt if these can be neatly categorized according to personality, faith development theory, temperament or age, or for that matter, sex, race, and class, although these particulars do influence our experience of each way. The variety of human responses to God and to various life circumstances suggests an infinite array of possibilities for faith renewal and restoration. The reflection questions at the end of each chapter can serve as conversation starters for your group. Group leadership can be lay or clerical.

For the past several years it has been my privilege to coordinate the Spiritual Formation groups required of first-year students at the Perkins School of Theology. Eight or nine students meet with a faculty member for an hour and twenty minutes each week throughout the year. Agendas usually include reflection on vocation, becoming acquainted with the Christian traditions of formation, and experiencing a variety of spiritual disciplines. These disciplines will include various ways to read scripture in a devotional manner, approaches to meditation, fasting, journaling, and appreciation of silence. One of the memorable experiences in some groups is the sharing of personal faith journeys. The majority of students are second-career persons. As we listen to each others' stories of faith we learn something about how God works in life, how we are repelled and compelled by God's initiative, how we resist and respond, and how faith is developed and restored in a variety of ways. Along with a number of students I have found these times to be deeply significant. I can imagine combinations of seminary students, faculty, and/or pastors using these chapters to generate lively discussions.

My Hope for the Reader

My hope in presenting this material is twofold. First, I hope you will become more aware of how faith can be revitalized, in your life and in the life of the church. God is not limited to the confines of human personality charts, nor to spiritual disciplines defined in conventional terms, significant as these may be.

My second hope is that these ways will encourage every reader to be a better neighbor. This is not a book about escapist, other-worldly spirituality. In each chapter I seek to demonstrate our God–neighbor connection. Biblical faith moves in the direction of a just society of harmony and well-being for all people and, so far as possible, for the creation itself and all its creatures. Spiritual formation in the biblical sense is to move in the direction of participating in this work of God in the world. Our vocation as Christians can be no less.

Language names and shapes reality and our perspective about life. Language that is not inclusive perpetuates a narrow and prejudicial interpretation of existence. In this book I use inclusive language for my own formulations. Quoted material is left in its original form.

Since Christian readers are familiar with the term "Old Testament," I use that term in referring to the Hebrew scriptures. Generally, I use the terms "faith renewal" and "spiritual formation" interchangeably, without technical distinction.

1

The Way of the Will: Preserving the Sacred Story

The winds of grace are always blowing,
but you have to know how
to set your sails to
avail yourself of
the breeze.

This assertion from an unknown source underlies a vast segment of biblical faith and spiritual formation. Clearly, the assumption is that in order to receive revelation the faithful must be intentional and deliberate in various disciplines. According to this tradition the order of the day is seeking structured means of faith renewal. "The way of the will" is the name I give to this approach.

The way of the will indicates a will-ingness to be exposed to the influence of transcendent reality. It embraces corporate worship and all intentional means of receiving a fresh offering of God's self-giving, such as personal prayer, meditation, scriptural reading, and fasting. The key is deliberateness and intentionality, since the way of the will is not restricted to rational or cognitive elements of experience. For example, a corporate worship experience may be very emotional, involving a wide range of feelings. Even so, the emotions experienced are the result of deliberately and intentionally seeking interaction with God. In other words, the way of the will does not describe the nature of the experience as much as it defines how one came to be in the experience in the first place.

It will quickly become obvious that the way of the will is everywhere present in both testaments: the temple and synagogue worship of Israel through centuries of change; the psalmists meditating on the mighty deeds of God; the house church in the New Testament; the prayers of the apostles in the Book of Acts. Both corporate and individual sails are set throughout scripture in order to be available to the winds of spirit and grace.

Today the way of the will in which the largest numbers of Christians are involved in a discernible manner is the Sunday service of worship by whatever name. It is that structured, intentional, deliberate time and place in which we hope and pray that the story of redemption and liberation will happen again, not just in general, but to each worshiper and to the church as corporate body.

In order for this recurring corporate way of the will to be a growing experience of faith renewal it is desirable to explore some ways of discerning what is happening in liturgical action. Because there are so many excellent resources available on individual ways of the will, such as prayer and types of meditation, I have oriented the two chapters concerned with the way of the will toward community. As you progress in this chapter, keep in mind your congregation's worship service and experience.

Liturgy: Remembering and Rehearsing
the Sacred Story

The word "liturgy" sounds arcane and academic. If we were to play word association, the related words which come to mind for a good many Protestants are frequently these: high church, formal, dull, or the apparently necessary parts of the worship service preceding or surrounding the sermon.

Suppose, however, we consider liturgy as expressions of our worship which connect us with the event of Jesus Christ, both on Sunday and during the week. Liturgy can be a virtual synonym for worship, or, perhaps more accurately, liturgy constitutes the "ingredients" of our worship. While we frequently image liturgy as a sequence of printed items, liturgical action may involve movement, spontaneity, silence, touch, and visual participation. Liturgy may be oral, written, or visible. All of these are means to provide a link and a continuation with the life, death, and resurrection of Jesus Christ. We could say it like this:

Liturgy remembers and rehearses the sacred story.
Liturgy preserves and participates in the sacred story.
Liturgy enacts and evokes the sacred story.

Liturgy is a movement from amnesia or forgetfulness to *anamnesis,* a remembering through which the past, so to speak, happens again or becomes current. Anamnesis comes from a Greek word describing the Hebrew way of remembering in which a past event "happens again" for today. We could say that liturgy is a way of remembering which rescues us from a kind of Alzheimer's of the soul. The theologian Harvey Cox has said that community depends on a corporate autobiography with a fund of remembrances.[1] Lacking this, community breaks down into an amorphous aggregate of individuals with no common link or story. When I read in the newspaper about an orthodox Jewish family celebrating the Sabbath by remembering the Exodus event of liberation thousands of years in the past, I think liturgy! When I go to the state fair and see a sign advertising Chinese acrobats—"They have been rehearsing for 2500 years"—I think of liturgy. We have been rehearsing for 2000 years! Liturgy is the crucial link without which we have no future as a faith community, having lost our connection with the past event out of which the community was created. When you worship on Sunday morning you intentionally "link up" with the sacred story, the root of our spirituality.

As a teacher of both preaching and worship I am eager for ministerial students to be grasped by the liturgical context of preaching. Preaching is itself part of the liturgy in which the Word of God is celebrated and re-presented. By seeing preaching as part of a total act of remembering, the preacher can experience freedom from egocentricity. There are other elements of liturgy which offer the promise and claim of the gospel! Thus, the preacher is free for each sermon's particularity, and does not have to cover all bases with every sermon. There is freedom to recognize the presence of God among the gathered people and God's many ways of self-giving in the total liturgy. The laity in turn will experience a greater sense of the priesthood of all believers and a recognition of the God-given gifts they bring to the liturgical interaction.

Liturgy as the Living Interaction Between God and People

As we continue our exploration of corporate worship as the way of the will, other vistas on liturgy beckon for our attention.

Liturgy is the living interaction between God and people

Gift of God	Revelation	God's Self-Giving
Work of the People	Response	People's Participation

Liturgical theologians often have made the point that liturgy is not only *about* God but is also *of* God. We point to this reality when we say that God speaks to us in scripture and sermon, or at least the sermon is intended to be the living voice or Word of God. Likewise, we can experience God in song and sacrament—indeed, in the total liturgical interaction.

Worship, then, is both God's revelation or self-giving and our responsive participation. We speak to God in our prayers, whether spoken or silent, and in our hymns and our offering. Worship or liturgical action is the give and take between God and the worshiping community.

Liturgy has often been thought of as the primary theology of the church, a theology rehearsed and enacted by the whole community. It becomes the community's catechism and basis of spiritual formation of the laity. I like to say that liturgy sows seeds in the soil of the soul, and that these seeds grow and have a life of their own in developing our faith! The sacred story and its symbols are remembered and rehearsed by more people in the structured, intentional manner of corporate worship than in any other activity of the church. John Weborg, a professor of theology at North Park Theological Seminary in Chicago, suggests that

what blues can be for blacks, the liturgy can be for Christians [of any race]. It collects the stories, the living human documents, that make up the story of our salvation. The liturgy makes these narratives available to generations yet unborn. It gives us the lines we are to know and enact, the play that God comes to see and hear. Liturgy maintains people in their heritage and challenges them to know and live out this faith.[2]

Liturgy as
Theological-Spiritual Profile

The Spanish philosopher Ortega y Gassét suggested that language is the acoustical profile of the soul of a people.[3] Language does reflect the culture of a people and something of the inner soul. It would be difficult to imagine Germanic people speaking Spanish as a native tongue, and conversely, it would seem strange for people of Hispanic heritage to communicate in German!

If we translate this into a liturgical context, we have this axiom: *Liturgy is the theological-spiritual profile of the soul of a people.*

The truth of this came to me with special force not long ago when I visited a Greek Orthodox church and a black United Methodist church on consecutive Sundays. The Orthodox service was characterized by the thirty-seven-page liturgy of St. John the Divine, the chanting of parts of the liturgy by the clergy, the use of incense, the kissing of the Holy Scriptures, and the centrality of the Eucharist (the Lord's Supper) which is intended only for "the faithful." The service at Warren United Methodist Church was much more informal in style and movement and featured rhythmic choir music and black or African American style preaching without sacrament.

Could these styles of worship be merged? It would be very difficult. Certainly on an occasional basis the two congregations could respond to novelty and new experiences of liturgy. The fact is, however, that the liturgical action in each case mirrors the theological and spiritual profile of the worshipers themselves. This is not to say that disparate liturgical forms cannot be joined. It is to say that to do so requires careful theological, liturgical and sociological analysis and planning. When we alter the ways of the altar we had best know what we are doing! People may not seem possessive about liturgy until someone attempts to make radical revisions.

Every worship service makes a theological statement. Worship is like an X-ray of the soul, or, in more up-to-date terms, it is like magnetic resonance imaging which probes inside the body and provides an in-depth picture. Liturgy reveals the makeup of the Body of Christ in a particular congregation. An astute visitor can make some preliminary formulations about a congregation after only three or four visits.

For example, we can size up a beginning analysis as to whether the congregation is primarily self-serving or oriented toward existing for the world. The content and wording of the liturgy and the substance of the preached word provide the clues. We can shape some tentative ideas about the role of women in the congregation.

The level of regard for children will be manifest. The architectural setting and the placement of pulpit, font, and table or altar will speak loudly concerning liturgical priorities. The theological-spiritual profile inevitably is revealed.

Liturgy as the Work of the People

I have already suggested that liturgy, that is, the various forms through which a community of faith expresses its public worship, is both God's initiative and our response. Historically, liturgy has often been referred to as the work of the people. This has been especially true since the sixteenth-century Protestant Reformation restored the New Testament emphasis on the people's participation. As we look at several interpretations of liturgy as the people's participation, we do well to remember that before liturgy is the work of the people it is the gift of God.

The Work of the People as Participation

Perhaps the most common notion of liturgy as the work of the people is the active involvement of the congregation during the time of gathered worship. We are likely to recall the various reforms of sixteenth-century Christian worship initiated by the Protestant movement. People began to worship in their own language rather than in Latin; psalms and hymns were sung by the people; the communion elements were received more frequently, including both bread and cup; and the recovery of preaching encouraged the people's understanding of scripture.

Whereas we sometimes distinguish between liturgical and non-liturgical services it is closer to the truth to distinguish between types and styles of liturgical services. A traditional "non-programmed" Quaker service, for example, is liturgical in a sense because there is quiet participation of the people. The liturgical action here may differ from a service of planned progression and vocal participation. But who is to say that inner or silent participation is any less authentic or "liturgical" than outward, audible participation which can be merely going through the motions? The way of the will embraces a great variety of liturgical intentionality.

The Work of the People as Planning and Preparation

In recent years the work of the people has come to include the involvement of the laity prior to the actual worship gathering. Following the Second Vatican Council (1962–65) the Roman Catholic Church began to give greater prominence to lay leadership roles in worship. Many Protestants followed suit, rendering the liturgy more "lay intensive," as in the early church. A dimension of greater lay liturgical leadership also involved the laity in worship planning and preparation.

Liturgy can become the work of the people as the people prepare prayers, calls to worship, visual arts, and work hand-in-hand with clergy in the overall preparation of the service. The specifics of this before-the-worship participation vary from place to place even within denominations. The preparation of communion elements by laity has been a long-standing tradition in several denominations. Today we hear of Bible study groups working with the preacher on forthcoming lectionary texts, thus influencing the preaching of the Word.

The preparatory work may be seasonal, such as Advent-Christmas or Lent-Eastertide. Or it may be a year-round structured committee. Whatever the specifics in a given situation, the involvement of lay persons preceding liturgical action is a recognition of the church as God's people rather than as the possession of the clergy. Paul Hoon, remarking about "The Nature of Liturgical Action," provides this insight:

The concept of the priesthood of all believers will come alive when liturgy is the people's work not only in the sense that they perform the action of worship, but also in the sense that they do the work of studying and planning for worship as well.[4]

The Work of the People as Presence and Practice

We have arrived now at the liturgical "bottom line." Liturgy as the work of the people is more than liturgical action on Sunday morning or in the gathered assembly whenever it may be. Liturgy is not something merely printed on an Order of Worship or limited to an uplifting experience in the sanctuary.

Liturgy is the work of the people in the world—at work, at home, in the community, and in the institutional church. Liturgical action begins in preparation and participation but it is not complete until it is acted out in the world by the body of Christ. The presence and the practice of the liturgy, such as confession, celebration, and commitment, constitute the true liturgical action. In other words the liturgy is our script to be lived out in the difficult and demanding arenas of daily life where it can make a difference in the world for which Christ died. The liturgy shapes and preserves the story of our lives. As one pastor likes to say in the Sending Forth statement, "Take this Word we have rehearsed today into your particular piece of geography in the coming week."

Liturgy as the story to be remembered and rehearsed and then lived out in the world provides a handle for interpreting the enormous significance of Christian liturgy. If both clergy and laity can grasp this understanding of liturgy it will give new vitality to our worship and at the same time make a liturgy-life connection that is indispensable for a faithful church. The whole liturgical action looks like this:

Before Worship	Planning and Preparation
During Worship	Participation
After Worship	Presence/Practice in the World

The liturgy, then, interprets my identity as a Christian. It becomes the ever-present story out of which I am called to live my life as a member of the body of Christ in the world. When we ask, "What is my life in Jesus Christ to be like in daily existence?" the liturgy replies, "Learn from me. Live me out in the world and your life will participate in the life and work of God."

Earlier I mentioned my experience at worship in the Greek Orthodox church. At the conclusion, everyone, both "the faithful" and visitor alike, proceeds to the front to receive portions of bread which have been blessed to be taken into the world. The bread is a tangible reminder of Eucharistic life in the world, both spiritual and physical dimensions. The Orthodox call this "the liturgy beyond the liturgy." Again, Paul Hoon:

Our traditional understanding of worship as restricted to the cultic gathering of the congregation at a designated time and place for rite and proclamation will no longer do. This is not what the New Testament means by worship. . . . The life and work of Christ are biblically understood in terms of both worship and mission, and cultic terms are interchangeably employed (especially by Paul) to apply to the totality of life, not merely to gathering for rite and cult.

In short, the thrust of our recovered understanding of the New Testament conception of worship moves us to a view of the Christian's life in its totality as a liturgical life, and in exploring this profound meaning lies the clue to overcoming the gulf between the Church's worship and the life her laity live in the world. . . .

The New Testament conception of worship as the unity of *leitourgia* and *diakonia,* of worship and service, must always be borne in mind.[5]

Specifics of the Script

I have referred to the sacred story as one manifestation of the way of the will, that is, the Good News of Jesus Christ in its total biblical framework. Further, I have alluded to liturgy as the bearer of that sacred story and thus as our script for daily living. What, specifically, does this mean?

When we pray the Lord's Prayer we pray for the coming of God's Kingdom in the here and now ("on earth as in heaven"). Biblical scholars have long been in agreement that the rule of God constitutes the core of Jesus' message. God's reign or rule is all-encompassing and has dominion over both individuals and society and its various structures. Mortimer Arias reminds us, "It embraces all dimensions of human life: physical, spiritual, historical, eternal. . . . It implies a total offer and a total demand. Everything and everybody has to be in line with it."[6]

The sacred story by which we as Christians understand ourselves and the world is a God-initiated story calling forth a covenant community existing as a sign of God's love and an advocate for a just world order. Christians, then, are called to follow in the footsteps of the Vulnerable-Victorious One who was anointed to "preach good news to the poor . . . / to proclaim release to the captives / and recovering of sight to the blind, / to set at liberty those who are oppressed, / to proclaim the acceptable year of the Lord" (from Luke 4:18–19).

This content is basic to our script, our story to live out, our "liturgy beyond the liturgy." Our liturgical action more than likely includes themes or motifs of celebration and praise, confession, and offering or commitment. How do these inform our work in the world?

Praise and gratitude are not merely Sunday morning themes in the service of worship. The weekly corporate celebration is part of our script for daily life. The Christian life is eucharistic, that is, based on thanksgiving because God makes new beginnings out of life's endings; God rules the world with truth and grace; God's irrepressible grace through the crucified–risen Lord enables us to live our lives, in spite of all the "in spite ofs"! Since we tend to forget and deny the reality of sustaining and renewing grace, we come again to corporate worship so that the word of grace once again can undergird a life of praise and thanksgiving.

Or let us consider the act of confession as part of the liturgy. Confession acknowledges that the values of our economic class, our political party, our social club, our national ethos are all under the judgment and correction of God. Confession is the liturgical action by which we recognize the sovereignty of God over all of life—past, present, and future.

But the action should not be left at the door of the church. Confession is a way of life in God by which we remain open to reconsideration, open to transformation, open to self-examination, in the light of the gospel. The honest recognition of one's condition is the beginning of health, and it is the truth to which Christian confession points. The future of any relationship depends on the possibility of amendment and reorientation. There is no "gospel lesson" more valuable than the conviction that God loves me enough to disturb me!

Liturgy brings us to commitment as well as to celebration and confession. Where there is grace, there is responsibility. To receive God's grace is to be free for others. Our offering on Sunday morning is more than placing a gift in the offering plate. Offering of self to others in the love of Jesus Christ is the very essence of our lives as Christians.

Liturgy, as we have seen, preserves and participates in the sacred story. Since the sacred story is rooted in Jesus Christ and in the message of God's rule, liturgy has a prophetic function to change us so that we become God's people changing the world. If liturgy is divorced from the realities of the world—injustices, suffering, starvation, widespread violence—it becomes an opiate instead of an interaction prompting us to participate in the purpose of God in the world. If liturgy involves us in the worth-ship of God, then surely it will involve us in the purpose of God. To say it another way, for Christians to take seriously the person of Jesus Christ is likewise to take seriously the purpose and work of Jesus Christ. As I suggest later (chapter 4 in particular), this might take the shape of caring service or work for a more just society.

Liturgy as the work of the people, in response to the gift of God, becomes our way of life as we leave the church parking lot to resume our daily tasks and responsibilities. The Christian life as liturgical life, as the liturgy after the liturgy, shifts into biblical gear. And that's an invitation "to do justice, and to love kindness, and to walk humbly with your God" (Micah 6:8).

In the preface I suggested that the way of the will is the most comprehensive and varied of the ways of faith, as well as the foundation of other ways in its corporate expression of worship. For that reason a second chapter, continuing the way of the will in its community expression, will explore further our sharing the sacred story.

QUESTIONS FOR REFLECTION

1. What strikes you as new or different in chapter 1 as to the interpretation of liturgy?
2. Does your service of worship reflect the theological-spiritual profile of the soul of the congregation? How so or not so?
3. What connections can you make between the liturgical actions of confession, proclamation, offering, and your life in the world?
4. What are the ways in which you experience liturgy as the work of the people in your congregation? prior to, during, and following worship?

In appreciation to the congregations
called Elma, Justin, St. Stephen, and Northaven
with whom I have shared sermon mentality and sacramentality.

2

The Way of the Will: Exploring Sermon Mentality and Sacramentality

And day by day, attending the temple together and breaking bread in their homes, they partook of food with glad and generous hearts.

Acts 2:46

This glimpse into the worship of the early church in Acts was to become a signpost for liturgical development in succeeding years. We see here two central foci of the way of the will as it was to unfold in various relationships in the church's corporate worship:

Temple/Synagogue → *scripture, psalms, prayer, spoken word or sermon*
Passover Tradition/Upper Room → *meal, table, acted word or Eucharist*

In the ministry of Jesus we read of his spoken message in Luke 4, based on Isaiah 61, at the synagogue in his hometown of Nazareth. From the tradition of the synagogue came "the sermon mentality" of the developing Christian movement. The spoken word would include scripture readings, the use of psalms and hymns, and the homily or sermon. Faith renewal, then, was dependent on hearing the Word. As the first Christians exchanged synagogue for church, the practices of the synagogue were transposed into the framework of the developing Christian faith.

Simultaneously the heritage of the upper room meal from the Jewish sabbath meal and the Passover tradition found its way into the house church of the first Christians. Over a period of time the meal was changed into eucharistic elements controlled by clerics and a developing sacramental theology. Faith renewal through the table was dependent on a range of senses including sight, touch, taste, and smell.

From these earliest liturgical beginnings, which preceded both scripture and doctrines *about* Word and Table, grew the normative worship tradition of the church. By the middle of the second century the church's practice of sermon and sacrament was clearly in evidence. One of our earliest records of Christian worship is from the hand of Justin Martyr in his first Apology, written in Rome approximately 155 AD.[1] Notice the liturgical action in this excerpt:

Second Century	*Today's Equivalent*
And on the day called Sun-day an *assembly* is held in one place of all who live in town or country, and the *records* of the apostles or writings of the prophets are read for as long as time allows.	*Gathering* *Scripture*
Then, when the reader has finished, the president in a *discourse* admonishes and exhorts us to imitate these good things.	*Sermon*

Then we all *stand up together and offer prayers;* and as we said before, when we have finished praying, *bread and wine* and water are brought up, and the president likewise *offers prayers and thanksgivings* to the best of his ability, and the people assent, saying the Amen; and there is a *distribution,* and everyone participates in (the elements) over which thanks have been given; and they are sent through the deacons to those who are not present.

Prayers of the People

Presentation of Gifts

Great Thanksgiving

Communion

And the wealthy who so desire *give what they wish,* as each chooses; and what is *collected* is deposited with the president.

Offering

He helps orphans and widows, and those who through sickness or any other cause are in need, and those in prison, and strangers sojourning among us; in a word, he *takes care of all those who are in need.*

Outreach

This fusion of Word and Table, of sermon and sacrament, became the most common form of worship known in the Western church. Indeed, according to James F. White, "From the sixth to the sixteenth century, the ministry of the Word and the eucharist became inseparable except on rare occasions such as Good Friday."[2]

Two caveats are in order lest the impression be given that sermon and sacrament co-existed in more or less equal prominence until the Protestant Reformation. During the Middle Ages the sermon degenerated and was treated as a mechanical device secondary to the sacramental system. There was emphasis on preaching at times through the mendicant orders (Franciscan and

Dominican friars dependent on alms), the Crusades, and at some universities. On the whole, however, the sacramental means were much more prominent than preaching.

The other caution concerning the inseparability of Word and Table is that for almost a thousand years the laity seldom received communion more than once a year, and even then, the bread or wafer only. Although the mass was celebrated regularly during which the priests partook of the elements, communion was infrequently received by the laity. Protestants take it for granted that the celebration of the Lord's Supper, Holy Communion, or the Eucharist is synonymous with participation in the bread and the cup by the laity.

The Protestant Reformation for the most part resulted in unbalancing sermon and sacrament in precisely the opposite direction, that is, the sermon became primary and the sacraments secondary. Luther's 1520 treatise *The Babylonian Captivity of the Church* attacked the premises and practices of the existing sacramental system. Regarding the mass itself Luther sought to restore the cup to the laity and to rescue the mass from its captivity as a human work offered to God. Although Luther's intention was to restore more frequent communion by the people on a faith basis, the results were quite the contrary.

This treatise represents a genuine paradigm shift, for it completely undercuts the ground on which the whole medieval sacramental system stood . . .

The final consequence was to move the central focus of Christian worship for Protestants from worship—which for lay people, had been almost entirely the sacrament—to one in which the sacraments became occasional intruders on a normal pattern of worship. No greater shift has ever occurred in Christian worship, either in East or West.[3]

One might say a long-range result of the Protestant Reformation is the triumph of the synagogue tradition of the spoken Word over the Upper Room tradition of the meal in developing Protestant traditions. Even so, the Wesleys, not unlike Luther and Calvin, also called for regular Communion. Indeed, John Wesley's admonition to Methodists in "the new country" was weekly Eucharist, but this fell by the wayside on the frontier for several reasons.[4] Over a period of time the Disciples of Christ and the Church of Christ, both of North American origin, insisted on weekly observances of the Lord's Supper, whereas most other Protestant traditions were content with less regular observance of the meal.

Since the Second Vatican Council, Roman Catholics and many Protestants have moved towards a recovery and restoration of Word and Table as known in the early church. The homily or sermon has been given more attention in the Roman Catholic Church and the sacraments of baptism and Eucharist have been more prominent in Protestant circles, especially in seminary training and in the development of liturgical resources by denominational sources. Word and Table can be said to be the most common or "normative" form of worship in church history, taking into account all Christians in all times and places. Thus what I call sacramentality and sermon mentality are in a process of restoration in relation to one another.

But just what is sacramentality and how is it different from yet similar to sermon mentality? What are we talking about or pointing to when we use terms like "sacramental theology" and "sacramental piety and practice"? Active church members, as well as clergy, frequently need guidance in coming to terms with these questions. Sacraments have to do not with so-called "high church" but to a significant degree with our basic understanding of worship throughout the history of the church.

Three levels of sacramentality have deepened my understanding and my experience of baptism and the Eucharist.

Cosmological/Creation–Centered Sacramentality

Sacramentality begins here: All life is holy and sacred. The creation itself is a sacrament of God, offering gift, promise, purpose, and providence. There is no distinction between sacred and secular, that is, the presence or activity of the Holy cannot be restricted to some discrete sphere or dimension of life.

Creation-centered sacramentality takes seriously a doctrine of creation. Albert Schweitzer would have called it reverence for life. The psalmist said it this way:

The earth is the LORD's and the fulness thereof,
> the world and those who dwell therein;
for [the LORD] has founded it upon the seas,
> and established it upon the rivers.
>> Psalm 24:1–2

The Psalmist echoes the Genesis statements "in the beginning God created the heavens and the earth" (Genesis 1), and "in the day that the Lord God made the earth and the heavens . . ." (Genesis 2).

Many Native Americans embrace a creation-centered sense of sacramentality much needed in our world today. In the film *I Heard the Owl Call My Name*, based on Margaret Craven's novel,[5] a young Episcopal seminary graduate is sent to a Native American people located on one of the islands off the Pacific Northwest mainland. He travels to his new appointment in a small boat guided by Jim, a young Indian from the congregation to be served.

As their conversation develops, Mark, the priest, asks Jim about the village population. Jim replies to the effect that whites are always asking the numbers question. How, he asks in reply, do you measure the wind or count the ripples on the stream or calculate the number of fish?[6] Jim's way of looking at the world introduces us to a sacramental perception. The land is holy. The streams are sacred. They reflect the purpose and providence of the Creator.

This sacramental view is further developed in an 1854 oration by Squamish Chief Sealth (spelled Seattle by early white settlers). The speech was given in his native language, Duwamish, addressed to the "great chief " in Washington D.C. on the occasion of the transfer of ancestral Indian lands to the federal government. The speech is entitled "If We Sell You Our Land, Love It." It speaks for itself. Here are some excerpts.

The Great Chief in Washington sends word that he wishes to buy our land. The Great Chief also sends us words of friendship and goodwill. This is kind of him, as we know he has little need of our friendship in return. But we will consider your offer. For we know that if we do not sell, the white man may come with guns and take our land.

Every part of this earth is sacred to my people. Every shining pine needle, every sandy shore, every mist in the dark woods, every clearing and humming insect is holy in the memory and experience of my people.

The red man has always retreated before the advancing white man, as the mist of the mountains runs before the morning sun. But the ashes of our fathers are sacred. Their graves are holy ground, and so these hills, these trees, this portion of the earth is consecrated to us.

We know that the white man does not understand our ways. One portion of land is the same to him as the next, for he is a stranger who comes in the night and takes from the land whatever he needs. The earth is not his brother, but his enemy, and when he has conquered it, he moves on. . . . He treats his mother, the earth, and his brother, the sky, as things to be bought, plundered, sold like sheep or bright beads. His appetite will devour the earth and leave behind only a desert.

The air is precious to the red man, for all things share the same breath—the beast, the tree, the man, they all share the same breath. The white man does not seem to notice the air he breathes. Like a man dying for many days, he is numb to the stench.

If we sell you our land, you must remember that the air is precious to us, that the air shares its spirit with all the life it supports. The wind that gave our grandfather his first breath also receives his last sigh. And the wind must also give our children the spirit of life. . . .

We will consider your offer to buy our land. If we decide to accept, I will make one condition. The white man must treat the beasts of this land as his brothers.

I have seen a thousand rotting buffaloes on the prairie, left by the white man who shot them from a passing train. [But] I do not understand how the smoking iron horse can be more important than the buffalo that we kill only to stay alive.

You must teach your children that the ground beneath your feet is the ashes of our grandfathers. So that they will respect the land, tell your children what we have taught our children, that the earth is our mother. Whatever befalls the earth befalls the sons of the earth.

This we know. The earth does not belong to man; man belongs to the earth. This we know. All things are connected like the blood which unites one family. All things are connected.

Whatever befalls the earth befalls the sons of the earth. Man did not weave the web of life, he is merely a strand in it. Whatever he does to the web, he does to himself.

It matters little where we pass the rest of our days. They are not many. A few more hours, a few more winters, and none of the children of the great tribes that once lived on this earth or that roam now in small bands in the woods will be left to mourn the graves of a people once as powerful and hopeful as yours. Men come and go, like the waves of the sea.

One thing we know, which the white man may one day discover—our God is the same God. You may think now that you own him as you wish to own our land, but you cannot. He is the God of man and his compassion is equal for the red man and the white. This earth is precious to him and to harm the earth is to heap contempt on its Creator.[7]

While fearing the intentions of white men, Chief Seattle nevertheless welcomed them and became a Christian. He died in 1866 and is buried by the small church on Bainbridge Island within sight of the modern city of Seattle.

Covenant-Centered Sacramentality

Judaism is the seedbed of Christian sacramentality. We could name covenant-centered sacramentality as the Jewish sense of the Divine revealed through earthen vessels. The physical becomes a vehicle, a conduit, an avenue of the spiritual, making the intangible tangible, the invisible visible, the ordinary extraordinary. This is the heart and soul of sacramentality.

The genius of Judaism is the holding in tension of the transcendence or otherness of God with God's concrete involvement in human history through things, objects, signs, and events—like burning bushes, rainbows, pillars of fire, manna, a stone at Bethel, and daily bread. These objects disclose divine will and presence, yet are never confused or equated with deity as in the idolatry of Baalism.

Anyone acquainted with Christian sacraments will quickly recognize the Jewish roots that undergird Christian development. The baptizing of Jewish converts with water (proselyte baptism) and the Jewish sabbath meal are the clear underpinnings of early Christian practice. In each case the universal is made known in the particular and the holy is revealed in concrete, earthy forms.

Christ-Centered Sacramentality

The fundamental sacramental notion of God revealed through finite form is basic to our faith, although there are Christians who still react to sacramental language as to something fearful or alien. What could be more sacramental than the Word Become Flesh? The incarnation is the very essence of sacramentality! Jesus Christ is the primordial and primary sacramental presence of God to Christians. Christian faith is by its very nature sacramental to the core.

Sacraments are intended to continue the ministry of Jesus Christ, not unlike preaching's intent to offer God's Word anew. Sacraments combine actions, words, and objects to be a sign of God's covenantal promise and claim. If we reflect with care we will realize that sacramentality and sermon mentality are perhaps more similar than different. In the spoken word there is action of a sacramental nature through the medium of preacher and Bible. Indeed, it is not uncommon to hear the phrase that the preacher of the sermon will "break the bread of life to us." Similarly, we can speak of the Word in the Eucharist. In fact, Paul exclaims, "As often as you eat this bread and drink this cup, you *proclaim* the Lord's death until he comes" (1 Corinthians 11:26; emphasis added). The word translated "proclaim" is the same word Paul uses for "preaching" or "proclamation" elsewhere (*katangello* in 1 Corinthians 9:14; Philippians 1:18, for example; also in other epistles or letters such as Colossians 1:28 and Acts 15:36).

Sermon Mentality

Whereas most Protestant traditions do not celebrate weekly Eucharist, preaching is the rule for most denominations.[8] There are church members in many denominations who would point to preaching as the most essential and least dispensable part of the worship service. This phenomenon is seen in United Methodism by the priority given to this function when ordained ministers are discussed by pastor-parish committees and district superintendents. My hunch is that this is not peculiar to United Methodists. The laity do not customarily say, "Send us a minister who can administer the sacraments well," or "who is a good administrator or organizer," or "who is a good teacher." What they say is, "Send us a preacher."

Why is this so? One can provide some superficial answers, such as the desire for a congregation "to look good" (or to sound good) in comparison to other churches. But the more profound answers have to do with the fact that hope springs eternal in the human heart. "Is there any Word from the Lord?" This ancient query from King Zedekiah to Jeremiah (Jer. 37:17) is contemporary as well as ancient. The plain fact is that there are hardy souls who long for the word of joy and love and hope, and, yes, of challenge. And once you have heard it you know you need to hear it again and again and again.

To be sure, there is a preaching mentality that wants a parental word of legalism and moralism. There are those who want to be homiletically spanked in order to make guilt-motivated changes of one sort or another. And there is something in most of us, whether lay or cleric, willing to settle for preaching limited to self-interest or at least to the confines of our personal stories, hopes, and ambitions.

Beyond these yearnings for scaled-down preaching, however, are subterranean desires in the majority of laity for the pulpit to declare the whole gospel. Even with our reservations there is a hope that our stories can be caught up in God's larger story of covenant and kingdom.[9] We want our lives to make a humane difference for others and to be more than self-gratification at the expense of others. We want our baser instincts challenged and our better natures strengthened and uplifted. Preaching is that liturgical action which seeks to interpret the written Word of God in its great wisdom and variety so that it becomes the true and lively Word for life today.

Many of us are aware that interest in preaching revived as a result of the sixteenth-century Protestant Reformation. The Word of God was above all a preached Word. Of course, not every Christian tradition today shares the exalted position of preaching articulated and practiced by the reformers and their followers. As I have indicated, the core of Quaker tradition provides a different view of preaching. The Disciples of Christ, while not disregarding the significance of preaching, would insist on the centrality of the Lord's meal. Some Episcopalians hold a similar view. However, the Constitution on the Sacred Liturgy arising from the Second Vatican Council has given the homily more prominence in the Roman Catholic Church than previously experienced.

Preaching has experienced many ups and downs throughout Christian history. The forms and styles and even the basic purposes of sermons have varied widely from age to age and place to place.

The fact remains, however, that sermon mentality remains basic to most traditions. It is through preaching that the church proclaims its faith to itself and to the world and interprets in every age the presence and purpose of God through Jesus Christ and the entire biblical tradition. "It provides a medium for revelation which enables the eternal Word to maintain its living, dynamic character and encounter our concrete situation."[10]

A Teaching Tool:
If You Had to Choose

Now that we have explored some dimensions of sacramentality and sermon mentality as expressions of the way of the will in corporate worship, I want to pose a question for your reflection. If at all possible, wrestle and discuss the question and your answer within a group. Share your experiences and listen to those of others in the group.

The question is this: If you had to choose between the sermon and the Eucharist for the rest of your life, which would you choose and why? If you choose preaching you will never again receive communion. If you choose the Eucharist, you will never hear another sermon as long as you live. Let us assume that the Eucharist includes scripture reading and accompanying liturgy of your choice. The same applies to preaching, that is, the service would include scripture and non-Eucharist liturgy. This question is merely a "teaser teaching tool" to assist in clarifying our priorities. By having to make even an imaginary choice we can probe our theological assumptions, our faith histories, and our liturgical "mentality." The imaginary choice will likely be difficult and, if processed in a group, you will surely hear how the option you surrendered is the chosen option of others. Then there can be an enrichment of shared experience and perspective.

My Previous Surveys:
If You Had to Choose[11]

Read this only after processing your own response.

In 1985 I posed the "if you had to choose" question to an unsuspecting group of twenty-four laypersons attending a consultation at Saint Paul School of Theology in Kansas City, Missouri. I suggested they think about it overnight.

Before I asked the question, we had studied a historical overview of liturgy. We had done a bit of updating, examining the post–Vatican II move toward recovery and restoration of Word and Table where the practice of combining them had been lost. I was curious to see whether there might be two or three "sacramental souls" in the midst of average Protestant midwestern lay people born and bred on the Word.

When I returned home for the evening I tried the question on my wife. I explained that choosing preaching meant never again receiving the Eucharist, while choosing the Lord's Supper meant never hearing another sermon. After reflecting a moment, she exclaimed, "That depends on who's doing the preaching!"

At the seminary the next morning I asked the members of the group to declare themselves and give their reasons. Twelve and twelve! I am still in shock, having expected an overwhelming majority for preaching. The Eucharist lovers gave reasons like these:

preachers come and go, sermons are good and bad, but the communion remains constant; at communion there is a more direct experience of Christ and of community. Indirectly, I perceived them to be saying that the Eucharist is less likely to be fouled up by the preachers! The sermon devotees sounded like this: preaching interprets the Bible for today and provides a range of themes and issues; the preached Word can make the faith current and relevant to the needs of our lives and community; preaching is essential for transmission of the faith from generation to generation.

After considerable discussion I suggested that we shift gears a bit: Would your decision be different if you were choosing for the church instead of for yourself? In most cases their decisions were the same, although one or two communion advocates said they might switch because the church's responsibility to evangelize would be more effective through preaching.

We discussed this at length and concluded the session with the assurance that the good news is that we do not have to make this terrible choice and that in Word and Table together the fullness of God's Word is offered. If there were those who experienced the choice as a simple one, I urged them to reflect carefully on the alternative easily surrendered. For most it was an awful choice, surely a healthy sign.

My curiosity was unabated and I was not content to let my research end. Was the surprising sacramental rating peculiar to this particular group of United Methodists? Did it portend a wider phenomenon within United Methodism and perhaps for other traditions as well? I tried the same question on a diverse group of United Methodist chaplains (hospital, prison, and military) in Texas, following similar historical preparation. To my amazement the results were exactly the same: fifty-fifty. One chaplain said that he had never heard a sermon which was as meaningful to him as the experience of the Eucharist. And when I suggested that we do not have to make the choice, another chaplain exclaimed, "What do you mean we don't have to make it? The Methodist Church made the choice many years ago, and the choice was that preaching is four times more important than the Eucharist!" (meaning that the United Methodist communion observance is usually once a month).

In 1986 I proposed the choice to a worship class at Perkins School of Theology. Twenty-six to four in favor of the Eucharist! By this time I had reversed my original concern and began to hope for a deeper sermon appreciation. Even in the preaching class of fifty-eight students the ratio was sixty percent for Eucharist, forty percent for preaching. A few would choose Eucharist for self and preaching for the church, but never vice versa.

As a professor of preaching *and* worship I remained neutral but urged deeper consideration on the surrendered option in each case. The question served as a challenging opening for examining the theology and history of Word and Table. Perhaps best of all, students shared with each other their own formation history in relation to Word and Table and defended their choice. Thus each student had to look at his or her own experience in light of others' experiences, as well as biblical resources and the church's varied tradition.

For some United Methodists the decision hinged on the selection of communion liturgy. The more recently used yet older and more joyous liturgy, traceable to Justin Martyr in the second century, would tilt them toward the Eucharist. But the heavily confessional liturgy inherited from Thomas Cranmer and the Reformation would lead them to favor preaching. It was our assumption in each group that the Eucharist would include some liturgical framework, including the reading of scripture.

In the past several years I have put the question to a number of groups, including pastors' schools and an assortment of lay groups. So far the Eucharist has always gathered at least fifty percent of the responses, and usually higher.

One can make several very tentative observations from these responses. While they represent opinions from both lay and clerical persons of diverse adult ages of both sexes, it is a small sampling mainly within one denomination. Very few persons from ethnic minorities were represented in the groups. Yet the issues raised may well be pertinent and provocative for other traditions as well, as a teaching and learning tool if nothing else.

It seems apparent that for many respondents who favored the Eucharist preaching has not been a significant factor in their faith formation, at least not consciously. For these people the more direct or experiential quality of the sacrament, as they put it, was more dependable and meaningful. This way of receiving God's self-giving was more attuned to the sensory than the cerebral, to the so-called "right-brain" dimension. Some insisted on Wesley's conviction that the sacrament was a converting ordinance as well as a nurturing one. Yet others pointed to the spoken word as basic to all other forms of communication, including the sacrament. "It is only because of interpretive words," they would say, "that one comes to an appreciation of the Eucharist."

These responses raise a number of questions. For example, do we believe that preaching can change life, or more aptly put, that through preaching God can profoundly transform, redirect, and sustain? Those of us who teach homiletics had *better* so believe and insist on the same as a growth pattern for our students! In an unending hunger for a word of hope perhaps the laity believe in preaching more than the preachers. What else explains why "we want a preacher who can preach" is almost always the primary concern when a minister is being sought? A pastor friend reminds me that since for most United Methodists preaching is much more frequent than communion, the pastor's leadership is likely to be more helpful or hurtful in preaching than in communion.

Another question is whether or not one's choice is related to particulars of the faith journey, especially aging. Several persons, both lay and clerical, indicated that whereas earlier in life they would have opted for preaching, at this later stage in life the Eucharist was a more powerful experience of faith renewal. It was as though they were saying something like, "The spoken word was indispensable to our calling into the faith, but now in later years words seem less important than the sense of divine and human relationship experienced in Holy Communion."

The fact that the imaginary choice between Word and Table was difficult for most respondents is an encouraging sign and may indeed signal a readiness to embrace both on a more regular basis.

While there are those in the church who believe that a stronger sacramental emphasis would detract from preaching, I strongly suspect this is not the case. As James F. White and others have so well demonstrated, the mutual reinforcement of spoken word and visible Word recovers the fullness of God's self-giving and of our normative tradition while offering a range of both experiential and intellectual means of receiving God's gifts basic to human need and to the mission of the church. When all is said and done, sacramentality and sermon mentality belong together.

QUESTIONS FOR REFLECTION

1. How is your present worship service parallel to the second century (Justin Martyr) service and how is it different? What has been added or subtracted?
2. What are your remembrances of Holy Communion or the Lord's Supper as a child and youth? Of preaching? Were these experiences positive or negative? These experiences may help us to understand "why and where we are" in relation to sacramentality and sermon mentality.
3. What are the personal and what are the social or corporate implications of the Eucharist?
4. Where did you and other members of the group come out with the imaginary choice between sermon and Eucharist, between Word and Table? What were the underlying issues?

3

The Way of Wonder: Discovering Spiritual Classics in Creation and Culture

The winds of grace are always blowing,
and sometimes you will be
utterly surprised.

God does not die on the day when we cease to believe in a personal deity, but we die on the day when our lives cease to be illumined by the steady radiance, renamed daily, of a wonder, the source of which is beyond all reason.

Dag Hammarskjöld[1]

In the first two chapters we explored some community dimensions of the way of the will—liturgical action and sacramentality–sermon mentality—in order to have a better understanding of corporate worship. The way of the will, we said, may be both corporate and individual and is characterized by intentional and deliberate seeking and searching for recovery and renewal of our faith. We set our sails, so to speak, in order to receive anew the gifts of God. Now we are ready to consider what might be called *unintentional* ways of faith renewal. Not everyone in the Christian tradition resonates with intentional–conventional means of personal spiritual discipline. The percentage of church members who sustain a regular practice of prayer (at least as generally defined) or Bible reading is likely quite low.

The legion of those who fast, who keep journals, or who practice regular devotional readings is probably even smaller. While I have not taken an extensive poll on such matters, conversations with church members of various denominations through the years convince me that frequently the so-called classical disciplines are not high on the list of personal priorities. I might add that clergy do not seem to fare a whole lot better in many cases. There are many more or less regular "churchgoers" (corporate way of the will) who are not regular practitioners of individual ways of the will.

Far be it from me to discourage conventional "inward disciplines"[2] which are part of our traditional spiritual formation as Christians. Indeed, as coordinator of the Spiritual Formation groups at Perkins School of Theology I regularly encourage seminary students to experience various kinds of prayer and meditation. In my judgment seminary students, if they are to accompany church members on the faith journey, need exposure to spiritual disciplines along with the scholastic-analytical and the practical-functional. The graduate or academic dimension and professional or applied training is best complemented by familiarity with the life of prayer which sustains and renews.[3] After all, whether lay or clerical, we minister out of our own faith.

However, there are many persons who benefit from a broader exposure to Christian traditions than the strictly intentional ways of the will even in its many variations. Some writers have sought to expand the possibilities of spiritual formation by matching prayer and spirituality preferences with personality or temperament.[4] The Myers-Briggs Type Indicator (MBTI), combined with temperaments of human behavior devised by David Kiersey, is used to connect and interpret forms of prayer with different personality types. This approach and others like it suggest that various methods of prayer are needed for differing temperaments.

These guidelines are not intended to be absolute or to be taken too literally. They can be useful within limits, although on occasion the categories seem somewhat akin to a spiritual horoscope in which I can find part of myself in each description. However, many people today, Christians included, do not find any method of intentional prayer meaningful. It is not just a matter of fitting the right prayer form or style to a particular personality. It is the issue of formalized prayer itself—if not the reality of it, then the ability to sustain an ongoing habit or discipline for it.

Fortunately our biblical tradition offers alternatives for those not able to matriculate in the school of intentional prayer. We might call it *unintentional* spirituality, or specifically in this chapter, the way of wonder. The way of wonder is not necessarily inimical to the way of the will, but it may be more accessible to brothers and sisters for whom conventionality is not always life-giving. As we shall see, however, the way of wonder is firmly rooted in our biblical and historical tradition.

The Way of Wonder in Contrast to the Way of the Will

If the Way of the Will Is . . .	*The Way of Wonder Is . . .*
seeking and striving	serendipity and surprise
intentional	integration
concentration and cultivation	creation centered
focusing	festal
deliberateness	delight
structured activity	sacramental attitude

In his book *Apology for Wonder* Sam Keen invites the reader to reflect on wonder in a number of helpful ways.[5] He suggests that we think in terms of ontologic wonder and mundane wonder. Have you ever marveled at the very fact of "isness," that is, that there is something rather than nothing, that there is created life rather than void? This mystery of being itself is what Keen calls "ontologic" wonder. "The primal source of all wonder is not an object but the fact that something exists rather than nothing."[6] The very notion can jar us, so vast and incomprehensible is the awareness.

"Mundane" wonder "is elicited primarily by *what* a thing is rather than *that* it is. . . . There could be no adequate catalogue of objects that produce such mundane wonder: a loved person, a gnarled tree, a beautiful stone, a miraculous event, and so on."[7]

Whereas the way of the will is intentional and deliberate, the way of wonder is quite the opposite. Wonder comes as surprise, not as the result of planning or deliberation. The experience of wonder may bring a sense of awe, or as we sometimes say, being wonderstruck. Silence, puzzlement, ambivalence, admiration and astonishment may be called forth as part of the wonder experience, as well as elements of fear and hope.

The temperaments of Ignatian (Jesuit) and Franciscan spirituality are sometimes contrasted by writers wishing to point to different styles of spiritual development and discipline. The Ignatian style generally corresponds more closely to the way of the will: orderly, well-planned, "a carefully organized regimen of striving toward a relationship with God."[8] Some would think left-brain, Apollonian, traditional. On the other hand Franciscan spirituality is usually characterized "by an attitude of openness and willingness to go in any direction that the Spirit calls . . . the whole of God's creation is a bible for the Franciscan temperament. . . ."[9] Franciscan spirituality "dislikes formal prayer and prefers a free-flowing, informal communing with God."[10] Insofar as these descriptions are accurate it is safe to say that there is an affinity between the Franciscan way and the way of wonder.

The Biblical Tradition of Wonder

Wonder is the beginning of wisdom in the same way as is the fear of the Lord. They may, in some way or other, be identical.

Cornelis Verhoeven[11]

The grace of God . . . is the whole giftedness of life, the wonder of life, which causes me to ask questions that transcend the moment.

Joseph Sittler[12]

Like the terms "revelation," "welcome," and "liberation," the actual noun "wonder" seldom appears in scripture. Yet its reality is almost everywhere present. If we think in terms of the related experiences of awe, surprise, and astonishment it is not difficult to detect the presence of wonder. Revelation—the revealing of the Holy or the Ultimate—occasions wonder with its ingredients of surprise, ambivalence, and amazement. For the Holy is both fearful and promising, repelling and compelling simultaneously. So it was for Moses before the holiness of the burning bush. So with Isaiah in the temple: "Woe is me . . . send me." And so it was with the shepherds keeping their flock by night.

We especially associate wonder with the celebration of Christmas. The concept and the experience of wonder permeates the Christmas story in both scripture and song. There is a child-like ambience of the birth narrative which cleanses and challenges our jaded, utilitarian world. As I recalled the presence of wonder in our hymns I rediscovered the many-splendored shapes of wonder that inform not just Christmas but the entire Christian story.

Here are a few examples which are recognizable to nearly all Christian readers.[13] The journey of wonder will take us through virtually the whole Christian year. (Italics, below, are mine.)

Birth   He rules the world with truth and grace,
and makes the nations prove the glories
of his righteousness, and *wonders* of his love,

and *wonders* of his love, and *wonders, wonders*
of his love.

(#246) "Joy to the World"

Passion   What *wondrous* love is this, O my soul, O my soul,
what *wondrous* love is this, O my soul! What
wondrous love is this that caused the Lord of life
to lay aside his crown for my soul, for my soul,
to lay aside his crown for my soul.

(#292) "What Wondrous Love Is This"

When I survey the *wondrou*s cross
on which the Prince of Glory died,
my richest gain I count but loss,
and pour contempt on all my pride.

(#299) "When I Survey the Wondrous Cross"

Resurrection   Christ is risen! Shout Hosanna! Celebrate this day
of days. Christ is risen! Hush in *wonder;* all
creation is amazed. In the desert all-surrounding,
see, a spreading tree has grown. Healing leaves of
grace abounding bring a taste of love unknown.

(#307) "Christ is Risen"*

Grace   Finish, then, thy new creation; pure and spotless
let us be. Let us see thy great salvation perfectly
restored in thee; changed from glory into glory, till
in heaven we take our place, till we cast our
crowns before thee, lost in *wonder,* love, and
praise.

(#384) "Love Divine, All Loves Excelling"

---

*Words by Brian Wren. Copyright © 1986 by Hope Publishing Co., Carol
Stream, IL 60188. All rights reserved. Used by permission.

These references to wonder and its derivative terms call our attention to the marvel and mystery of God's grace and to the exhilaration of human response encompassing awe, amazement, and astonishment. This prevailing scriptural sense of wonder at the surprising, interceding, and sustaining presence of God is usually engendered by the seemingly ordinary vested with the extraordinary. Perhaps a stone at Bethel. A balm in Gilead. A child born to peasant parents. A wash basin and towel. A loaf of bread. A simple chalice. The wonder of a wandering rabbi long since alive on a global basis through a body two thousand years old and still counting. No wonder there is wonder alive. It goes back to the very beginning.

The presence of wonder in scripture is not difficult to locate. In fact the Scriptures begin with the promise of purpose and the assurance that creation itself reveals the good: "And God saw everything that he had made, and behold, it was very good" (Genesis 1:31). The twenty-fourth psalm continues the theme: "The earth is the Lord's and the fulness thereof, / the world and those who dwell therein; / for he has founded it upon the seas, / and established it upon the rivers" (vs. 1–2).

The nineteenth psalm tells us in vivid imagery that God is revealed in creation:

The heavens are telling the glory of God;
    and the firmament proclaims his handiwork.
Day to day pours forth speech,
    and night to night declares knowledge.
There is no speech, nor are there words;
    their voice is not heard;
yet their voice goes out through all the earth,
    and their words to the end of the world.
Ps. 19:1–4

In Psalm 150 both creation and culture (in the forms of music and dance) are means by which God is known and praised:

Praise the Lord!
Praise God in his sanctuary;
    praise him in his mighty firmament!

Praise him for his mighty deeds;
    praise him according to his exceeding greatness!
Praise him with trumpet sound;
    praise him with lute and harp!
Praise him with timbrel and dance;
    praise him with strings and pipe!
Praise him with sounding cymbals;
    praise him with loud clashing cymbals!
Let everything that breathes praise the LORD!
Praise the LORD!

As indicated through the hymns cited earlier, the New Testament is replete with occasions of wonder and awe from birth announcements and narratives all the way through the passion narratives and the amazement of the resurrection accounts.

Expanding Horizons for Spiritual Classics

Christian spiritual tradition has long identified spiritual classics, great literary treasures that have nourished and guided Christian seekers through the centuries. These writings represent a broad range of spiritual insights and practices from Roman Catholic, Orthodox, and Protestant sources. The following are some of these great classics from literature:

Confessions, of St. Augustine (fourth century)
On Loving God, by St. Bernard of Clairvaux (twelfth century)
Revelations of Love, by Julian of Norwich (fourteenth century)
Talks of Instruction, by Meister Eckhardt (fourteenth century)
The Imitation of Christ, by Thomas à Kempis (fifteenth century)
Interior Castle, by St. Teresa of Avila (sixteenth century)
The Dark Night of the Soul, by St. John of the Cross (sixteenth century)
Treatise on the Love of God, by Frances de Sales (seventeenth century)
The Journal of John Woolman (eighteenth century)

A Serious Call to a Devout and Holy Life, by William Law (eighteenth century)

A Testament of Devotion, by Thomas Kelly (twentieth century)

Waiting on God, by Simone Weil (twentieth century)

Contemplative Prayer, by Thomas Merton (twentieth century)

Mere Christianity, by C. S. Lewis (twentieth century)

Many other names can be counted among the authors of spiritual classics. Contemporary additions might include *Life Together* by Dietrich Bonhoeffer, *With Head and Heart* by Howard Thurman, and some of the writings of Henri Nouwen. Whether or not a certain document becomes a classic is a matter of opinion, although the test of time and the breadth of use are significant factors.

One must ask, however, why spiritual classics should be limited to literature, that is, the written word. Why not include music and other art forms? Why not natural wonders that bring forth awe and reverence? Furthermore, although a classic is by usual definition widely accepted and appreciated, why should we not embrace personal "classics" that probe the soul and offer an experience of wonder and renewal?

The tradition of spiritual classics needs to be expanded beyond widely accepted literary gems to include natural and artistic wonders which feed our souls. The Western mind has frequently deceived itself into believing that reality does not exist unless recorded in writing. For example, the daring exploits of Polynesian seafarers were not believed in the West for centuries because they were preserved in oral stories, chants, dances, and sculptures instead of in written accounts. I will explore expanding the horizons for spiritual classics under the genres of creation and culture.

Wonder from Creation

I have long realized that for me there are natural wonders which come as messengers of life in profound ways. The experience will sometimes defy a satisfactory explanation. For example, I will be driving on the highway when suddenly there appears in the distance a high-flying formation of Canadian geese. I am deeply moved. I am not sure why. But it is revelation. Perhaps they communicate mystery and transcendence. Maybe it has to do with "coming home" or journeying away from home.

The geese in their regal flight seem to be saying, "We don't exist for you. We have our own lives that you don't know about. You would be less without us. Respect us and thus find greater depth of life and being. Look and listen up, and be present to that which is not created by you." The Canadian geese speak a word of grace and mystery to me. That word is a spiritual classic. Grace in creation.

In a somewhat different way the Maroon Bell Peaks near Aspen, Colorado, constitute a spiritual classic for me. My friends know that I am an unrepentant, compulsive, "Rocky Mountain high" addict with probably the world's largest collection of Maroon Bell slides. It is a holy place of renewal for me. Past family and friendship associations here are combined with the ever-new experiences of sun and shadow in the valley and on the mountains and the unpredictable combinations of wildflowers. The reflection of the peaks on Maroon Lake. The sound of the rushing mountain stream accompanied by the dainty, ever-present Chiming Bell flower. The beaver dams and the wildly scooting miniature marmots. The way of wonder is cleansing and healing. A spiritual classic for me.

In the introduction I suggested that the various ways of faith renewal complement and interact with one another. Since I return to the Maroon Bells from time to time, there is a sense in which the way of the will, intentional and deliberate, is merged with the way of wonder, as I sit once again at their majestic feet as pilgrim and learner. The sanctuary has moved out of the church building into the wildlife sanctuary so that church and creation are united in wonder and praise and adoration. Spirit and matter become one in the mystery of givenness. As one writer put it, "All of creation is smeared with the ointment of divinity. We live in an anointed world."[14] The genes of Francis of Assisi arise again in the creation way of wonder.

In our consumer-oriented society the gift of wonder from creation breaks through our utilitarian mode of existence. We relearn there is that which does not exist for our domination or possession but in its own createdness. There is life and being to be "respected and relished in its otherness."[15] Wonder frees us to enjoy and appreciate the unproductive and thus to be present to being as well as doing and striving. For Thomas Berry, "the universe is the primary revelation of the divine, the primary scripture, the primary locus of divine–human communion."[16]

One can make a case today for the eclipse of wonder by science and its dizzying discoveries in genetics, microbiology, astronomy, and other areas. But one can make an equally strong case for the widening mystery occasioned by science, both in the mystery of the known and in the sense that most new advances in knowledge uncover how much more we still do not know. The scientific method itself can become a closed and short-sighted view of life if seen as the only way to arrive at truth, but science itself can add to the mystery and wonder of life. Indeed, wonder is the link between the genuine religious spirit and the scientific mind not totally defined by the scientific method.

Wonder From Culture

A spiritual classic is an event, experience, or source that profoundly illuminates our existence and calls us to dimensions of depth, healing, and wonderment.[17] Such an event may come from culture as well as from creation or nature. Paul Tillich spoke of religion as the expression of ultimate concern as well as having a set of beliefs and symbols in which this concern is manifest.[18] This broad concept of religion as a dimension of depth intersects the narrower sense of religion as a set of beliefs centering in the existence of God with intellectual and practical consequences. To speak about religion and art, he suggested, is to speak in terms of both the broad and the narrow concepts of religion.

It follows, on the one hand, that religious art may express the larger concept of religion, that is, an expression of ultimate concern. On the other hand, religious art may refer to traditional religious symbols, such as pictures of Christ, the virgin and child, and/or the saints. Or as Tillich put it, one needs to consider the religious dimension in non-religious art and the non-religious dimension in religious art.

In 1955 Tillich gave a lecture at Drew Theological Seminary titled "Existentialist Aspects of Modern Art."[19] Four levels of the relation between religion and art are articulated by Tillich in the lecture. His reflections have been widely read and debated. Obviously it is one typology among many and provides limited illumination. Art historians have claimed that the levels, which Tillich later changed to dimensions, do not speak to a broad spectrum of Western art. Tillich's references to art in this lecture are almost always to paintings, although his four levels or dimensions are applicable to a variety of art forms and expressions. Like all interpretations, Tillich's view or aperture is highly subjective and open to challenges from various directions in both art and theology.

Nonreligious Style, Nonreligious Content

Tillich uses the term "style" to indicate that there is something breaking through the surface from the depths. "The piercing of the surface" was a phrase he used frequently. Whenever this happens, he insisted, we have a style that is religious even if there is no religious content depicted. By religious content he means traditional symbols, such as Jesus, the disciples, the saints—in other words, visual representations where identity or source is more or less unmistakable.

The first level, then, is usually called secular art. Insofar as it expresses any ultimate concern it does so indirectly. Nor does it deal with religious symbols or rites. Level one is made up of landscapes, human scenes, portraits, events, and all kinds of scenes on the level of secular human existence. In this level he cites "The World Upside Down" by Jan Steen and "Return of the Prodigal" by Rubens.

Religious Style, Non-religious Content

Here there are no sacred scenes in terms of content. Tillich calls this the existential level. Van Gogh's "Starry Night" points to the depths of reality and goes below the surface, according to Tillich. It is well known that for Van Gogh the presence of the divine was evident in the stars and in the everyday life of the peasants whom he served as minister. Picasso's *Guernica,* named for the small Basque village destroyed by saturation bombing in the Spanish Civil War, "shows the human situation without any cover."[20] "Although it has no religious content, it does have religious style in a very deep and profound sense."[21]

Tillich contrasts works by Chagall and Chirico and Picasso—works of a religious style in his judgment—with the sentimental Jesus portrayals by Hoffman which are commonly thought to be very religious. Religious style "puts the religious question radically, and has the power, the courage, to face the situation out of which this question comes, namely the human predicament."[22]

Nonreligious Style, Religious Content

For Tillich the art of the High Renaissance typifies level three. Reflecting on several Madonna and Child paintings (Raphael, Fouquet, Rubens), Tillich asserts that the beauty and harmony revealed may be wonderful to look at but they do not reflect the reality of life. "Religious content in itself does not give a religious picture, and many of those pictures which you find in the magazines of the churches . . . are of the same character. They have religious content but no religious style."[23]

Religious Style, Religious Content

"Is such a religious art possible today?" is the question Tillich raises about level four. From the distant past Tillich points to El Greco's Crucifixion, and a yet earlier picture of the late Gothic period,

Grünewald's Crucifixion on the Isenheim Altar (now in the Unter-linden Museum, Colmar, France). He then cites as another candidate a modern Crucifixion by Sutherland. These paintings, according to Tillich, attempt to reformulate traditional religious content in a style understandable to our time. Tillich seems ambivalent as to whether even these examples are capable of uniting style and content in a truly religious way.

Application of Tillich

It has long been recognized that art can serve a religious function by interpreting the present age, challenging existing norms in a prophetic manner, and enlivening our conscience. The fact that tyranny seeks to silence the artist is not accidental whimsy. Tillich's category of religious style, nonreligious content has been particu-larly significant for me in the way I view the world. Through this aperture Tillich reminds us that religious language, such as sin and grace, points to reality and is transparent to the reality itself. In other words, a novel, a play, a film, music, a painting may reveal the human condition and possibilities thereof without necessarily using traditional religious words, images, or forms.

For example, the flute often reveals to me a sense of mystery and beauty for which I have no explanation. For me, James Galway on the flute is likely to be "a religious experience," a spiritual classic if you will. There is something about the flute that is haunting and playful in a way that touches an archetypal nerve with me. And I experience this as one who does not read music and who has never played a musical instrument.

Tillich's religious style, nonreligious content provided me a new set of ears and eyes. Profound dimensions of sin and grace, of alienation and community, of guilt and forgiveness, are uncovered in some novels, plays, and films.

Although we frequently insist that God's Word is in conflict with the dominant culture, offering an alternative vision, it is also the case that God's Word may come from culture as well as the church.

This is not acculturation but a recognition that God works through many diverse sources and resources to speak and demonstrate the truth. "By men of strange lips / and with an alien tongue / the Lord will speak to this people" (Is. 28:11), such as Samaritans, poor and rich outcasts, and suffering servants.

The film *The Bicycle Thief* was a more profound influence on my understanding the power of systems than all the books I read in business school, although by the time I saw it I had the advantage of theological study and reflection, including Tillich! The plot is roughly this: In postwar Italy, after many days of waiting in employment lines, a man at last lands a job putting up billboards. He hocks his family's meager possessions in order to acquire the one thing necessary to keep the job: a bicycle. On his first day on the job the bicycle is stolen. The rest of the film consists of his attempts to recover the bicycle. He acts responsibly throughout, but to no avail. In final desperation, facing his family's hunger and eviction from their small apartment, he himself becomes a bicycle thief. He is caught on the spot and humiliated in front of his son, whose presence at the scene is unknown to him.

This film became a classic for me in interpreting the limits of economic systems and in deflating the notion that if we just try hard enough, things will surely turn out all right. The film is a profound commentary on human struggle and hope and how pressures can erode or even destroy the integrity of good intentions. Provocative questions are raised about social justice and social services, issues that are inextricably bound up with the rule of God.

Who can forget the powerful sense of rediscovered community in *Babette's Feast?* The vulnerable images in *The Pawnbroker?* The powerful commentary on sanity and insanity in *The King of Hearts?* The acceptance of all life at the conclusion of *Zorba?* The profound friendship between two men in *Dersu Usala?* The lostness, yet glimpse of grace in *Death of a Salesman?*

While I have applied Tillich's categories of content and style to wonder from culture, his categories can also be applied to wonder from creation or nature. The Maroon Bell peaks, mentioned earlier, reveal a religious style, non-religious content in terms of Tillich's categories. In the imagery of the 24th psalm they tell the glory of God and proclaim God's handiwork. They "pour forth speech" and "night to night declare knowledge." Their "word" unfolds the beauty of creation, the power of the creator, the equality of all human beings, and offers a restorative therapy to the soul.

Wonder and Jesus Christ

I am sometimes asked—indeed, I ask myself—"Would you see the implications offered in creation and in culture if you had not first been exposed to interpreting the world through Jesus Christ?" Since the Christian community has always undergirded to one degree or another my understanding of self and the world, it is impossible for me to answer the question with certainty for myself. This much I can say for myself: Jesus Christ is the lens through which I perceive life. The Christian faith gave me a way of interpreting the world. The Word gave shape to my value system. Although theologians have used the term "common grace" to indicate a grace or presence available to everyone in nature, it can also be argued that the heavens are telling the *glory* of God more than the *will* of God. The late theologian Joseph Sittler put it this way: "My theology is not one derived from nature; it is a theology of the incarnation applied to nature."[24]

However, it is clear to me that other human beings experience the way of wonder quite apart from Christian faith. Indeed, many persons of other religious faiths have come to the experience of wonder in their own terms. Many Buddhists, for example, have a deep sense of awe and interconnectedness with the universe itself. Those of us who are Christians have much to learn about care for the earth and environmental reverence. The comedian Dick Gregory has said, "There isn't a Catholic moon and a Baptist sun. I know the universal God is universal. . . . I feel that the same god-force that is the mother and father of the Pope is also the mother and father of the loneliest wino on the planet."[25]

It would be absurd to claim that Jews or Muslims or Buddhists, for example, have less capacity to wonder or to delight in the serendipity and delight of the God-bearing revelation of creation or of some dimensions of creative art (note the psalms from Judaism quoted earlier in this chapter). The Christian faith has no corner on the market of profound religious sensibility and sensitivity. All that I can claim is the personal affirmation that Jesus Christ has been *my way* of being opened to the way of wonder which from time to time and place to place invites me to the renewal of what Tillich called ultimate concern.

Wonder and Love of Neighbor

Is there any guarantee that the way of wonder will enlarge our capacity for justice and for being a more loving neighbor? Cannot wonder become merely a private aesthetic experience titillating our sense of awe or surprise, or even an escape into our own sphere of privileged enjoyment?

There is no guarantee that the way of wonder will deepen our ethical commitments, but neither is there assurance that every Sunday worship attendance will bring about greater sensitivity to the class, race, sexual orientation, age, and nationality of our many and varied neighbors. Sunday worship has opened my eyes and life to my neighbor in many ways. I can assert that it is the true intention of Christian worship to do so. But the fact remains that racism, sexism, nationalism and classism are alive and well in the church in spite of God's Word of unconditional love which offers to free us all for others.

Indeed, Wade Clark Roof and William McKinney, in *American Mainline Religion*, show that going to church in America is seen as conformist behavior often associated with conventional values and attitudes.[26] For example, the religious population is less tolerant in regard to civil liberties than the nonreligious. Persons with no religious preference are more supportive of black rights. Also, my "environmental" friends assure me some surveys suggest that the more frequent the church attendance, the more abominable the level of sensitivity to environmental issues. This offense leads to the joke that less regular church attendance might be efficacious for environmental perspective, but I continue to hold out hope for the relationship between liturgy and a life sensitive to both neighbors and creation! In fairness it also needs to be said that other surveys indicate that churchgoers contribute more to humanitarian causes and are more stable in work and family relationships.

Wonder can and should lead us to make connections with all human beings. We do not have to reflect at length to realize that the wonders of creation are intended to link all human beings together as recipients of grace. Native Americans sometimes say that they do not have to join hands when in a circle to experience community or a common bond. They are already joined by the earth. Dick Gregory is right. The moon and the sun are not denominational. Furthermore, the wind is not Christian, the clouds are not Hindu, the rain is not Jewish, the stars are not Islamic, the trees are not Buddhist, the rivers are not Shinto, the air is not Confucian. The clear implication of all nature is the universal quality binding us all together. If the ozone layer is destroyed, what will religious labels mean?

The same connection with all human beings is implied in many expressions of art. Music in fact is called the universal language. Recently a Soviet jazz pianist came to Dallas and improvised with a group of local musicians. None of the Americans could speak a word of Russian and vice versa, but what music they made together!

One does not have to be a practitioner of any certain religion to appreciate a grand jeté in the dance or to be moved by Picasso's *Guernica*. No prescribed theological or philosophical background is necessary to marvel at the beauty and power of the Taj Mahal or of Chagall's windows in the Fraümunster cathedral in Zurich or of Michelangelo's sculpture of David in Florence. While these artistic wonders do not spell out ethical relationships in words, they imply that all human beings "are caught in an inescapable network of mutuality, tied in a single garment of destiny."[27]

A sense of sacramental wonder about the world and life within it is available to all human beings. And this means that God—the Divine Reality—is loose in the world!

QUESTIONS FOR REFLECTION

1. What signs of wonder from creation are spiritual classics for you?
2. What expressions of culture or art have fed or continue to feed your soul?
3. What other expressions of "religious style, non-religious content" came to mind?
4. How do you see the relationship of wonder and justice?
5. What do you think these examples of wonder in God's world mean to a person who professes no religious belief of any kind? Do you expect the experience is different from those who profess religious belief?

In appreciation of Fr. Daniel Sanchez
and the courageous members of
Maria Madre de los Pobres, San Salvador

4

The Way of Witness: Renewing Faith Through Compassion and Justice

The winds of grace are always blowing,
and sometimes you will meet God
and neighbor together
in the wind.

One act of solidarity or love means more than a thousand books
of theology.

Gustavo Gutierrez[1]

We have been exploring the way of the will and the way of wonder.
Now we are ready to consider yet a third dimension of faith renewal,
the way of witness. While the doing of faith may be a consequence of
faith, it can also be a deepening and strengthening of faith. Witness

to be sure can be the result of faith, so to speak, but it can also be the recovery of faith. Holiness of heart ordinarily leads to holiness of life, to cite John Wesley, but it is also true that by the grace of God involvement in holiness of life can lead to holiness of heart, a cycle of interaction.

The Way of Witness Contrasted with Other Ways

If the Way of the Will Is . . .	*The Way of Wonder Is . . .*	*The Way of Witness Is . . .*
Concentration and cultivation	Creation-centered	Commitment and compassion
Intentional	Integration	Implementation
Seeking and striving	Serendipity and sacramental	Serving
Focusing	Festal	Forgetfulness of self

I want to emphasize again that these ways of faith renewal are not mutually exclusive but rather interactive and mutually supportive. They are distinguishable but in the final analysis inseparable in terms of the basic root of each one. But it is true that one or the other may speak to us in special ways at certain times in our lives and that we have an inclination or disposition toward one more than another.

Retracing Some Biblical Landscape

Faith comes alive and God seems real when we are doing the work of God. As with any newly acquired language faith can slip away from us when not practiced and used. This is true whether we describe faith as basic trust system or belief system or a combination of both. As I have listened to the experience of others through the years and as I have reflected on my own experience, I am convinced that faith often becomes stronger and is re-created and re-formed as a result of acting it out in ministries of service, compassion and justice. As we shall see, there is no guarantee that action produces a stronger faith, but this is likely to be, and frequently is, the case.

The notion that God becomes real when we are about the work of God will not seem strange or startling to those who know the biblical tradition. Consider just these few reminders among countless available examples:

Woe to him who builds his house by unrighteousness,
    and his upper rooms by injustice;
who makes his neighbor serve him for nothing,
    and does not give him wages; . . .
Did not your father eat and drink and do justice and righteousness?
    Then it was well with him.
He judged the cause of the poor and the needy;
    then it was well.
Is not this to know me?
    says the LORD.

Jer. 22:13, 15b–16

Jeremiah is holding before us a typical biblical insistence that we come to know God in doing justice related to the cause of the poor and the needy. This is not the only way we know God but we are unlikely to know God at the deepest level apart from the reality of justice's gifts and demand.

Isaiah offers a similar viewpoint in chapter 58 which marks a radical reinterpretation of Israel's observance of fasts. After return from exile the people are without vision and the nation languishes in gloom. We are told in the following chapter (59:14) that truth has fallen in the public squares. Thus the people, seeking the favor of God, humble themselves with fasting, sackcloth, and ashes.

But God does not acknowledge the fast. Indeed, God calls for righteousness, and thereby transforms the meaning of fasting from self-abasement and self-pity in outward piety to self-giving in ethical relationship.

Is not this the fast that I choose: to loose the bonds of wickedness,
    to undo the thongs of the yoke,
to let the oppressed go free,

and to break every yoke?
Is it not to share your bread with the hungry,
and bring the homeless poor into your house...?
Then shall your light break forth like the dawn,
and your healing shall spring up speedily....
If you pour yourself out for the hungry
and satisfy the desire of the afflicted,
then shall your light rise in the darkness
and your gloom be as the noonday....
you shall raise up the foundations of many generations;
you shall be called the repairer of the breach,
the restorer of streets to dwell in.

Excerpts from Isaiah 58:6–12

In this passage it is only in the doing of the faith that Israel will experience the presence of God ("then you shall call, and the Lord will answer ... 'Here I am.'" v. 9). Only when justice is acted out in the common life of the people will there be the *shalom* and wholeness from God.

Surely for Christians the clearest and most unmistakable connection between faith acted out in compassionate self-giving and the God made real is in the Last Judgment account in Matthew 25. There is major irony in the fact that today many religious workers who have given their lives for working among the poor are accused of consorting with communism. Interesting, isn't it? Jesus Christ tells us that it is not communists that we meet in caring about broken and marginalized people but Christ himself.

The familiar parable of the Last Judgment in Matthew 25 needs to be close to our hearts and minds. There have been many interpretations of this text. But the one consistent and unyielding theme in them all is that Christ is met in the needs of our neighbors. The reality of God is not separate from the basic needs of human beings for food, drink, and clothing, for hospitality and remembrance in difficult times. Like the story of the Good Samaritan this text reminds us that we sometimes "spiritualize" God's presence to the extent that God is no longer connected with basic daily human issues and problems. To the contrary, it is in binding up bodily wounds, welcoming the stranger, and providing food and drink that we meet God head-on in direct encounter. Do we want God to seem real? We need to listen and respond to this text!

One more biblical account will suffice. I have long regarded the Zacchaeus narrative in Luke 19 as a window of opportunity for affluent Christians throughout the world. Here, Jesus befriends not a poor outcast but a rich outcast. Notice that Jesus invites himself into Zacchaeus's life—the way it happens for all of us. Notice further the response of the crowd as they grumble about Jesus going into the house of a sinner. And notice finally the transformation of Zacchaeus and Jesus' response:

And Zacchaeus stood and said to the Lord, "Behold Lord, the half of my goods I give to the poor; and if I have defrauded any one of anything, I restore it fourfold." And Jesus said to him, "Today salvation has come to this house, since he also is a son of Abraham. For the Son of man came to seek and to save the lost."

Luke 19:8–10

Salvation today! Zacchaeus, having been found by God, has now found himself *and* God. God has become real because Zacchaeus has acted upon his newfound faith. He is turned inside out and is lined up with a cause greater than himself. His statement of restoration to others is extravagant and beyond self-protection since as a rich tax collector in a thriving, major city he has probably defrauded just about everyone through an unjust system.

These passages offer challenge and gift to both individuals and to our nation. How can God seem real to us if we are not committed to the work of God in acts of mercy and concern for others? Robert McAfee Brown has pointed out that the Last Judgment parable in Matthew 25 is addressed to the nations of the world.[2] Can God seem real to the citizens of a nation whose priorities reflect commitments to weapons instead of human needs—food, housing, and safe environment?

The biblical tradition is clear that to be saved is to be sent. The consistent biblical emphasis is on the action of God in drawing human beings out of narrow private worlds into the larger story of

God known as covenant and kingdom or rule.[3] Biblical faith means special responsibility rather than special privilege, as the latter is usually defined. This responsibility includes receiving the gifts of others as well as offering the gifts which God has given to us. These are some contemporary recommendations for the Way of Witness:

Personal References for the Way of Witness

He comes to us as One unknown,
without a name,
as of old, by the lakeside,
He came to those men who knew Him not.
He speaks to us the same word:
"Follow thou me!"
and sets us to the tasks which he has to fulfill
　for our time.
He commands.
And to those who obey Him,
whether they be wise or simple,
He will reveal Himself in the toils,
　the conflicts, the sufferings which they shall pass
　through in His fellowship,
and, as an ineffable mystery,
they shall learn in their own experience
　Who He is.
Albert Schweitzer[4]

If you in this country keep working in whatever ways you can for the crucified peoples of the earth—in the United States, in El Salvador, wherever—your lives will have more meaning; your faith will be more Christian; your hope will be stronger.

Jon Sobrino, S.J.[5]

Joseph Kordick is a former Ford Motor Co. executive from Michigan. He gave up that position a year ago to become a volunteer helping terminally ill people through the process of dying.

He also volunteers with the United Way and a Florida prison ministry. He serves on the administrative board of his new church home, Aldersgate United Methodist Church, in Palm City.

"I've searched the Bible for eleven months during my retirement, and I haven't found anything that contradicts my understanding that loving, caring and sharing are the ways to live our lives," said Mr. Kordick.

He has embodied that belief in his support of the eight patients he has helped in those eleven months. His most recent patient was a young man who died from AIDS in November.

Mr. Kordick is among a dozen retired executives who are to be profiled in a forthcoming national magazine article.

Of that dozen—all wealthy former executives who once wielded considerable corporate power—only he and two others expressed satisfaction with their retirement, Mr. Kordick said.

The fulfilled three are devoting their retirements to the service of others, he explained.[6]

It is not possible to live as a Christian without taking risks. If you live your whole life without ever taking risks for your faith, of what value is it?
Ignacio Martin Baro (murdered by the Salvadoran military)[7]

I was in the church for thirty-three years and had not met Jesus Christ until I began ministry with the homeless.
Arris Wheaton (minister to the homeless)[8]

What gives me hope is the community doing the will of God. Jesus died for his children and that is what we will do if we must. It is through suffering and giving ourselves to others that God is present.
Carlos (member of El Salvador resettlement village)[9]

O Divine Master, grant that I may not so much seek to be consoled as to console, to be understood as to understand, to be loved as to love. For it is in giving that we receive; it is in pardoning that we are pardoned; and it is in dying that we are born to eternal life.
From the prayer of St. Francis of Assisi

I hope you come to find that which gives life deep meaning for you. Something worth living for—maybe even worth dying for—something that energizes you, enthuses you, enables you to keep moving ahead. I can't tell you what it might be—that's for you to find, to choose, to love. I can just encourage you to start looking and support you in your search.
Sister Ita Ford in a letter to her niece on her niece's sixteenth birthday (Sr. Ford was raped and murdered by Salvadoran death squads in 1980)[10]

In recognizing and commemorating the lives of martyrs, like Archbishop Oscar Romero the people of El Salvador have a liturgical custom of proclaiming *Presente,* meaning that the remembered one is truly present in their midst. This is done through chanting *Presente* as the liturgical presider calls the name to be remembered. The foregoing extracts testify to the fact that Jesus Christ is *Presente* through our participation in the work of God in the world.

Jesus' central message was the rule of God over all of life. The Kingdom represents the work or action of God in history. Mortimer Arias, in his *Announcing the Reign of God,* provides a helpful summation of Jesus' message.

The kingdom of God, announced by Jesus, is multidimensional and all-encompassing. It is both a present and a future reality. It has to do with each individual creature and with the whole of society. It was addressed initially to "the lost sheep of Israel," but was destined for "the whole world" and to "the end of the earth." It embraces all dimensions of human life: physical, spiritual, personal and interpersonal, communal and societal, historical and eternal. And it encompasses all human relationships—with the neighbor, with nature, and with God. It implies a total offer and a total demand. Everything and everybody has to be in line with it: "Turn away from your sins and believe the Good News" (Mark 1:15, TEV) of the Kingdom of God.[11]

Every time we pray the Lord's Prayer we pray for the will ("kingdom") of God to be done *on earth* as in heaven. This means that we pray for a world of wholeness and justice in which there is equitable distribution of goods, care for the earth and its environmental systems, humane economic and political systems, and regard for the dignity and rights of all human beings. Thus, to be spiritual or religious is not just a matter of observances and disciplines but also participating in the rule of God. A friend of mine put it this way: "If we are not responsive in some way to the suffering of the world around us, Jesus Christ will take his life and give it to someone else." To be "in Christ" is to be in his work. And it is in and through the work of Christ that Christ can be formed in us over and over again. We might call this inductive faith or action-developed faith. Instead of commitment following from certain beliefs or doctrines, the reverse can take place. The acceptance of Jesus as Lord begins with the practice of faith in action. This taste of God's rule is followed by embracing some of the other means of grace that support grace in action, such as corporate worship, sacraments, prayer, scripture.

Whether we begin with verbal commitment or with doing the faith, some of our most profound spiritual exercises are to be found in extending a cup of water to parched lips, working for adequate housing, and accompanying others on the hard part of their journey. We might even be so moved by these experiences that they become for us *spiritual classics!*

The Way of Witness Working in Diverse Ways

I have been lifting up the renewal of faith through doing the work of God or, stated otherwise, participating in the kingdom of God. But what does this action look like and where does it take place? What do these rather general-sounding realities look like when seen in the specific?

Some time ago, after about thirty years in the ordained ministry, I came to the conclusion that the laity has either the easiest or the toughest job in the church. Which it is depends on each person. There certainly is nothing difficult about coming to worship more or less regularly, dropping some money in the plate, serving on an occasional committee and refraining from becoming a regular participant in mortal sins. But suppose you take your baptism with utter seriousness. Suppose you connect your baptized faith with its full implications to your life. What then?

Then you begin to realize that the loving, learning and liberating capacity of the laity is the greatest single resource God gives to the church. Then you begin to be aware that the promise and the claim of the Gospel have jurisdiction in every area of your life. And this translates into four contexts or settings with which most laity must contend.

Institutional Church

Ministries within the institutional church constitute one significant dimension of lay ministry. In some eyes these responsibilities—committee work, care for property, worship leadership, teaching, music ministry, visitation—may not be as "missional" as others we will mention. But in truth these are genuinely significant ministries. They need to be done well and faithfully. When they are not, everyone pays a price. In fact, some members are at their best in doing God's work in the institutional church.

Committees and councils perform what may be termed "indirect" people ministries. Their work may revolve around budgets, programs, or property, but everyone is affected for better or worse. The purpose of these support ministries is to enable the church to engage in its wider ministries to the world. Other ministries within the church are "direct" people ministries. These include visiting members who are sick or in special need, teaching ministries, or assisting in the leadership of worship. If there is no ministry to people already in the church (that is, members), there most likely will not be a sustained ministry from and beyond the church.

Community

By community I mean local, regional, national, and/or global. The church is not merely a consumer of the gospel, but a sign of the gospel and an advocate for the gospel. The struggle of most churches is similar to that of individual church members: finding the time, energy, and resources to be outward bound, to reflect that Christ died not for the church but for the world.

A simple yet profound story makes the point. A certain church experienced a dwindling membership due to a changing neighborhood and an economic depression. Many people moved out of the area. The church's struggle was tough. But other members remained for a variety of reasons. The church carried on. In the process of struggle to be in ministry an elderly woman had this to say about her church: "In and through this difficult time we learned that we come to church not only to be fed but to feed others. I've been here a long time, and it's the most exciting thing that ever happened in our church."

To feed others means that the church's role on behalf of the community always includes the proclamation of the gospel, that is, the unconditional promise and claim of God's love. Laity are inevitably part of this proclamation through the lives they lead and through their various efforts to engage others in the work of God through the gospel invitation and mandate.

As a result of the gospel's invitation and demand the church's engagement in the community can take at least two shapes. One is the alleviation of suffering and the other is the elevation of suffrage.

The alleviation of suffering is what Peter Berger called "Christian diaconate," "the helping outreach of the Christian community to individuals in distress—those suffering from illness, poverty, or other personal difficulties."[12] This can cover an incredible range of "doing the work of God" either as individuals, task groups, or ecumenical efforts related to hunger, housing, health care, AIDS, the aging, children, suicide prevention, and prison ministries. Obviously the specifics will vary with rural and urban settings and with the particular issues and needs in a given area.

The elevation of suffrage is what Berger calls "Christian action," "any attempt not only to deal with individuals, but also to try to modify the social structure itself."[13] The elevation of suffrage suggests the work of the church on behalf of social justice, that is, for human rights and dignity in our various social, political, and economic systems, all of which are under the rule of God's sovereign love. We need to recall that the prophet Amos said, "Let justice [not charity] roll down like waters . . ." (Amos 5:24). The alleviation of suffering, on the other hand, is more akin to charity and social service. Both constitute an expression of love for neighbor grounded in God's love for us all.

These community ministries extend the church beyond itself into local and global realities. They may be short-lived or ongoing for years. They may call for prophetic risk in taking unpopular stands. Whatever the specifics the laity is involved. We are now beginning to see why the laity could have the toughest job in the church. And the plot will thicken.

Family and Home

Maybe your most important ministry is learning to be a parent. You may be a parent to one or more children, a parent to a bedridden or Alzheimer's parent, or a single parent (who constitute at least 20 percent of all families in the United States). Maybe your domestic family now is just yourself, either as a surviving spouse or a single person. Longevity, along with other factors, has changed our definition of family in the last several decades. In chapter 1 I spoke of living out the liturgy in the world. What does it mean to live out confession, celebration, and commitment on the domestic scene?

The church is one of the few agencies having access to families and thus to persons at various age levels. Our deepest emotions and strongest hopes are frequently involved at home. Much is at stake for society in the stability and creativity of marriage and family, as well as the well-being of single persons. For these reasons the church has an unusual opportunity to assist people to mature in relationships and to better grasp family dynamics.

There are many resources at our disposal. For some families with adults and children the Sunday worship experience may be one of the few shared activities. The sacred story is remembered and provides a framework of vision and values for life. In many communities a variety of resource people are available for the educational ministry of the church. And the pastoral work of both laity and clergy can offer support in times of trouble and sorrow. Applying our understanding of faith to our most intimate relationships is not easy but it can be immensely rewarding.

Work

What does it mean for advertising agents, truck drivers, computer analysts, stockbrokers, farmers, salespeople to take the gospel seriously at work? This is where it is especially difficult to relate the gospel to daily life. As a clergyman I can at least relate a good deal of my daily activity to some dimension of the gospel. Pastoral work includes calling in hospitals, offering hope or a listening ear in counseling, working on a lesson or sermon, preparing to administer the sacrament, and the like. We all know that pastors can go stale or get lost in routine but there are discernible connections with faith. As a teacher I prepare lectures, counsel with students, and try to do my part in the overall service of the seminary. I can "theologize" this. But what if I were a taxi driver or a bellman in a local hotel? Or a domestic maid? Or a sanitation worker? The theologizing gets tougher.

Most of our seminary students today are second-career persons. They come from all walks of life. Naturally they are enthusiastic about the call to ordained ministry that compelled them to uproot self and family and head for seminary. I like to ask them, "What do you see as Christian ministry in the setting or position you've left to come to seminary?" If they have no answer, I tell them they have work to do. By the time they graduate from seminary they will need sensitivity, if not an answer, to the question. Otherwise they will be in a poor position to empower the laity. How can a minister implement ministry not even imagined or conceived?

There is not room here to develop a vision of work ministries for laity. There are many excellent sources available.[14] Suffice it to say that much work needs to be done for most laity to make connections between their faith and their work. Many laity initially think this involves only something about evangelizing co-workers. I am certainly in favor of sharing our faith with others. But what about ministries of presence, of listening, of advocacy, of fairness? There are faith-related possibilities in work but they vary greatly according to circumstance.

It is not my contention that every lay person should be actively engaged in all four settings. Retirement, health, personal circumstances, and other factors will influence or determine our ministry settings. I do believe each person is called to find his or her challenge of ministry and to develop and give that gift to others as

God calls each of us to do. Our ministries are frequently more faithful and more effective when clearly focused and practiced.

There are some persons who due to health constraints are unable to be in worship or in the wider community of activity and work. I do wish to affirm their ministry of prayer and example for others. I owe more than I can say in print to many shut-ins and convalescents whom I was privileged to visit during my seminary days and through fifteen years of local church pastoral ministry. They have handled limitations with grace and have taught me invaluable lessons of faith and courage. Perhaps their ministry is the toughest of all. In many of these courageous souls I have encountered the living Christ and my faith is the better for it.

I suspect that many denominations have vows of membership something like the United Methodist Church. In so many words, we promise to uphold the church with our prayers, gifts, services, and attendance.[15] In my mind this type of vow, unless interpreted by a sophisticated theological mind, tends to be weighted toward the institutional church side of ministry. As I have already said, this is one of four crucial settings for lay ministry, and if it is not taken seriously we are going to have a quickly crippled church. But it is only one out of four. Vows of church membership should point to all four settings of ministry as possibility and challenge as appropriate. As it is, our vows may promote an insular and narrow concept of the church's ministry.

The Two Sides of Witness: Exhaustion and Exhilaration

I expect that long before this point you have raised the question, "You make it sound as though the way of witness is some kind of certain upbeat, life-saving experience of faith renewal. But what about burnout? What about exasperation and exhaustion and wondering if it's all worth the effort? When do we talk about discouragement in and about the whole process?"

Now it is time to reflect on both sides of the way of witness. I've been careful to avoid suggesting any guarantee of faith renewal and deepening, yet until now I have addressed the biblical and contemporary "positives" of commitment to compassion, justice, and love.

There is no question that Christian ministry in whatever form or ecclesiastical framework can lead to alienation, cynicism, and emotional and physical depletion. Anyone who claims otherwise is naive, inexperienced in the faith, or given to Pollyanna analyses of ministry.

There are many discernible reasons for exhaustion in doing the work of God. Some reasons are hidden in the complexities of our emotional and spiritual makeup. Sometimes we allow unrealistic expectations consciously or subconsciously to demand measurable results, or perhaps demonstrative recognition. However, a great deal of ministry is not easily tabulated in tangible measurements. Recognition is often hidden in the values of the work itself.

Neither visible improvements nor ready rewards are likely to be forthcoming in ministry with Alzheimer's or advanced oncology patients. Prison ministries do not usually yield easy successes. Work with refugee asylum cases is a very low-percentage ministry in terms of court victories. When our compassion begins to wear thin, it may be time to switch gears to the way of the will for replenishment of faith. Perhaps the Eucharist or sermon or song will refresh us for the struggle. Or if circumstances permit we might open ourselves to surprises from creation or the wonder of art in various forms. Yet again, as we shall see in chapter 5, there may be recovery through the welcome of significant others, either individually or in a group. I have heard more than one person say, in effect, "To continue in the struggle for justice I need some sense of inner serenity and strength."

In peace and justice issues, as well as in many individual ministries, victories can be few and far between. Seemingly impossible tasks call for our dedication: world disarmament, equitable distribution of the world's goods, the elimination of torture, racism, sexism, and ageism, the protection of the environment. It has been said many times that social activists of the sixties burned out because they did not have sufficient faith or spiritual roots. I do not know to what extent this is true. What I do know is that we are not engaged with these issues just because the percentages are in our favor.

Insofar as we are able to be sustained in these seemingly intractable matters it is because God keeps calling us back and calling us forward in God's love. If we stay on with the impossible it is because with God all things are possible and because there are colleagues whose spirit ministers to ours. On many occasions I've realized that the people with whom I have been privileged to associate in peace and justice issues have made it all more than worthwhile.

Even so there are times when our faith energy and our physical energy are depleted. We may need to retreat for a while and resume the struggle later, or we may need to give ourselves to ministry more compatible with our physical and emotional requirements. There are times, and we do well to recognize them, when we are not strong enough to handle much in the way of risk and vulnerability. This is no cause for guilt or shame. Christ himself needed time away now and then to collect himself and to sort out the direction of his life and ministry.

Sometimes our spirits decline because we have fallen victim to a paternalistic attitude toward those whom we seek to serve or care about. Many of us who have been privileged to travel in El Salvador have received lifelong gifts of love, courage, joy, and hope from *campesinos* who live in poverty, under constant threat of harassment and death from the Salvadoran military. And how many times have we had the experience of visiting a critically ill friend and discovering that we were the recipient of ministry, rather than the minister?

There is yet another reason why doing the work of God can exhaust and exasperate us. It has to do with the nature of the gospel itself. We serve the vulnerable–victorious Lord. The gospel inevitably exposes us to personal risk. How many times have we heard someone say, "I tried reaching out and I got hurt. I tried being vulnerable and I got ripped off. I tried being Christian and I got taken advantage of." The fact is that piety does not insure personal protection. Even as we insist that vulnerability is to be freely chosen on behalf of others and not forced on us by others or by a masochistic understanding of the gospel, the gospel taken seriously still means risk at some point or another.

Scripture is full of stories in which God's favor leads to more difficulty, not less. Uncertain journeys ("Noah, make yourself an ark . . ."); civil disobedience ("Shiprah and Puah, disobey Pharaoh by letting the male Hebrew children live"); terrifying responsibilities ("Moses, go down to Egypt to Pharaoh and bring forth my people"); overwhelming duties ("Jeremiah, you are appointed a prophet to the nations"); astonishing and uncertain futures ("Mary, the Holy Spirit will come upon you and you will bear a son who will be called Son of the Most High").

The gospel also exposes us to the suffering of others. A seminary student once remarked that theological education is like having all your nerve endings exposed. You can never be the same again because you are made aware of injustice, pain and hurt as never before. There is given to us (inflicted upon us?) a heightened awareness and sensitivity calling us to lean into the world's sorrow and pain.

The Suffering Servant–Risen Christ taps many nerves in our lives. For some the journey into the world's suffering and cruelty is too much to bear. A friend once raised the question about preaching, "How do we know when too much light is revealed, destroying personal defenses and rendering people emotionally destroyed or damaged?" Sometimes the constant invitation and demand for self-giving vis-à-vis the gospel becomes a vehicle for self-punishment or the grounds for letting others take advantage of us.

The truth is that the gospel is unsettling to us all. At times we ask, "How can we really celebrate when so many are in misery and possibly without hope?" The gospel's commitment to justice can so command our allegiance that we are tempted toward hatred for those who oppress justice, unless we remember the command to love.

In the final analysis we are led back to the Amazing Grace and trust in that grace. In the final analysis we are led back to the theme of faithfulness, knowing that we live and move and have our being in God's world and thus in God's unconditional and everlasting love. The way of witness is neither less nor more than the way of Jesus Christ. It does not promise ease, success, or victory in terms of the world. It does not guarantee emotional or physical health, even if there are many who in fact may be healthier due to their faith. The way of witness offers the recurring possibility of giving and receiving in the way of Christ, and thus participating in the life of God.

QUESTIONS FOR REFLECTION

1. What are some of your experiences in which God became real in the doing of God's work?
2. Can you recall times when the way of witness wholly exhausted you and drove you into other ways of faith renewal?
3. How do you see your own ministry in the four contexts suggested in this chapter?

5

The Way of Welcome: Experiencing God in Others

The winds of grace are always blowing,
and they carry the presence of God
in relationship with others
(sometimes friends,
sometimes strangers).

The gospel is a saving event that occurs in human relations and is not a body of knowledge for mere verbal transmission.

Reuel L. Howe[1]

The way of welcome is the presence of God in human interaction and relationships. This notion should not seem strange to persons of biblical faith. God frequently speaks and acts through human relationships in scripture. Indeed, the New Testament proclaims that God is fully known in a person of history, Jesus of Nazareth. As has often been said, in the New Testament God is revealed not in a doctrine, an idea, or a philosophical principle, but in a flesh and blood person.

Once again it may be helpful to compare and contrast.

If the Way of the Will Is . . .	*The Way of Wonder Is . . .*
seeking and striving	serendipity
intention	integration
concentration and cultivation	creation-centered

The Way of Witness Is . . .	*The Way of Welcome Is . . .*
service	significant others
implementation	interpersonal
commitment and compassion	community and connectedness

The God and Neighbor Connection

"All real life is meeting."[2] This well-known phrase from the Jewish philosopher Martin Buber provides the foundation for whole fields of theological, philosophical, and psychological inquiry and wisdom. Life is relational, connectional, and grounded in community. Studies abound in the crucial significance of human touch in the initial stage of life. If we are not welcomed into the world by loving care expressed in touch and spoken word, our development is likely to be difficult and uncertain. Paul Tillich said that we speak and relate only because we already have received words and relationship.

Recent prenatal studies emphasize the relation of the fetus to the psychological and emotional condition of the mother. Thus, even before we are born our womb environment is relational and highly important for our future. A friendly and caring welcome into the world is a grace on which we are dependent from our very beginning and for a good beginning at that.

The sacrament of infant baptism, which I like to call our "I.D.

card," proclaims the unconditional grace of God for the child and in one way or another proclaims the inclusion of the child in the Christian community. At the same time the congregation in most denominations responds with a welcome that includes a commitment or pledge of Christian nurture and example in concert with the parents of the child. In a sense the congregation becomes an agent for the grace of God and an advocate for the gospel in the ongoing nurture of the child.

In this covenant, then, the church sees the image of God in the life of the child and the growing child might well see the image of God in the body of Christ, that is, the body of believers. The scriptures have an intriguing (and sometimes disturbing!) way of seeing God and our neighbor as inseparably bound to each other. For example, recall the account in Genesis 32 of Jacob's nocturnal wrestling match in the wilderness near the river Jabbok. Elie Wiesel, the Holocaust theologian, compares this enigmatic narrative with a mystical poem, mysterious from beginning to end, in which every question brings forth another.[3] God and humanity seem inextricably bound to each other. The text uses the word *ish*, "man" (also translated "someone" by some scholars). According to Wiesel, the Midrash and its commentators elevate the naming of the wrestling partner to the rank of angel.[4] And Jacob asserts, "I have seen *God* face to face, and yet my life is preserved" (Gen. 32:30; italics mine). Earlier in the text the wrestling partner confirms Jacob's appraisal by asserting, "You have striven with God *and* with men [sic], and have prevailed" (v. 28; italics mine).

In the very next chapter Jacob and Esau have their encounter after many years of separation. In this emotional reunion Jacob declares: "For truly to see your face is like seeing the face of God, with such favor have you received me" (33:10). Combined with the wrestling encounter in the previous chapter, these narratives suggest that to wrestle with God is to wrestle with human relationships, and vice versa. The two cannot be separated.

The classic Christian expression of the inseparability of God and neighbor is declared in the parable of the Last Judgment in Matthew 25 (see chapter 4). We are told by Jesus that what we do or do not do "to one of the least of these" we do or do not do to Jesus himself. When we welcome the stranger, we welcome Jesus Christ. When we are insensitive and rejecting of those in need, we reject Christ himself. For those who acknowledge that Jesus is the Christ, that is, a decisive expression or incarnation of God, the connection is unmistakable.

These initial reflections suggest the possibilities for perceiving God's presence in our neighbor and our neighbor as an instrument of God's presence.

The remainder of this chapter will focus on three dimensions of the way of welcome: the grace of God in personal friendship; the grace of God in Christian community; and the grace of God in strangers. While the emphasis in this chapter is on our formation through both personal and group relationships, it will be obvious that the way of welcome intersects with ways already mentioned. Again, the various winds of grace and ways of faith are inseparable but distinguishable.

The Grace of God in Personal Friendship

To be a friend may mean to be the most important person in the world to someone else over a period of years.[5]

To imagine life without friends is next to impossible for most of us. Profoundly unfortunate is the person who has not known the acceptance, support, generosity, loyalty, and trust which is found in the give and take of friendship. Sometimes friends have comforted us, sometimes clarified important personal matters or issues, sometimes confronted us with a fresh dimension of truth, and of course, occasionally deeply disappointed us as we have them.

Whatever mysteries and unexamined features there may be connected with friendships, one fact is clear: our lives more than likely have been immeasurably enriched and strengthened by friends. In *Just Friends: The Role of Friendship in Our Lives*, Lillian R. Rubin provides this overview of the role of friends:

Whether child or adult, it is friends who provide a reference outside the family against which to measure and judge ourselves; who help us during passages that require our separation and individuation; who support us as we adapt to new roles and new rules; who heal the hurts and make good the deficits of other relationships in our lives; who offer the place and encouragement for the development of parts of self that, for whatever reasons, are inaccessible in the family context. It's with friends that we test our sense of self-in-the-world, that our often inchoate, intuitive, unarticulated vision of the possibilities of a self-yet-to-become finds expression.[6]

A few verbal and written statements stick with us from the very first time we hear or read them. Such is the case with Reuel Howe's statement at the beginning of this chapter. It stood out for me above everything else in his book *The Miracle of Dialogue.* Important as are preaching and naming the gospel in words and other forms of verbal transmission, there can be no substitute for love and acceptance in the incarnational form of significant others, whether family or friends.[7]

The grace of God represented in friendship takes many forms. Sometimes the word of forgiveness. Sometimes a sustaining and loving presence. Sometimes encouragement to risk for others and thus a confirmation of the gifts God has given. Sometimes just being with another in mutuality of interests and enjoyment. In friendship there is grace shared in both giving and receiving. We become and remain selves only in relationship.

Most of us can name one or more significant other(s) through whom God's grace has come in crucial ways. Maybe one or both parents or relatives who affirmed our selfhood. Perhaps a teacher who opened a whole new vista of life. Or a friend with whom we have been able to share deeply. A spouse as best friend through the years. Perhaps a mosaic of these and other gifts of relationships. And perhaps we also have been on the giving end of these "saving events," for friendship has to do with being a friend as well as having friends.

As we are open to the presence and saving action of God by

intentionality (the way of the will), through a stance toward the creation (the way of wonder), and through doing the work of God (the way of witness), so the way of welcome bids us to experience the grace of God in human relationships. We cannot force friendship, much less the nurturing and sustaining action of God therein, but we can encourage the risk of giving and receiving in friendship which opens the door to God's grace.

If all real living is meeting, as Buber pointed out, then in ways beyond our calculation God is present. Friendship can be a vehicle of grace, pointing beyond itself to a more ultimate Presence. Friendship embodies acceptance, thus affirming a sense of "somebodiness" in a disposable culture. When we define spiritual classics, we should point beyond great literature to the great moments of life-giving relationships which are with us and in us all of our days. These relationships are basic to our development as human beings. Their importance is underscored when death separates a friendship and we feel the irreparable void as though part of ourselves has died.

In these paragraphs I am using the term "grace" to indicate "a saving event that occurs in human relations," a saving event or a series of events without which we cannot form a sense of self and personal identity. At its best the grace or saving event in human relations points us in the direction of "being for others" out of gratitude to God for the gift of life. And this leads us to the second emphasis of this chapter.

The Grace of God in Christian Community

The Holy Spirit touches the human spirit through certain kinds of old friends.[8]

In Christian community God seeks to give direction, definition and disclosure to relationship. In spite of the critical importance of friends there is no guarantee that friendship involves anything remotely close to a value system characterized by religious sensibility. For example, friendship among skinheads, or neo-Nazis, to use two among many possible illustrations, can hardly be referred to as the grace of God in the same sense as friendship with some genuine sense of religious values. Friendship that functions as a protective circle of selfishness with no concern for public good hardly qualifies as relationship rooted in the Torah or in Jesus Christ.

In Christian community personal identity is not defined by self-fulfillment as such, but by becoming our deepest and truest selves for God and for others. In living our lives for justice and love inherent in the rule of God, we come to know God, life in the world, and ourselves at the deepest level.

The term "welcome" does not appear in the Old Testament and only infrequently in the New Testament. Almost the same can be said about the word "hospitality," although it and its derivatives do appear a number of times in the New Testament. But both terms denote key customs and realities in both testaments.

In Romans 15 Paul, speaking to some internal problems in the church, urges the members to "welcome one another, therefore, just as Christ has welcomed you, for the glory of God" (15:7). It is not unusual for Paul to address quarreling factions and a judgmental attitude in the church with an appeal for generosity and magnanimity based on God's acceptance of each person. Earlier in the epistle he has reminded his flock that Christ died for the ungodly while they were yet sinners. Paul is not here arguing for uniformity but for generosity of spirit amid sharp differences of opinion and practice. John Wesley, in his sermon *Catholic Spirit,* urged his followers to love alike even if they could not be of one opinion or thought.

The theme of welcoming each other is closely related to the biblical practice of hospitality. In chapter 12 Paul has provided some directions for Christian life in the body of Christ. Included is the call to "contribute to the needs of the saints, *practice hospitality*" (v. 13; italics mine). God's hospitality is an essential part of Jesus' message as it reflects the divine generosity. The parables of the Good Samaritan and the prodigal son suggest the extravagant nature of God's welcome and hospitality.

The New Testament message of welcome and hospitality was not an idle theoretical matter. In the first century Christians were often in need of hospitality. Many inns were often either disreputable or beyond the means of Christians on the road. Travel was risky and uncertain at best. Jesus and the early disciples and missionaries were dependent on hospitality for daily care and lodging. In this historical setting hospitality was the chief bond between churches.

In the New Testament church the work of hospitality was obviously the task of the whole congregation. Care for other members of the body of Christ, whether local or itinerant, was not primarily the responsibility of clergy as we have tended to make it in our time. If the New Testament practice of hospitality is translated today to mean the care and nurture of the Christian flock, then we need to return to the paradigm of the early church to fully recognize and unleash the gifts of the people of God.

When we hear the term "pastoral care" we most likely think of the work of the clergy. They carry out the hospital-ity calls and visits. Why? Because congregations hire or accept appointed clergy to do the work of caring. This narrow paradigm of "clergy equals pastoral care" is being rethought today. More churches are waking up to the fact that the loving, learning capacity of the laity is the most important gift God gives the church. Hospitality is increasingly seen as the calling of the whole people of God inherent in the sacrament of baptism. Recently an ordained minister told me about the most exciting new ministry in the congregation he serves: the ministry of communion bearers. It seemed to come about from pragmatic necessity rather than theological reflection, but at least it is happening. The clergyman discovered that he simply could not take the Eucharist to all the people in the hospital or who were convalescing at home from various debilities. So now eight to ten laypersons have been prepared to be communion bearers to those unable to come to the worship service. Following the worship service when the Eucharist is celebrated the lay bearers gather for a brief time of prayer and sending-forth. They represent the congregation as they go forth to extend the hospitality of Jesus Christ to hospitalized persons. The Eucharistic experience has been greatly enriched for both the lay communion bearers and the lay recipients. Other acts of lay outreach can be encouraged in denominations in which by church law laity do not offer communion.

In the giving and receiving of welcome and hospitality, we meet the living Christ. The hospitality of the church has been a key factor for many of us in shaping our selfhood and our values. But when I say church I'm not speaking of a theoretical or amorphous entity. I'm talking about flesh-and-blood brothers and sisters whose welcome and witness individually and collectively have shaped the very core of my life. As Dietrich Bonhoeffer put it, "God has willed that we should seek and find God's living Word in the witness of a brother."[9]

In June 1959 I was appointed to a "vacant lot" on the east side of Dallas to start a new congregation. I served as pastor for eight years in the congregation that became St. Stephen Methodist Church. In the early days of the congregation a small group of women began to meet to play bridge. Soon the husbands became part of a monthly dinner meeting in one of the homes. Eight couples. Thirty years later the group still meets on a regular basis. We seldom play bridge anymore. (Some of the group, but not all, look back and playfully say "that was when we had no depth"!)

Children have grown up. Grandchildren have been born. Many changes have occurred. Some of us have moved away and then moved back and today we are scattered throughout the Dallas area. Still we meet. When one of the group asked at one of our meetings, "What keeps this group together?" another replied, "We all agree on everything." We broke up in wild laughter.

In May 1988 we lost our first member to death. When we gathered after her death we wistfully said, "We're still a bridge group . . . a bridge over time and a bridge over troubled waters." In May 1989 two of the husbands died within a week of one another. These were the most difficult funerals at which I have ever officiated, but they were true celebrations of lives that were self-giving in the best sense. Still we meet. Now I'm teased as being the "oldest living groupie." What keeps the group together? Shared memories and experience. Concern for each other. Desire to support each other. Humor amid situations of pathos. Freedom to differ amid mutual appreciation. We will continue to dwindle over the years but in the meantime we rejoice in life and give thanks that love is stronger than death. I call it Christian community.

Friendship in the Christian community is based on the Word made Flesh. My baptism continues to tell me my basic identity and purpose in life. I was baptized into the Word but it happened through family and friends who were my parents and my pastor. Nurture came through church school teachers who served as friends in the faith. I am indebted to countless brothers and sisters past and present for touching me with the living Word of loving encouragement and correction. Ultimate vision and meaning have come my way through the church, and that means through human beings caught up in the Word. No one could ever convince me that God is not at work through the welcome and hospitality of friends in the Christian community.

The way of welcome and hospitality releases us from loveless-ness and loneliness. As we have been welcomed and affirmed, we are freed to reach out to others. Every preacher knows that sermons proclaiming God's love already have two strikes against them if the person in the pew has been shortchanged on the experience of being loved and affirmed by others. Naming is important but cannot substitute for the reality. The way of welcome is the experiential base for God's saving grace. In the Christian community it is, we hope, both named and experienced.

The Grace of God in Strangers

> Every friend we now cherish
> was once a stranger.

"In our world the assumption is that strangers are a potential danger and that it is up to them to disprove it."[10] Few readers would disagree with these sentiments. Newspapers and television bombard us constantly with the latest acts of violence, sometimes by persons who are strangers to the victims and other times by acquaintances or even family, as is the case with domestic violence. We hear of children swept off the street by an unknown assailant. Homicides of every description flood the news. Robberies and thefts abound. The escalation of crime creates an "on-guard," wary mentality.

The grace of God in strangers? We will want to look closely at what we mean by strangers, the implications of welcoming strangers, and how the grace of God might be present. Some strands of biblical tradition can serve as our guide.

The entertainment of a stranger as a guest was recognized as a sacred duty in the Mediterranean world. In the Old Testament the Deuteronomic requirements call upon the Israelites to love the sojourner because "the LORD your God . . . loves the sojourner, giving him food and clothing" (Deut. 10:17–18). After all, the passage continues, "you were sojourners in the land of Egypt" (v. 19). A sojourner in Israel was an "almost" Israelite, dependent on the bond of Israel's hospitality, bound by Israel's regulations, yet a person not indigenous to Israel. To this day the seder feast of Judaism is not complete without a guest to share in the occasion.

In the New Testament the teachings of Jesus provide a profound dimension to the concept of welcoming the stranger. Again and again the outcast is embraced in the love of God, an insistence that reaches its most poignant power in the parable of the Last Judgment: "I was a stranger and you welcomed me" (Matt. 25:35).

Words of *xen-* stem in New Testament Greek can mean "foreign" or "strange" but also "guest." Our word "xenophobia" comes from this Greek root and indicates an irrational fear of strangers. Some sources claim that xenophobia is the most widespread form of racism in today's world. Love of the *xenos* is a special form of love of neighbor. In the Matthew 25 parable (vs. 31–46) Jesus himself is the *xenos* (stranger), so that "in the most alien of aliens Jesus himself is loved."[11]

Welcome or hospitality overcomes the alienation between the world of difference and thus makes "a world of difference" based on friendship. God's unconditional love or *agape* is the ultimate source and motivation for welcoming the stranger.

When we think of ourselves as welcoming strangers we probably think mostly of the risk for us. But the biblical tradition brings yet another twist in claiming that in the act of welcoming we may receive more than we give. "Old and New Testament stories not only show how serious our obligation is to welcome the stranger in our home, but they also tell us that guests are carrying precious gifts with them which they are eager to reveal to a receptive host."[12] The author of Hebrews lifts up this truth: "Do not neglect to show hospitality to strangers, for thereby some have entertained angels unawares" (13:2).

Welcoming the Stranger Today

When we consider the story of the Good Samaritan for today we know instinctively that its application has to do with more than assisting a wounded person on the highway. It is a narrative of extravagant love involving a hero alien to the Israelites. In the "reversal style" typical of so many biblical stories, there is unlimited risk which offends our prudent self-protection. And by a Samaritan, of all people! The implications reach far beyond the road from Jerusalem to Jericho in the first century (see Luke 10:29–37).

In a similar way the biblical tradition of welcoming strangers is a much broader concept than "who's coming to dinner" or how we respond to a street person's request for a handout. As we translate from biblical times to our culture, welcoming the stranger has to do with our basic attitudes and actions toward those who are unlike us, at least on the surface. It has to do with experiencing the world of difference and whether or not we are open to receiving the gifts that marginal people have to offer. It has to do with the way we respond to those whose positions or actions we abhor. It has to do with our willingness to expand our horizons of learning and our openness to listen to those who are not supposed to have anything to say worth hearing.

Perhaps I can best bring this home by sharing some of my own faith pilgrimage. Welcoming the stranger for me has been a series of eye- and ear-opening connections with persons who do not represent the dominant white male culture. Several vignettes will make this evolutionary journey yet more specific.

Vignette One

A ten-day trip for a lifetime, we called it afterwards. Twelve of us travel to El Salvador on an educational seminar. Our group sees the poverty of the people and hears story after story of oppression and harassment, even bombing, by the Salvadoran military. We worship with a Roman Catholic congregation in a structure built by the people. Afterward the priest and the lay leaders tell us of the community's work. This includes reading and interpreting the Bible in terms of the reality of the people and leading workshops in practical skills like sewing and in improvements in health, housing, and literacy. Anyone organizing for decent living conditions is considered subversive by the treasury police. Four of the police, armed with automatic rifles, appear at one of the barrio worship services attended by members of our seminar group. The lay people tell us, "Those who meet to discuss the Word of God are watched. Sometimes as a result of evangelization you can disappear and end up in a trash dump. We are called agitators and subversives."

One more thing from this vignette. Members of the parish offer us food and drink amid their poverty. There are some meals that one does not forget. As they welcomed us as strangers, we welcomed them into our hearts and lives. What gifts they offered us! Friendship. Food. Faith. Hope. Love. Strangers no longer strange.

Some of our group return home saying that for the first time they know what it means to be born again. Another wears a cross for the first time, a small black cross worn as a daily reminder of the crucifixion of the people taking place in the country called The Savior. I come home with a renewed sense of "apostolic compulsion," a term I had long forgotten, yet now remembered from seminary. Only at the price of my soul can I not fulfill my unwritten covenant with the people of El Salvador to speak out on their behalf.

Vignette Two

In the class of eleven students there are four white males, one male from another continent, two African-American males, one Hispanic male, and three white females. MN-7300 we call it, otherwise known as one of the second-year preaching units at Perkins School of Theology. I playfully call the unit "How to Preach Prophetically and Keep Your Appointment—Hopefully!" In the process of the semester the group playfully calls itself "the radical preaching group."

Our particular interest is developing our concern and our talents for a pulpit sensitive to the social conscience of the Bible. As we discuss and hear sermons related to refugees, people with AIDS, peace with justice, violence in our society, race relations, the prison system, persons with handicapping conditions, we realize that to consider issues is to consider people. Especially suffering people. Especially strangers or those whose world is not our daily world, yet *is our world.* In the movie *A Dry White Season*, an affluent Afrikaner family struggles to relate to the oppression and injustice of the system toward their black gardener and his family. The Afrikaner's wife says to her husband: "This is *their* problem." The husband replies, "No, this is *our* problem, too." Our homiletical homework connects us with people frequently invisible to us. As we interpret the conditions of suffering people, so we exegete the gospel's gift to and demand of us all.

There is more. The more is the variety of experience resident in the class. To some extent it is a microcosm of the world. The women tend to see from a different perspective. Do you males see how Abraham made Sarah expendable in Egypt (Gen. 12)? The ethnic and international students bring their perspective born of experience. Is the leper in Mark 1 no more than an individual in need or does he represent in today's message the masses of invisible *campesinos* in Latin America? We get in touch with what we bring to the text. We experience conflict in interpretations and in different views about inclusive language. All in all it is a great learning possibility, not like when I was in seminary. We were nearly all white males without the agitating benefit of other points of view! I keep repeating, "Remember, God loves us enough to disturb us. And believe it or not, that blessed disturbance is our profoundest hope." We might even learn to welcome strangers and thus angels unaware.

Vignette Three

It is the 1970s. I begin to read all kinds of so-called liberation theologies—feminist, African-American, and Latin American. I want to listen to these theologies representing the underside because I am convinced that my relationship to Jesus Christ is closely connected with the outcast, the poor, the downtrodden, the relatively invisible. The themes of liberation theologies—dignity, freedom, peace with justice, release from cultural stereotypes, humane systems, inclusiveness, a global perspective—all rooted in the rule of God, are deeply rooted in the prophets and in Jesus Christ.

These readings build on many experiences during the sixties with blacks or African-Americans in civil rights activities. I get a view into the world of the black community by listening and conversing and by participating in neighborhood and church partnerships. I realize a deep affection for black worship—the lively music, the powerful choirs, the rapport between preacher and people.

I begin to see from the viewpoints of people previously unheard. I look then and now at my society and see what a white male world is producing—billions for military hardware, decaying urban areas, manipulation of financial institutions, Contragate and drug scams, bankrolling a brutal and corrupt Salvadoran military. I recall the statement of a sister who said she has never been made to feel afraid on the street by the presence of women. I see the environment in critical distress from all kinds of pollution.

So I say, "We need some new approaches." We need a new order, a new dispensation of priorities that are humane and life-giving. Perhaps if we learn to welcome the strangers, those who are unlike the dominant culture, we will forge a future worth having. So I'm a perpetual student seeking alternative visions and possibilities. Some of them seem to be coming from "the other side." I believe it is the movement of the Holy Spirit in our time of history.

Vignette Four

Recently I've been exposed to a variety of environmentalists. Some are Christian, some are Buddhists. It continues to be an education. Why is it so difficult for people, including myself, to get excited about and committed to environments? Maybe the threat does not seem immediate even when it is. Maybe the destruction of the ozone layer is so terrible and irrevocable a prospect that we cannot bring ourselves to feel concern and to act. Maybe some other causes seem more focused and manageable.

But I tell you this. The smug assumption that we Christians do not really have much to learn from brothers and sisters in other religions is out of date and flat wrong. For example, some of our Buddhist friends have long maintained a deep love and respect for the earth. By and large the track record of Christians on the environment leaves much to be desired. For that matter, we can discover an environmental future by traveling into the past and listening to generations of Native Americans. If we do not welcome the worldview of those who are "strangers" to our dominant society, our children may not have a world to view. Chief Seattle's speech (cited in chapter 2) is a place to start. Paul warned us a long time ago that God will destroy the wisdom of the worldly wise and thwart the cleverness of the clever. It is happening today.

Vignette Five

One of our favorite vacation sites is Aspen, Colorado. We've returned there again and again. On this occasion my wife and I are at the Aspen Art Museum reading about a sculpture by Ann Sperry called *Sometimes It Takes Forty Years.* The sculpture itself is in the pond at the Aspen Music School. The story behind the sculpture intrigues us. It seems that the artist was visiting Stuart Mace, a longtime area resident known as an environmentalist, among other things. As they walked in the valley Mace discovered a plant he had never seen in his many years in that area. He said it takes just the right conditions of climate and moisture and seeding for that plant to grow. "Sometimes it takes forty years," he said.

And so it is with certain areas of our own growth. Some things take longer than others due to the absence of just the right conditions. Sometimes the right conditions involve knowing "the stranger" as a human being instead of a statistic or a stereotype. When that happens it can be a freeing experience for all concerned.

In our society gay and lesbian persons have been treated as strangers not to be welcomed. For a long time I was aware that while I wanted my words and actions to be clear on behalf of liberation and justice for heterosexual ethnic minorities, women, and people of the so-called Third World, I remained silent for the most part when it came to gays and lesbians. The journey looks like this: As a pastor in the 1960s and early '70s I become increasingly aware of mistreatment and injustice toward gays and lesbians. I start to ask myself why the church has been cruel and rejecting in many ways when we profess love for all people. Later as a seminary administrator and now as a seminary professor I am present at convocations where I hear that capable and committed lesbians and gays are fired from their staff positions. I think, "The church should do better than this. Why are we treating persons of different sexual orientation as lepers when Jesus receives the stranger of every description?"

Along the way I read a variety of views, but more importantly I converse with professed gays and lesbians. As a heterosexual I become aware that there is as much difference of personality, lifestyle, and values within the homosexual community as within the heterosexual. I reflect on the fact that through personal friendship I now know that many gays and lesbians are as committed— sometimes more so—to peace and justice, to love for the earth, to qualities of compassion and mercy as are my heterosexual friends. Regardless of sexual orientation and regardless of views on issues, we are *all* children of God and loved by God.

Presently I am connected through worship and commitment with a United Methodist congregation where I was pastor from 1967 to 1973. The church has received a number of professed gays into membership. I am convinced that those members who have indicated being disturbed by the presence of our new members have not had or made the opportunity for personal conversation and friendship with gay persons. The fact is that our congregational life is enriched through their gifts to the music ministry, occasional participation in the children's sermon, and human friendship.

What is clear to me is that the gospel calls us as grace-dependent sinners to welcome the stranger. There is no warrant in the life or message of Jesus for self-righteousness; there *is* warrant for hospitality and friendship. It is time for the church to cease rejecting persons because of their sexual preferences and to speak and act a clear word of justice, love and welcome in the name of Jesus Christ, the champion of those regarded by the society as outcasts and lepers.

Vignette Reflection

The gospel itself is a stranger in our world. There was no place in the inn, so the Stranger was born away in a manger. There was no place at home in Bethlehem, so the Stranger became a refugee fleeing Herod's oppression. There was no place in the Nazareth synagogue for this One set for the fall and the rising of many in Israel, so the hometown Stranger was cast out of the synagogue and out of the city. There was no room in the religious establishment, so the Stranger who welcomed strangers was despised and rejected. There was no place in the centers of political power for the Prince of Peace and the Champion of Justice, so the whole battalion of soldiers stripped the Stranger and put a scarlet robe upon him and put a crown of thorns on his head and put a reed in his right hand. Kneeling before him they mocked him, spat upon him, and took the reed and struck him on the head and led him away to crucify him.[13]

The gospel of strangers, of those from "the other side" or "the underside," can liberate us from our narrow perspective and our many prejudices. Strangers can challenge our attachment to the values of the dominant culture and lead us into a deeper participation in the kingdom or rule of God in our time. My most profound epiphanies over the past quarter century usually have resulted from connections with the "unlike me" people through literature, lectures, and personal engagement. Along with the Bible, for devotional purposes, I read such material as *The Gospel in Art by the Peasants of Solentiname*.[14] This punctures the presumptions of much academic theology and exposes me to a commonsense gospel interpretation in words and in art by people of different color, nationality, class, and circumstance. I read *I Dream A World, Portraits of Black Women Who Changed America*. This book, named after Langston Hughes's poem, is particularly exciting to me because it is the work of a white male photographer who spent two years photographing and interviewing 75 extraordinary black women. His experience parallels my own:

In 1982 I read *The Color Purple* by Alice Walker. Her fiction opened my eyes to the reality of the lives that some women have lived. I realized that while white male society was driving down the boulevard of opportunity with only an occasional traffic light to contend with, these women reached their goals by traveling a circuitous path adjacent to that boulevard, a pathway cluttered with the obstacles of racism, poverty, sexism, and more, making their route all but impassable. Her writing brought me out of my own narrow world and into the world of black women. When I finished reading, my world was not the same.[15]

To welcome the stranger is to challenge the convenient and conventional presuppositions of the dominant culture. Exposure is not an easy or necessarily comfortable journey. But it can give depth, development, and direction to our lives.

In a racist, heterosexist, class-injured world, God is likely to meet us often in images associated with children, poor women, black, brown, yellow and red women, lesbian women, battered women, bleeding women, and women learning to fight back. . . . Dark images. Like Mary's poor little boy,

God is seldom welcome in reputable places. The story is not a nice one. Good theology is not respectable.[16]

The very metabolism of the gospel is a stranger on Main Street and sometimes in First Church: "God chose what is foolish in the world to shame the wise, God chose what is weak in the world to shame the strong, God chose what is low and despised in the world . . . to overthrow the existing order" (I Corinthians 1:27–28 RSV/NEB).

QUESTIONS FOR REFLECTION

1. Who are the strangers you have difficulty receiving? Why are they more difficult to receive than others?
2. What ways do the Old and New Testaments provide for us to welcome strangers today?
3. What determines whether we see a teenage member of a racist or violent gang as just that, or as a lonely adolescent caught in a system?

With gratitude to Maude McElvaney,
whose prayerful spirituality has always had the credibility
of connections with people of all races, nations, and stations.

6

The Way of the Whisper:
Validating
the Still, Small Voice

The winds of grace are always blowing,
and sometimes that grace is
more discernible in the
sound of silence.

Now a word was brought to me stealthily,
　　my ear received the whisper of it.
Amid thoughts from visions of the night,
　　when deep sleep falls . . . , dread came upon me, and trembling,
　　which made all my bones shake.
　　　　　　　Eliphaz's experience, according to Job 4:12–14

Sometimes we believe that God's still, small voice is speaking to us
one-on-one. How do we know—or can we know—if the "word" we

are hearing is from God? After all, biblical accounts of God addressing human beings directly are not hard to come by. And after all, people claim all kinds of things coming from direct action by God.

Heretofore I have suggested different yet related ways by which faith can be restored and strengthened. Although the initiation of God's grace always precedes our response in one way or another, grace does call forth a response, whether by the intentional way of the will, the surprise of wonder, the result of witness, or the experience of welcome.

In this chapter, we will consider yet another visitation of grace and receptivity to revelation. This way is direct experience or encounter with what we believe in a given circumstance to be the presence or Word of God or, as some would say, the direct impact of the Holy Spirit. Our journey in this chapter will include a look at some biblical accounts of individuals said to have experienced God in immediate revelation, apart from their deliberate attempt to be present to God, apart from any action on their part, and apart from immediate interpersonal relationship. This personal encounter with God in the way of the whisper (as I call it) is hardly without vexing dilemmas. We will take a look at some of these problems and proceed to consider some tests of validity as we ask, "How might we know if God's Word is addressing us in a given situation?"

Before proceeding, it is worth noting that every major religious tradition speaks of direct encounter with "the wholly other." According to Frederick J. Streng, one of the four traditional ways of being religious is the "personal apprehension of a Holy Presence."[1] Thus, while chapter 6 centers on the Jewish–Christian witness, the subject matter is by no means limited to these traditions.

Close Encounters of a Biblical Kind: From the Old Testament

One does not travel far in the Old Testament before discovering divine–human encounters of a one-to-one direct fashion. The genre of literary style and form varies greatly in these stories but they have in common a word from God to a person or group of persons. To put it bluntly, God is portrayed as talking to someone; this someone hears what God says (either correctly or incorrectly!); and this someone frequently responds to God in dialogue or becomes a vehicle for God's Word to someone else—to Pharaoh or to the nation of Israel, for example.

As soon as we complete the first paragraph of Genesis God starts talking. Every remaining paragraph in the first chapter begins: "And God said" or "Then God said." To whom is God talking? To Godself? To creation? To the reader? The Genesis 2 creation story, actually considerably older than the Genesis 1 account, provides the initial words of command to the humans (Adam and Eve) concerning appropriate conduct in the garden of Eden. Chapter 3 blossoms into full-scale conversation between God and man and woman, to say nothing of the slick-talking serpent. Further on we pick up the dialogue between God and Cain, and before long the extended give-and-take between God and Noah. God tells Noah to make an ark of gopher wood. Detailed instructions follow. Noah, go into the ark. Noah, go forth from the ark. God promises a covenant with Noah and Noah's family and all living creatures. A universal covenant!

The extended patriarchal–matriarchal narratives which present countless episodes of God's encounter with persons are launched in Genesis 12. Again, God is talking. "Now the Lord said to Abraham, 'Go from your country and your kindred and your father's house to the land that I will show you' " (12:1). In chapter 17 God's words of covenant and assurance are addressed directly to Abraham.

As we reflect on these encounters, and others to come, many concerns could rightfully engage our interest. We could center on the content of the divine–human encounter. We could consider the historical circumstances, the literary form of the stories, and questions of origin and authorship. However, my primary interest in this chapter is to invite you to look at the many and varied settings of God–human conversations to see what we might learn about our relationship with God today. What do those stories tell us about revelation? How are we to interpret stories that picture God talking with persons, and persons talking with God? Does God talk directly with people today as of old? If so, what images and words would we use to say so? And how might we know? Before we venture some replies, let us look at some more close encounters.

Few biblical encounters are better known than the dramatic episode of God and Moses in Exodus 3. Subject of countless sermons and songs of liberation, this high drama of the burning bush, holy ground, and call for deliverance captures our imagination and deepens our sense of mystery. Few conversations in the entire Bible are more commanding in their presentation of one-on-one give-and-take between God and human. "Moses, Moses!" Like many if not most divine–human encounters in the Bible, a mission, a task is laid by God upon the unsuspecting human recipient. When God appears, someone is about to be sent. Then, more often than not, human resistance: "Oh, my Lord, send, I pray, some other person" (Exodus 4:13). Then divine insistence and ingenuity (in this case, God's call to Aaron, Moses' brother). And so back to Egypt and "let my people go" as a result of personal encounter. God talk leads to God walk!

In these encounters we see all the ingredients of person-to-person relationship and communication: invitation, challenge, assurance, interruption, prodding. God speaks. God acts. Is God seen? Let's look again.

As the Hebrew Bible moves into the stories of kings, judges and prophets, we hear over and over, "The word of the Lord came to——" and "Thus saith the Lord." Here are just a few typical examples of persons naming their reception of revelation:

And there [Elijah] came to a cave and lodged there; and behold, the word of the Lord came to him . . . "What are you doing here, Elijah?"
1 Kings 19:9 (Note that the Word of the Lord here is a question, similar to the Genesis 3 question directed to Adam, "Where are you?")

And I heard the voice of the Lord saying "Whom shall I send, and who will go for us?" Then I said, "Here I am! Send me." And the Lord said, "Go, and say this to the people. . . ."
Isaiah 6:8–9

For thus said the Lord God, the Holy One of Israel, "In returning to rest you shall be saved; in quietness and in trust shall be your strength."

Isaiah 30:15

Now the word of the Lord came to me saying . . . then I said . . . but the Lord said to me . . .

Jeremiah 1:4–7

And [the Lord] said to me, "Son of man, stand upon your feet, and I will speak to you." . . . And I heard him speaking to me . . . And he said to me, "Son of man, I send you to the people of Israel. . . ."

Ezekiel 2:1–3

The word of the Lord that came to Hosea. . . . The word of the Lord that came to Joel. . . . Now the word of the Lord came to Jonah. . . . The word of the Lord that came to Micah. . . . The oracle of God which Habakkuk the prophet saw.

From the beginning of each of these biblical books

I have referred to these encounters as divine–human events. Actually, as you may have noted, divine–male encounters is more accurate. The patriarchal recording of history did not preserve women's stories of revelation and characteristically interpreted God's communication as occurring with men only. Exceptions are few and far between. Even longtime students of the Bible are usually shocked to discover that God is portrayed only on a few occasions as addressing women, including through the medium of an angel. The very few Old Testament examples include Hagar in Genesis 16 and 21 and Samson's mother in Judges 13. Even in this story the woman is never named, as is her husband, Manoah, and he becomes central to the ongoing communication with the angel.

Close Encounters of a Biblical Kind:
From the New Testament

What about personal encounters between God and persons in the New Testament? Since the sign of God's presence is experienced in the ministry of Jesus Christ, the other signs of immediate revelation between God and persons are almost entirely to be found in the announcements of birth and resurrection, with the exception of Acts. In other words, in the New Testament witness God meets human beings through encounter with Jesus Christ. Thus, it is primarily before Jesus' birth or related to the birth and after his death—but before the resurrection encounter—that God's revelation is directly and immediately perceived according to the gospel witness.

A brief word concerning angels is in order here. Generally speaking, angels in the biblical material are messengers of God sometimes appearing in human-like form. Their functions include conveying God's mandates, announcing special events (such as forthcoming births), protecting the faithful, and serving as instruments of divine displeasure.

In the first two chapters of Matthew an angel of the Lord appears three times to Joseph in a dream. In sequence, the angel, a symbol of God's presence and word, informs Joseph of Mary's forthcoming delivery of Emmanuel through action of the Holy Spirit, later warns the family to flee to Egypt due to Herod's wrath, and finally beckons the family to return to Israel at the safe time.

Similar stories are to be found in Luke's prenatal narratives. In Luke 1 an angel identified as Gabriel appears to Zechariah in the temple and announces the coming birth of John to Zechariah's wife, Elizabeth. In the same chapter Gabriel appears again, this time to Mary in Nazareth. Gabriel announces that Mary's favor with God will result in her giving birth to a son who will be called holy. The angels aren't through yet. We remember them well in song, scripture, and sermon: "And the angel said to [the shepherds], 'Be not afraid; for behold, I bring you good news of a great joy which will come to all the people; for to you is born this day . . .' " (Luke 2:10–11). And you know the rest.

The gospels, each in its own variation, portray a divine message given to the women who were the first to come to Jesus' burial place. The good news of the risen Lord is announced to the women by angels in Matthew 28 and John 20, by a man in a white robe in Mark 16, and by two men in dazzling apparel in Luke 24.

The Acts of the Apostles gives us many accounts of God's

presence through the Holy Spirit to individuals and to the church. These episodes remind us in some ways of the Old Testament stories where God is present in Word but not in visible form (except through angels). In Acts the Holy Spirit turns up again and again, and not infrequently, angels—God's messengers—make their appearance. Once again the Invisible One speaks and is heard.

Here are some examples from Acts in which God is heard sometimes through the words of angels and sometimes through the words of the Holy Spirit:

And they were all filled with the Holy Spirit. . . .
                                   Acts 2:4

At night an angel of the Lord opened the prison doors and brought them out and said, "Go and stand in the temple and speak to the people all the words of this Life."

                                   Acts 5:19–20

In Acts 9 a blinding light bursts forth and a voice speaks to Paul on the road to Damascus. "Saul, Saul, why do you persecute me?" (v. 4). The voice (identified as Jesus) gives directions to Saul. The story continues with the Lord appearing in a vision to Ananias. "Rise and go to the street called Straight . . ." (v. 11) is the Lord's command.

In Acts 12, similar to the account in Acts 9, an angel of the Lord appears to Peter in prison, saying, "Get up quickly" (v. 7). Peter's chains fall off and he is led to freedom by the angel.

In the church at Antioch the Holy Spirit appears during a time of worship and fasting and says, "Set apart for me Barnabas and Saul for the work to which I have called them" (Acts 13:2).

In Chapters 18 and 23 the Lord speaks to Paul words of encouragement. "Do not be afraid, but speak and do not be silent; for I am with you . . ." (Acts 18:9–10). "Take courage, for as you have testified about me at Jerusalem, so you must bear witness also at Rome" (Acts 23:11).

Dilemmas in Close Encounters

The passages of direct encounter between God and humanity, whether in the Old or in the New Testament, raise a number of questions for today. The plain, unvarnished truth is that people in our time who claim to have visions or to have heard divine voices or who speak of "appearances" are often regarded as either mentally suspect or religious charlatans. People who claim a "pipeline" to God through personal conversation or private visitation from divine headquarters are likely to be regarded as candidates for psychological reconstruction. And as we all know our mental institutions as well as our city streets are not without those who hear the voice of God or who are convinced that they speak for God because God has given them a message to bear.

If you saw the film *Oh God* you have an idea of our predicament. The assistant manager of a grocery store has a series of auditory and visual experiences in which he is addressed by God (in the human form of George Burns). He goes through experiences that many of us know something about: "How do I know you are God? . . . I don't understand anything. . . . I can't take this job (spreading the Word). . . . I feel like an idiot. . . . I'm not crazy."

As he begins to be faithful to "the vision," his wife goes through a whole gamut of responses: concern for her husband's mental health (she suggests a holiday); doubt, despair, embarrassment, denial, and sarcasm. To the public he is a sideshow in the news, a laughingstock, a nut who claims he has talked to God and in turn been addressed by God. (Just for fun but for education, too, try Jeremiah 20:7–9).

The dilemma is well stated in this manner: "People who have a personal experience of the holy are faced with a real dilemma: How do they talk about it? When they personally experience the Holy Presence, they are filled with awe in response to the strange and sometimes extrahuman qualities that confront them. However, the experience can only be communicated to others through human symbols, actions, or ideas."[2]

Oh God points out the predicament for us today of the direct God-connection inherent in the biblical tradition. Our faith is based on the conviction that a reality we call God in the English language does in fact communicate directly with human beings. We believe that God is revealed to us in a variety of ways, or we might say that God speaks to us. On one hand we may want to dismiss the biblical language of angels, appearances, direct communication from God as absurd. "This stuff is for either crazy folk or gullible ones," some are tempted to exclaim. On the other hand the God–human (described in scripture as essentially God–man) communication, as we see in the foregoing examples, is a staple of biblical witness.

The biblical witness of direct encounters with God, the Word of the Lord, the Holy Spirit, poses yet another problem. How does one know if the revelation is from God? How does one know if the message has been heard and interpreted correctly? And how does one distinguish between a word from God and the workings of one's own imagination or conscience?

What is going on in these many direct encounters of biblical witness? Did God communicate differently then than now? Were biblical characters "tuned in" in ways we are not? Or has the Bible simply used transcendent language (God, angels, Word of the Lord, Holy Spirit) in place of creative human religious imagination?

Toward Interpretation for Today

One of the most highly regarded Old Testament scholars of the past fifty years is Gerhard von Rad. In his book *The Message of the Prophets* he reflects on prophets who provide us with insights into how revelation is to be interpreted.

We would be mistaken for a number of reasons if we attempted to make easy comparisons of our time and circumstance with those of the prophets. Even so, their reception of revelation, as suggested by von Rad, does provide some clues as to how we might interpret the biblical tradition of close encounters for today.

On one point, however, there is universal agreement, that visions and auditions came to the prophets from outside themselves, and that they came suddenly and completely without premeditation.

It is impossible exactly to separate out visionary experiences which were genuinely ecstatic from other forms of the reception of revelation. Yahweh had assuredly more ways than one of communicating with the prophets, but it is hopeless to try to gain clear ideas about the psychical side of the processes. . . . There were also revelations which took the form of an auditory experience and nothing more. . . . On the other hand, we have good reason to believe that the prophets were also given inspiration in which no kind of change came over their ordinary consciousness, that is to say, in which the revelation was a mental process. This is probably so in the great majority of those cases in which the prophet speaks only of the word of Yahweh which had come to him. Nevertheless, even here the element of "event" which the revelation had for the prophet ought not to be overlooked. *It is not simply a matter of mental perception, but of the "coming" of the word of Yahweh, and, consequently, even with this quite unsensational form of revelation the prophets never lost the feeling that there was something strange in the experience.*[3]

Von Rad suggests that revelation involves both inspiration from beyond oneself and mental process within the self. This I can begin to understand. A word comes upon us out of the events of life itself. It comes as a gift and may be in the form of a question, an assurance, a challenge, a task. The incoming gift becomes a convincing and convicting occasion of disclosure and discovery. I like to say that I have been addressed by "the not-me, the not-you, and the not-all-of-us-put-together."

Yet this immediate and direct sense of having received a word not my own is neither apart from the receiving mechanism of my own imagination nor is it apart in the wholistic sense from the tradition of the community of faith. Even the inspiration of the prophets interacts with the existing tradition, both oral and written, to form a fresh and particular word for a particular and unrepeatable moment of history. Revelation does not occur in a void, but intersects with what has already been given to us in the way of imaginative perception and through the already existing religious tradition.

At the risk of sounding too clerical, for at least a moment I want to connect the biblical witness of direct encounter with the process of call into ordained ministry. Over a period of six months in the early 1950s I wrestled with a sense of being called into ordained ministry. There were no angelic appearances, no remarkable visions, no audible words from an unseen divinity. But I was convinced that there was a word being addressed to me as surely as audible words and visible appearances.

The occasional thought became an obsession, an undeniable pull. It became destiny, meant-to-be-ness. Exactly as von Rad put it, "It is not simply a matter of mental perception, but of the coming of the word of Yahweh, and consequently, even with this quite unsensational form of revelation the prophets never lost their feeling that there was something strange in the experience."[4]

In the Spiritual Formation groups at Perkins School of Theology we have opportunity to listen to student experiences of coming into preparation for ordained ministry. We learn something about the various ways in which God is experienced. One student shares an abiding sense of God's presence and growing conviction of a call to ordained ministry. Another reflects on a sense of deeper meaning for the use of talents already given. The language may not call forth images or experiences of literally hearing or seeing God, yet God through faith is seen and heard. The reality of revelation is parallel to the biblical witness but the language and the images are today's as would be expected. The biblical language of angels, appearances, and God speaking directly as though literally audible need not be discarded as hallucinatory or the result of a hyper-religious imagination.

In biblical witness there are several recurring features of revelation which can be instructive for us today. One is that direct encounters know no limitation of place or person. God communicates in dreams (Joseph), at the altar in corporate worship (Zechariah), in the home (Mary), at work (shepherds in the fields), on the road (Saul), at a burial site (the women), and in prison (the apostles). No one, regardless of societal place or stature, has a monopoly or even a claim on the surprising activity of God. This knowledge is critical for us today.

Another frequent feature of God's visitation is the connection with mission. To be favored with a visit from the Lord is to be commissioned. The words that recur again and again are "go" and "arise." And many are those who would just as soon not be so favored—Moses, Jonah, Jeremiah, Job, Paul (formerly Saul), to name a few. The history of the church is replete with persons who became convinced that they had been visited from on high, answering a call to serve others in faraway places or to respond to desperate need under their own noses. When God moves in, we are likely to be commissioned to move on or out. The visitation of grace may not be tidy, is seldom without a measure of ambiguity on our part, and is likely to complicate already complicated lives, even as assurance of God-with-us is given.

Testing the "Word of the Lord"

It is time now to bring our deliberations on close encounters closer to home. We have considered a number of biblical examples in which God has addressed individuals or groups personally in a direct or immediate fashion. Some dilemmas posed by these accounts were lifted up, followed by several clues for translating these encounters into contemporary idiom and language.

All of this leads us back to the questions raised early in the chapter: How do we presume to know if and when God is addressing a word to us? We know that the authority of divine approval or sanction has been used and misused in many ways. Are there ways we can test our perceptions of "the still, small voice"?

At the outset a caution needs to be named. We will be walking on tricky terrain. There are no surefire means by which we can eliminate an element of ambiguity. Revelation is not a matter of dogmatic truths or laws dispensed in computer-like fashion. Revelation is a matter of faith and ongoing discernment. Those who want absolute certainty look to revelation as a substitute for faith instead of the ground and motivation for faith. We cannot prove that God spoke to Moses or to Mary or to us. But we can live by faith in the assurance of what we believe to be God's grace experienced again and again.

What then, are some ways of testing and discerning a visitation of the still, small voice? How might we recognize the whisper of the Holy Spirit? Be aware now that some tests will be more relevant for a given situation than others. In other words, not every test will be fitting for every circumstance.

There are, I'm sure, many intimations of direct encounter. I will suggest six for your consideration and reflection.

Community Wisdom

On many occasions I have found it helpful to call upon the insights of the collective wisdom of others in the faith community to assist me in reflecting on my own experience of the Holy. I might share my struggle in coming to grips with a particular circumstance with several friends and colleagues. It may be that they can deepen or clarify my perspective. "How do you see God's interaction in this situation?" I might inquire.

"Where there is no guidance, a people falls; but in an abundance of counselors there is safety" (Proverbs 11:14). Frequently those who know us well know our propensities for rationalization, for self-elevation, or perhaps our proclivity to self-abasement, as the case may be. By exposing our journey to others we draw informally on the tradition of spiritual guidance in which members of the faith community wrestle with discerning the action of God in life.

When I look back on my six months "wrestling with God" in connection with my ordained ministry decision, I do so with considerable amazement. As far as I'm concerned my decision was the right one for me. But at the time I regarded the decision to be "between me and God," so that I consulted virtually no one else. I think the reason was probably because I did come to a point where

I felt "sure beyond being sure" and proceeded to make the decision. But I must say that I have experienced very few times in life with such a low quotient of ambiguity. Over a period of years I have learned to test out more of my journey with others and have found my life enriched thereby. Of course there is no guarantee in the response of others, but it does usually enrich the decision-making process.

Since from a Christian standpoint we regard the church as the Body of Christ, and thus as an intended sign of the presence and action of God, it should not seem strange to us to check out our perceptions of God's presence in our lives with sisters and brothers of the faith. In the concern, comfort, and challenge of one or more brother and sister we stand a good chance of coming to grips with the voice or vision of God in our lives.

Our perception of the Word of the Lord is inevitably shaped by our experience of the community of faith. Revelation cannot occur apart from a total context of all that we have known in life, and certainly seldom if ever apart from the faith tradition as we have come to know it. This is to remind us that revelation is inevitably a conditioned experience. For this reason it has become important from my standpoint to consult and be open to the counsel of "strangers" as I defined them in the latter part of chapter 5. As the Word of God shapes the community of faith, so the community inevitably shapes the Word in its specifics, its priorities, its nuance of gift and demand. To hear the whole counsel of God I need to be receptive to the whole people of God.

Unfortunately, however, community wisdom as perceived in terms of denominational law and practice may in fact constitute a roadblock to the workings of the Holy Spirit. The arduous and continuing history of women's struggle for acceptance in ordination is ample testimony to this dilemma.

Fruits of the Spirit

Sometimes it helps to ask of a pending decision and its relation to God's action, "What are the ethical implications? How does it affect other persons, especially those most in need?" But also it is wise to ask, "How will a certain decision or proposed action affect my sense of self and my relation to others?"

In his letter to the Galatians, Paul, wishing to expound on Christian freedom from the law, speaks of the fruit of the spirit as love, joy, peace, patience, kindness, goodness, faithfulness, gentleness, and self-control (5:22–23). Obviously those are quite general and need to be supplemented in the situations of oppressed peoples by such fruits as self-respect, dignity, justice, and freedom.

Testing fruits of the spirit encourages us to think about the consequences of decisions and actions we may be considering. There was a time many years ago when my political stance was uninformed by my theological position. But I began to compare the two and saw that I needed to test my politics by my theology. My politics was centered in my own vested interests, whereas my theology kept pointing to the claims of others. Applying something like the fruit of the spirit, I began to see that I had been asking the wrong question. Instead of "What's in it for me and my class, race, and sex," the question became "How does it affect marginal people and thus all of us?"

If it is God speaking to us or appearing to us, we cannot be satisfied to be either the oppressor or the oppressed. If it is the whisper of the Holy One impinging on our life, chances are a more profound moral and ethical stance is making the claim upon us along with the assurance of participating in the very life of God. The way of the authentic whisper will lead us to be better neighbors one way or another.

Sustained Longevity

It could be the voice of God calling when a certain conviction stays with us for a long time, withstanding changing circumstances and a range of resistances on our part. No guarantee, you understand, just a possibility. The vision may come and go, may be sublimated and go underground for awhile or even back and forth many times. But if it keeps resurfacing and will not go away, it might be the way of the whisper. Especially this might be the case if the vision challenges you to an unmanageable task or a cause greater than yourself on behalf of others.

I am not talking about going to seminary, necessarily, although you could be led in that direction, as I was. I am thinking about the commitments of many lay persons through the years who have worked on behalf of battered women, refugees, the Special Olympics, AIDS patients. I'm thinking about courageous laypersons who have been emboldened by the pugnacious presence of a still, small voice, sometimes named and sometimes not, to make risk-filled decisions at work which were not in their own best interests.

Presently I am committed to an ecumenical task in Dallas in which I once would not have imagined myself involved. Part of the time I do not even want to do it. But in spite of myself the vision keeps coming back, exciting me again. And again. Slowly I have become convinced that the whisper has spoken a word that will not let go. So I am hooked. I may be deceiving myself but it seems like a claim from beyond myself that will not let go. It keeps coming back as sustained gift and claim. Do you know what I mean?

What Else Is Happening?

As mentioned earlier, revelation always occurs in a context. Sometimes when people have consulted me about whether a certain experience represents the call or pull of God in their life, I ask, "What else is going on in your life?" It is difficult to make certain connections between life experiences, but it may pay to try.

If a person begins to rely on God or Jesus for every decision, it is important—maybe crucial—to have a sense of what else is going on. It could be a deepening of religious commitment. It also could be the sign of a frightened, fragile self-seeking security and stability.

If a person wants to know if it is God's will that they do this or that, it could be helpful to explore some background in the way of history, feelings, and what seems to be at stake. We in the ordained ministry have a joke about preachers being offered a so-called more prestigious church. Somehow that larger church *must* be the will of God and so we humbly submit to it! My point is that we can always find a way to convince ourselves that what we want or what we deem to be in our best interests is somehow the will of God. No less a personage than Martin Luther reminded us that the human mind is a factory that produces idols.

My purpose here is not to "psychologize" our experiences but rather to recognize that life is multi-layered. Diverse conditions of the self can lurk beneath the surface of our religious language and longings. We do well to cultivate some awareness of this fact.

Watching and Waiting

Testing the spirit surely involves watching and waiting "in the means of grace," as John Wesley put it. The black church speaks of "putting your hand in the hand of God." The long tradition of spiritual guidance would focus on discerning the spirit's presence in a person's life. The Quaker tradition would talk of centering and the inner light.

All of this is to suggest that some of the other ways of faith mentioned in earlier chapters can help us discern God's action and its implications for our lives. The way of the will, with its deliberate seeking, might lead us to an intensive time of personal prayer, scripture reading, meditation, fasting, as well as renewed alertness in corporate worship.

There are times when prayer as a time of quiet listening has been especially helpful to me in sorting out where God is in my life and where I am with God. I like the description of prayer as the willingness to be influenced by God. In the quietness of listening there can be a kind of emptying which prepares the way for receiving the still, small voice.

The themes of watching for the signs of the times and waiting on the Lord for inspiration and/or clarity will not seem alien to ears attuned to the biblical witness.

A Sense of Otherness and Oddness

In speaking of the prophets' reception of revelation, von Rad spoke of visions and auditions "from outside themselves," and further, of the feeling "that there was something strange in the experience."[5] This is an inevitable test of the visitation of grace, especially in the sense of immediacy.

Here we have to know ourselves well to have a sense of what is innately "me" at a given time and what appears to be "from the outside," even though these can seldom if ever be neatly divided. The gospel is a stranger to this world, as I pointed out in chapter 5. Grace accompanies us, yet is not of us. Grace comes to us, yet comes from beyond us. There is a foolishness of the gospel not extrapolated from the world around us.

Who among us believes that Noah would build an ark on his own, and by his own volition put up with all the smelly animals, unless they were included in divine covenant? Do any of us think that Moses, weak of spirit and weaker yet of public eloquence, according to his own perception, would dream it up on his own to liberate a nation of slaves? And would Shiprah and Puah have defied Pharaoh apart from the conviction of divine inspiration? And what brightest and best dreamed up a crucified, humiliated Messiah contrary to almost the entire preceding religious tradition?

Note that the otherness spoken of here has to do with the content of the message as a mysterious and wondrous gift, not with peculiarity of style such as speaking in tongues or other characteristics not amenable to community testing and edification.

No matter how it happens to us, the gospel often comes as the reversal of human wisdom. After all the first will be last, the last first. Every valley lifted up, every mountain made low. The humble exalted, the exalted humbled. Saving your life is losing. Losing is gaining. Crazy stuff. A perceived Word needs to be tested from time to time in the ways of testing suggested here. But if it is not there to test, then God is "not present," there has been no whisper, and the still, small voice is silent. At least for now.

QUESTIONS FOR REFLECTION

1. What visitations of grace have you experienced from "the still, small voice?"
2. Which of these forms of testing have assisted you in discerning the action of God in your life?
3. What other forms of testing not mentioned in this chapter have you or others used?
4. Should we seek to interpret God's will for us in every important decision? How would you define "important"? Do you see this approach in the New Testament?

In memory of many shut-ins and convalescent parishioners
who have borne witness to God's presence
in the Way of the Whirlwind.

7

The Way of the Whirlwind: Birthing Hope and Love in the Storm

The winds of grace are always blowing
and sometimes we do not know
what to name the
whirlwind.

The gospel is not a palliative to help us escape the pain of life, but the way to transform suffering into the birth pangs of something new.

Henri Nouwen[1]

I went to seminary as a second-career student fresh from Continental Oil Company. I have never forgotten the first day of the first class. There we were, greenhorn first-year students, waiting for the professor to enter the classroom. His reputation had preceded him; he was known as a tough old no-nonsense character.

In he came, walking around the room, staring at us, not saying a word. Talk about intimidation! Finally he opened his mouth. We leaned forward in anticipation to hear the first words of our formal theological education: "If you've never been to Waxahachie, you've never been to Waxahachie, but you will."

Silence.

I don't know what my classmates thought but I was thinking, "*This is theological education? I left a good job with Continental for this?*" All of us who were native Texans knew that Waxahachie was that county seat some thirty miles south of Dallas, known for its famous old courthouse with the gargoyles and other carvings. But what did Professor Joseph Matthews mean, "If you've never been . . ."?

He kept repeating the enigmatic phrase every so often all through the semester. Never did tell us what it meant. Didn't have to. Our neophyte theological brains finally figured out that Waxahachie was Professor Joseph Wesley Matthews' code word for "the up-against-it," nowhere-to-turn situation, an undeniable limit confronting us.

The Old Testament doesn't mention Waxahachie, but it does give us the term "whirlwind." Usually it denotes a windstorm or destructive wind connected with turmoil, tempest, and calamity, but not always. Elijah went up by a whirlwind into heaven (2 Kings 2:11). In the book of Job God answers Job out of the whirlwind on two occasions (38:1 and 40:6). In Job 27 the whirlwind strikes in the night to carry off the wicked man (v. 20). And in chapter 37 the whirlwind is pictured as the power and majesty of God through natural wonders, as similarly used in Psalm 77:18.

In other places the whirlwind seems to be an instrument of God's judgment on Israel, on other nations, or even on individuals who scoff at the ways of the Lord. Examples can be found in Proverbs 1:27, Isaiah 29:6, Amos 1:14, and Hosea 8:7 ("they sow the wind and they shall reap the whirlwind"). Contemporary theological writers, such as Langdon Gilkey, have used the term whirlwind to indicate historical ferment, turbulence and upheaval, and the resulting theological response.[2] These works reflect on the changing shape of history in which the foundations of religious thought are called into question, offering a reconstruction of theological thought and language deemed appropriate for our time.

The way of the whirlwind as used in this chapter refers to the experience of sorrow and wound, a metaphor for the unwanted, the devastating, the seemingly unmanageable, the Waxahachie experience, in Joe Matthews's terminology. It calls us to a choice or a life situation we did not seek, a time of trial and tribulation. Although this usage of the term whirlwind will differ in some respects from some of the Old Testament references, there is a common denominator: God will be understood to be in the whirlwind.

In order to lay the groundwork for the way of the whirlwind we need first to take at least a brief look at the matter of theodicy, that is, the issue of the goodness of God in the face of evil. This is a risky venture since there are few issues more complicated or more controversial from a theological standpoint. And it might as well be said at the outset that "telling and sharing the story," as suggested by Holocaust theologian Elie Wiesel, is more convincing and life-giving in the midst of actual circumstances than any rational analysis.

God's Impartiality

In much of the ancient world trials and tribulations were seen as the direct judgment of God on human beings, a perspective not exactly missing in our own time! If you were afflicted, it was because you had sinned or done something to bring this misfortune on yourself. If you were blessed, it was because you were righteous or in correct relationship with divine power. Not surprisingly, scripture offers several perspectives for consideration, and again unsurprisingly, these views of theodicy are in conflict.

The Old Testament itself suggests viewpoints at variance with each other. Passages in Deuteronomy for example, Deut. 7:13, indicate God's reward of blessing in terms of "the fruit of your body and the fruit of your ground . . . the increase of your cattle. . . ." At the same time there is clear warning that failure to keep the commandments will result in destruction (vs. 9–10). Yet the book of Job, in spite of Job's well-meaning friends' words to the contrary (see the words of Eliphaz, Job 4:7–9), calls for a no-easy-answer theodicy in which God finally appears to Job in a whirlwind, suggesting something of the "wrestling-God" of Jacob, and thus a God who engages us and is present with those who suffer.

In the New Testament two viewpoints inform our reflections on theodicy. One is Jesus' insistence that God makes the sun rise on the evil and on the good and sends rain on the just and on the unjust (Matthew 5:45). The context of this statement is that our love for neighbor is to be impartial as God's love is impartial, that is, not determined by whether or not the neighbor is in good standing with us. There is, then, an impartiality of God's providence in which the mechanistic reward-and-punishment theodicy is rejected. This can be plainly said: The wicked may prosper in the terms of this world, and the most devout lover of God and humanity has no protection against cancer. You can multiply this example many times over with little effort.

But there is another experiential truth that exists side by side with this impartiality of God's providential love. We can name it as God's involvement in our suffering and distress as compassionate companion.

God as Compassionate Companion in Suffering

Passages in both testaments encourage us to think of God as compassionate companion, counselor, and comforter in the midst of the whirlwind rather than as the cause of suffering. To say it another way, God is experienced in these passages as presence in the whirlwind rather than as punisher.[3]

In previous chapters we have considered several visitations of grace and varieties of faith response: meeting God in the intentional way of the will; encountering God through the surprise of wonder; God becoming real to us by our doing God's work; God manifest in personal relationships; and God revealed in the still, small voice of direct personal encounter. The remainder of this chapter seeks to lift up the presence of God through the whirlwind in selected scriptures and in contemporary personal and collective experience.

No better advice can be given than to urge us to avail ourselves of the psalmist's profound experience in the whirlwind, that is, to hear the story again. Virtually every lamentation finds its way to praise in due time. Listen to these words "from out of the depths":

I waited patiently for the LORD;
    [The LORD] inclined to me and heard my cry.
[The LORD] drew me up from the desolate pit,
    out of the miry bog,
and set my feet upon a rock,
    making my steps secure.
[The LORD] put a new song in my mouth,
    a song of praise to our God.
Many will see and fear,
    and put their trust in the Lord.

                    Psalm 40:1–3

Read Psalms 73 and 77 in their entirety. They are sublime testimonies to the recovery of faith in the midst of the whirlwind.

And out of the whirlwind come these New Testament statements of faith:

Who shall separate us from the love of Christ? Shall tribulation, or distress, or persecution, or famine, or nakedness, or peril, or sword? . . . No, in all these things we are more than conquerors through him who loved us. For I am sure that neither death, nor life, nor angels, nor principalities, nor things present, nor things to come, nor powers, nor height, nor depth, nor anything else in all creation, will be able to separate us from the love of God in Christ Jesus our Lord.

                    Romans 8:35, 37–39

Blessed be the God and Father of our Lord Jesus Christ, the Father of mercies and God of all comfort, who comforts us in all our affliction, so that we may be able to comfort those who are in any affliction, with the comfort with which we ourselves are comforted by God. For as we share abundantly in Christ's sufferings, so through Christ we share abundantly in comfort too. If we are afflicted, it is for your comfort and salvation; and if we are comforted, it is for your comfort, which you experience when you patiently endure the same sufferings that we suffer.

Our hope for you is unshaken; for we know that as you share in our sufferings, you will also share in our comfort.

For we do not want you to be ignorant, brethren, of the affliction we experienced in Asia; for we were so utterly, unbearably crushed that we despaired of life itself. Why, we felt that we had received the sentence of death; but that was to make us rely not on ourselves but on God who raises the dead; he delivered us from so deadly a peril, and he will deliver us; on him we have set our hope that he will deliver us again.

2 Corinthians 1:3–10

These forebears in the faith encourage us to be open to God as the compassionate companion, counselor, and comforter in the midst of suffering and devastation. They experienced God as Emmanuel—God with us—not as cause of their suffering. In the case of the Psalms we see intensely personal struggles, yet journeys related to the community of faith. The psalmist (Ps. 73) enters the sanctuary and is surrounded by the holiness and wholeness of God and by comparison perceives the emptiness of the way of the wicked. In another instance the psalmist (Ps. 77) is so troubled he cannot speak until he lets the tradition of the community touch his life again. As he looks beyond his immediate circumstance and calls to mind the deeds of the Lord in both nature and in Israel's history of liberation from bondage, his faith is restored and his life is connected again with God's larger story.

In the Romans and 2 Corinthians passages Paul reverses our usual and natural human tendency. Instead of distress and tribulation resulting in separation from God, Paul speaks of an inseparable connection with the love of God in Jesus Christ. Instead of the absence of God, Paul rejoices in the discovery of deliverance by and dependence on God. These biblical affirmations in the midst of the whirlwind can offer encouragement and hope in difficult circumstances for which there are no easy answers in our lives today.

The Way of the Whirlwind:
Personal Circumstance

Some years ago the congregation where I served as pastor sponsored a Sunday evening series in coping with various losses and situations of grief. You might say it was an exploration of the whirlwind—its meaning, its difficulties, its implications for the individual and for the faith community as an agent of compassion. We asked the participants to share the experience of loss as they were willing, and to indicate what attempts on the part of others were helpful or destructive.

Frequently the most meaningful forms of compassion mentioned were simply presence, perhaps a brief word, and a caring touch or embrace, especially if offered over a period of time so as to sustain the compassion. The least helpful attempt at caring tended to be those times when friends said, "It was the will of God," especially if the loss were that of a loved one.

As the Sunday evening group reflected on these words, we came to the conclusion that people genuinely wanted to be helpful but did not know the best way. The "will of God" statement, we decided, is an attempt to say that what happens occurs within the loving providence of God, that it will be all right even when it's not all right. Unfortunately, the "will of God" way of trying to offer solace sounds like God was the cause of the loss instead of companion in the loss.

The Christian faith has always claimed that healing and redemptive possibilities can come out of human suffering. This has to be articulated with care lest legitimation be given to suffering itself. There is enough suffering in the world without Christian theology or faith adding to it. We need to call people out of circumstances of suffering where possible, yet be an agent of healing compassion in the midst of suffering where needed. To say that suffering is by its nature redemptive is to encourage or acquiesce to oppression. To say that there is no possibility in suffering is to condemn those whose suffering may be inevitable or unchangeable for the time being.

Carter Heyward, a lesbian feminist theologian, offers a word of clarity about healing as a process of finding or creating redemption in suffering:

To struggle against the conditions that make for or exacerbate suffering, and to do so with compassion—"suffering with" one another—is how we find redemption in suffering.[4]

The redemption in suffering associated with Jesus Christ resides in the fact that he struggled "against the conditions that make for or exacerbate suffering." Whether we are talking about the suffering of a family member or friend with a serious illness, or the suffering of an oppressed people, the redemption in suffering comes from the sharing of that suffering. In other words the best case for God's love is made in compassionate presence and sharing rather than rational arguments, although we do our best to explain and interpret.

By redemption is meant a transformation of spirit, a deepening of relationship, a level of courage and sharing that is freeing in spite of pain and sorrow, and the assurance that God is in the whirlwind as compassionate companion. Such assurance is expressed in these testimonies of faith from the black Christian tradition: "I know that God works in everything for good and reserves the right to squeeze a final blessing out of anything."[5] And similarly, "God can make a way out of no way . . . trouble does not have the last word."[6]

The Way of the Whirlwind: Collective Circumstance

By collective circumstance I mean a situation where a group of people is forced into suffering by the oppression of others. The whirlwind here is an identifiable historical reality, such as the oppression of black people in South Africa and in the United States or the vast human rights violations against the people of El Salvador by their own military forces.

It has been my privilege to be a visitor to one of the many

Salvadoran resettlement villages. The people in this particular settlement had returned to their original homesites after several years in the Mesa Grande refugee camp in Honduras. Their former homes and chapel had been destroyed by ground and air attacks by the Salvadoran military. Their story is one of immense suffering and tribulation, yet of incredible courage and determination.

The people, numbering approximately 1000, had rebuilt sixty homes in the wilderness. No one was to move from their provisional structures (bare huts) into the completed homes across the river until all homes were completed so that all could move together in solidarity. These peaceful *campesinos* were our hosts for a memorable meal of consecrated bean soup and tortillas.

When we asked the source of their hope despite their unrelenting vulnerability to the military, they spoke of the experience of the crucified–risen Christ in the solidarity of their own community. And they besought us to be their voice to our government in urging the cessation of U.S. funding to the Salvadoran military.

For communities of faith in Central America, the story of the crucified Messiah has not led to an acceptance of suffering as some kind of divine will, or of oppression as inevitable. Precisely the opposite. The Crucified One is seen as God-in-solidarity with the plight of the poor, the Liberator who accompanies the people as one who also was oppressed by political and military power. For the Crucified One is also the Risen One who brings hope with solidarity.

Lutheran Bishop Medardo Gomez tells a story about a six-foot rough cross, painted white, resting in a corner of the sanctuary of Resurrection Lutheran Church in San Salvador. A year ago, during a service, the congregation wrote the structural sins of society on the cross in black lettering: the children of the poor who die from malnutrition and other correctable diseases without seeing a doctor, the systematic torture of political prisoners, and many other sins.

"When the church was raided in November, the cross was taken as evidence of subversive material," Bishop Gomez relates. "It was held prisoner for three months by the treasury police until we recently got it released." The cross is a symbol of the prophetic work of the Lutheran Church that continues despite threats and pressure from the government.[7]

A similar theme is evident in these excerpts from a 1989 Holy Week homily offered to the people of war-ravaged Calavera in the Morazan province by Fr. Miguel Ventura, a representative of the Christian base communities of El Salvador:

A few days ago, I visited the village of Junquillo, near the Torola River. That community suffered a terrible bombing attack on March 8. A bomb fell two yards from one of the houses, destroying it completely. Five people died, and five others were seriously injured.

I arrived in the community four days after the bombing and met the family members of the victims. I saw the pain in the eyes of the father. Three of his children had been killed and three others injured. None of us could have been there without feeling his anguish. We can all understand the pain of that father.

But in the midst of that pain, and in the midst of a home which was completely destroyed, we saw another aspect of suffering. The community had gathered to share in the family's grief. One of those present said to me, "In our community, all of us have been touched by this tragedy. All of us carry this cross, and we can rise above the suffering."

I believe there are no wiser words than these. They showed me in a powerful way that as a community, we can overcome all the barriers that separate us from each other and confront any trial.

On this night of resurrection, we must understand that we are not walking toward death, but advancing day by day toward life. Christ seems defeated but rises again on the third day. His enemies place guards around his tomb to deny his resurrection. But Christ rises up victoriously and says with a loud voice: "The God of life has the last word!"

You, brothers and sisters, are the living testimony that Christ is the last word, that your profound faith is the last word. We are gathered as a people of God, as a church of pilgrims, in the midst of this martyrdom, proclaiming that the God of history and the God of resurrection has the last word![8]

Out of the whirlwind of terror and oppression, whether in El Salvador, South Africa, Liberia, Lithuania, or elsewhere, God raises up the communities of faith, hope, and love who defy human oppressors and human limitations. The God of the Cross shares in human suffering; the God of Easter calls for new life in both spirit and historical circumstance and for an end to oppression.

God's Partiality

Earlier in this chapter I lifted up the New Testament insistence on God's impartiality in the sense that the rain and sun come to both the just and the unjust. But it is also true that there is a Divine *partiality* in which God takes sides in relationships of the oppressed with oppressors. Medardo Gomez expresses this truth when he says that the parents of several children will give special attention and care to the one with the greatest need. The parents do not love the child in need more than the others but instead identify with the particular hurt or deprivation.

Similarly, in scripture God is lovingly partial to the hungry, the homeless, the sick, the poor. New Testament examples include the Magnificat (Luke 1:46–55), Jesus' sermon at Nazareth (Luke 4:18–19), the Parable of the Last Judgment from Matthew's gospel (cited earlier), and the many stories of Jesus' identification with marginalized people in the healing stories.

God does not punish us by bringing suffering to us or to our loved ones (impartiality), but God does create the world in a way in which our free will, if and when abused, can bring terrible suffering to ourselves and others. God comes as companion in suffering (involvement), and according to scripture, is partial to the disinherited. And this presence of the crucified God-with-us is always pointing toward the Risen God of hope and deliverance.

Transformation out of the Whirlwind

One must not speak glibly of "growth" that comes out of the whirlwind. Even so, history and experience reveal that trial and tribulation can be the occasions of a more profound view of life and corresponding commitments. The marine explorer Jacques

Cousteau tells us there are some forms of rare marine life which can be seen only in the depths. Perhaps discovering certain depths of life in terms of profundity and ultimate trust in God are more likely through the way of the whirlwind even though we would not choose such either for ourselves or for others.

In his book *Lament for a Son* Nicholas Wolterstorff exclaims in his grief, "I shall look at the world through tears. Perhaps I shall see things that dry-eyed I would not see."[9] When I look at the world through the lens of suffering, both mine and that of others, I see a different terrain than when I look through the lens of striving for status and success.

How many people have seen into the heart of matters by the unfriendly way of the whirlwind? How often I have read stories of heart attack victims in recovery (or those with a similar specter of limitation and finitude) wax poetic and passionate about new priorities, the cherishing of time, and the intention to smell the flowers.

And how many times have we heard people say that their suffering has sensitized them to similar journeys of others? There is of course no guarantee in this respect, but the reality of suffering can create a common ground of experience and a new depth of compassion. Think of the organizations which have sprung up composed of those who have suffered the same or similar fates— parents of children who have been victims of violence, adult children of alcoholics, and adults whose children have experienced a particular disease or illness, for example. If the whirlwind leads us to be better neighbors and more compassionate human beings, surely our suffering and that of our loved ones is finally not in vain.

I lost count many years ago of the numbers of persons who, in the midst of devastating loss, have spoken of gathering a strength not their own. Again, there is no guarantee that the whirlwind will result in such an experience and there surely is no genuine short-cut through the realities of grief with its many emotional ups and downs. Even so, countless persons describe their experience in words like these: "I didn't think I could get through this in one piece, but somehow I have discovered resources I didn't know I had." Sometimes the resources named are the presence and support of neighbors and friends in a way never known before. Sometimes the resource is named as the presence of God as compassionate companion in the midst of the whirlwind.

After all, the Christian movement was born in and out of the grave. Our most fundamental metaphor is that God brings new beginning to all of our endings, hope out of despair, healing out of brokenness, life out of death. The Vulnerable-Victorious One seeks to transform the whirlwind into "the birth pangs of something new."

QUESTIONS FOR REFLECTION

1. In times of experiencing the whirlwind what meant the most to you in terms of compassion and support? What was least helpful?
2. In the discussion of theodicy which issues are the most troublesome? Which most helpful?
3. How could your congregation strengthen its ministry to people caught up in the whirlwind?

Notes

INTRODUCTION

1. I am indebted to Dr. Lindsey Pherigo, emeritus professor of New Testament, Saint Paul School of Theology, Kansas City, Missouri, for introducing me to this term in a lecture at Saint Paul in the early 1980s.

2. Arthur Green and Barry W. Holtz, trans., and The Hasidic Masters on Contemplative Prayer, eds., *Your Word Is Fire* (New York: Schocken Books, 1977), p. 47.

Notes

CHAPTER 1

1. Harvey Cox, *The Seduction of the Spirit* (New York: Simon & Schuster, 1973), pp. 115–118.

2. John Weborg, "How Does a Liturgy Mean?", *The Christian Ministry* (May–June 1989), pp. 8–10.

3. Quoted in a lecture at Southern Methodist University by Professor Luis Martin.

4. Paul W. Hoon, *The Integrity of Worship* (Nashville: Abingdon Press, 1971), p. 338.

5. *Ibid.,* p. 54.

6. Mortimer Arias, *Announcing the Reign of God* (Philadelphia: Fortress Press, 1984), p. xv.

CHAPTER 2

1. "First Apology," 67, *Early Christian Fathers,* Cyril Richardson, ed., p. 287. Referenced from *Introduction to Christian Worship,* James F. White (Nashville: Abingdon Press, 1980). Emphasis added.

2. James F. White, *Introduction to Christian Worship* (Nashville: Abingdon Press, 1980), pp. 125–126.

3. James F. White, *Protestant Worship* (Louisville, Ky.: Westminster/John Knox Press, 1989), pp. 36–37.

4. The relative infrequency of communion on the frontier was caused largely by the lack of elders to preside, by the informality of the environment, and by influence from other Protestant traditions.

5. Margaret Craven, *I Heard the Owl Call My Name* (Garden City, N.Y.: Doubleday, 1973).

6. *Ibid.,* p. 22. In the book the village is described as follows through the young priest's memory of his bishop's description: "The myths are the village and the winds and the rains. The river is the village, and the black and white killer whales that herd the fish to the end of the inlet the better to gobble them. The village is the salmon who comes up the river to spawn. . . ."

7. "The Unforked Message of Chief Seattle," in Gamalier, *Flesh and Spirit: A Religious View of Bicentennial America* (Washington, D.C.: Community for Creative Nonviolence, 1976), pp. 72–73; also quoted in *Alternative Celebrations Catalog* (Bloomington, Ind.: Alternatives, 1978), p. 61.

8. The traditional Quaker service is an exception although today there are increasing numbers of "programmed" Quaker congregations that resemble "mainline" Protestant worship in a number of ways.

9. In William K. McElvaney, *Preaching from Camelot to Covenant* (Nashville: Abingdon Press, 1989), a conceptual and practical foundation is

provided for interpreting and preaching God's Word in accordance with the social conscience of the Bible.

10. Clyde Fant, *Preaching for Today* (New York: Harper & Row, 1975), p. 26.

11. Adapted with permission from William K. McElvaney, "Having to Choose: Word or Table?" *The Christian Ministry* (May/June 1989), pp. 14–15.

CHAPTER 3

1. Dag Hammarskjöld, *Markings* (New York: Alfred A. Knopf, 1964), p. 56.

2. See Richard J. Foster, *Celebration of Discipline* (New York: Harper & Row, 1978). Contents include "The Inward Disciplines," namely, meditation, prayer, fasting, and study.

3. See "Spirituality for O'Hare Airport," in William K. McElvaney, *The People of God in Ministry* (Nashville: Abingdon Press, 1981) for a further interpretation of spirit language, some brief historical background of Western spirituality, and assessment of the resurgence and reawakening of spirituality today.

4. One example is *Prayer and Temperament* by Chester P. Michael and Marie C. Norrisey (Charlottesville, Va.: Open Door, 1964).

5. Sam Keen, *Apology for Wonder* (New York: Harper & Row, 1969).

6. *Ibid,* p. 22.

7. *Ibid.,* pp. 22–23.

8. Michael and Norrisey, *Prayer and Temperament,* p. 48.

9. *Ibid.,* p. 70.

10. *Ibid.,* p. 72.

11. Cornelis Verhoeven, *The Philosophy of Wonder* (New York: Macmillan Publishing Co., 1972), p. 42.

12. Joseph Sittler, *Gravity and Grace* (Minneapolis: Augsburg Publishing House, 1986), p. 4.

13. All examples from *The United Methodist Hymnal* (Nashville: United Methodist Publishing House, 1989).

14. Lee Van Ham, "Praying With Trees," *The Christian Century* (September 27, 1989), pp. 839–840.

15. Sam Keen, *op. cit.,* p. 30.

16. Thomas Berry, "Our Children: This Future," *the little magazine,* vol. 1, number 10, p. 10; quoted in Matthew Fox, *Original Blessing* (Santa Fe: Bear & Co., 1983), p. 36.

17. The late theologian Paul Tillich was fond of using the term "dimension of depth."

18. This section is adapted from William K. McElvaney, "Analogies: Preaching and Tillich's Levels of Relation between Religion and Art," in an unpublished collection of papers of the Annual Meeting of the Academy of Homiletics (December 1989).

19. While this lecture was given at several institutions, Carl Michalson as editor included it in *Christianity and the Existentialists* (New York: Charles Scribner's Sons, 1956), pp. 128–147.

20. Michalson, ed., *Christianity and the Existentialists,* pp. 134–135.

21. *Ibid.,* pp. 136–142.

22. *Ibid.,* pp. 142–143.

23. *Ibid.,* pp. 143–144.

24. Sittler, *op. cit.,* p. 67.

25. Quoted in Fox, *Original Blessing,* p. 67.

26. Wade Roof and William McKinney, *American Mainline Religion,* chapter 6, "Mainline Morality," (New Brunswick: Rutgers University Press, 1987).

27. Martin Luther King, Jr., "The Man Who Was a Fool," in *Strength to Love* (Philadelphia: Fortress Press, 1963), p. 70.

CHAPTER 4

1. Quoted in *Sojourners* (April 1990), p. 16.

2. Robert McAfee Brown, *Unexpected News* (Philadelphia: Westminster Press, 1984), pp. 135–136.

3. See McElvaney, *Preaching from Camelot to Covenant.*

4. Albert Schweitzer, *The Quest of the Historical Jesus* (New York: Macmillan Company, 1968), p. 403.

5. Fr. Jon Sobrino, colleague of the six Jesuits murdered November 16, 1989, at the University of Central America, San Salvador. These words were spoken at an Interfaith Prayer Service, San Francisco, December 1, 1989; reported in *Sojourners* (February/March 1990), p. 6.

6. Excerpts from the "Faith at Work" section, *The United Methodist Reporter* (December 22, 1989). The article, "Retired Ford Exec. Finds Joy in Helping Others," was written by Cynthia B. Astle.

7. Fr. Ignacio Martin Baro, murdered by members of the Salvadoran military, November 16, 1989. Verbal statement to visiting group.

8. Arris Wheaton, seminary student, reflecting on his ministry with homeless people under the bridges near downtown Dallas. Verbal statement to the author and to various groups.

9. Carlos, member of resettlement village, El Salvador. Verbal statement to visiting group.

10. Read in a vigil service for El Salvador, March 1981, Kansas City, Missouri.

11. Mortimer Arias, *Announcing the Reign of God* (Philadelphia: Fortress Press, 1984), p. xv.

12. Peter Berger, *The Noise of Solemn Assemblies* (Garden City, N.Y.: Doubleday & Co., 1961), pp. 140–144.

13. *Ibid.,* pp. 144–147.

14. A few examples are George Peck and John S. Hoffman, ed., *The Laity in Ministry* (Valley Forge: Judson Press, 1984); William Diehl, *Thank God It's Monday* (Philadelphia: Fortress Press, 1982); James C. Fenhagen, *Mutual Ministry* (New York: Seabury Press, 1977).

15. In the *United Methodist Hymnal* (1989 ed.) the liturgy of reception can also read: "Will you be loyal to the United Methodist Church, and do all in your power to *strengthen its ministries?*" (italics mine).

CHAPTER 5

1. Reuel L. Howe, *The Miracle of Dialogue* (New York: Seabury Press, 1963), p. 149.

2. Martin Buber, *I and Thou* (New York: Charles Scribner's Sons, 1958), p. 11.

3. Elie Wiesel, *Messengers of God* (New York: Summit Press, 1976), pp. 106–109.

4. *Ibid.,* p. 107.

5. Martin E. Marty, *Friendship* (Allen, Tex.: Argus Communications, 1980), p. 98.

6. Lillian Rubin, *Just Friends: The Role of Friendship in Our Lives* (New York: Harper and Row, 1985), p. 13.

7. I have chosen to focus on friends rather than family because friendship is chosen whereas family is a given and because much more is written on family relationships. Rubin's *Just Friends* offers insightful comparisons and contrasts, especially chapter 2, "On Kinship and Friendship," pp. 15–33.

8. Marty, *op. cit.,* p. 161.

9. Dietrich Bonhoeffer, *Life Together* (New York: Harper & Brothers, 1954), p. 23.

10. Henri J.M. Nouwen, *Reaching Out* (Garden City, N.Y.: Doubleday, 1975), p. 49. For our purposes I especially recommend Nouwen's section, "From Hostility to Hospitality."

11. Geoffrey W. Bromley, *Theological Dictionary of the New Testament* (Grand Rapids: William B. Eerdman's Publishing Company, 1985), p. 663.

12. Nouwen, *op. cit.,* p. 47.

13. A paraphrase of Matthew 27:27–31.

14. *The Gospel in Art by the Peasants of Solentiname* (New York: Orbis Books, 1984).

15. Brian Lanker, *I Dream a World* (New York: Stewart, Tabori, and Chang, 1989), p. 10.

16. Carter Heyward, "The Power of God-with-Us," *The Christian Century* (March 14, 1990), p. 278.

CHAPTER 6

1. Frederick J. Streng, *Understanding Religious Life* (Belmont, Calif.: Wadsworth Publishing Co., 1985), p. 25.

2. *Ibid.,* pp. 39–40.

3. Gerhard von Rad, *The Message of the Prophets* (New York: Harper & Row, 1967), pp. 39, 47; italics mine.

4. *Ibid.,* p. 47.

5. *Ibid.,* pp. 46–47.

CHAPTER 7

1. *The Christian Century* (October 2, 1974), p. 908.

2. For example, *Naming the Whirlwind* (New York: Bobbs-Merrill Co., 1969), and *Reaping the Whirlwind* (New York: Seabury Press, 1976), both by Langdon Gilkey. See also *The Whirlwind in Culture,* Donald W. Musser and Joseph L. Price, eds., (Oak Park, Ill.: Meyer-Stone Books, 1988).

3. A Christian concept of theodicy has usually claimed that suffering is not directly willed by God but is a consequence of human freedom and finitude, and that God suffers with us and can draw good from evil. It has generally been held that natural disorders, such as disease and natural catastrophe, reflect an imperfect creation groaning in travail for redemption. Creation is viewed as good—even very good—but as imperfect.

4. Heyward, op. cit., p. 278.

5. Nicholas C. Cooper-Leuter and Henry H. Mitchell, *Soul Theology* (San Francisco: Harper & Row, 1986), p. 21.

6. James H. Cone, *Speaking the Truth* (Grand Rapids: William B. Eerdmans, 1986), p. 141.

7. The newsletter *Crispaz* (April 1990), p. 13.

8. Quoted from *Sojourner's* (April 1990), in *Perspective,* number 25 (April 4, 1990), published by the Office of the Chaplain and Covenant Community of University Chapel, Southern Methodist University.

9. Quoted in *The Christian Century* (April 11, 1990), p. 359.

DATE DUE

GAYLORD			PRINTED IN U.S.A.

bishop he might alienate the people pushed to the margins of society. But, after his colleagues encouraged him, he accepted the episcopacy, with the proviso that he would *not* be given preferential treatment over the poor, the weak, the downtrodden, the exploited.

In his first pastoral letter, he wrote the following:

> If it is the first and the most imperious demand of a bishop's duties to be a prophet, and if being a prophet means to tell the truth to the people, if to be a bishop means to be the voice of the weak and the voiceless, then, now that I am fully in possession of this priestly office, I can no longer keep silence with a good conscience [see pp. 109ff.].

In the gigantic landmass of the prelature of São Félix, there are four pastoral teams at work, each with a handful of collaborators. Their first concern is for the health needs of the people; by their loving care to persons in misery they give a credible witness to the good news, the gospel. When Dom Pedro is away, Sister Irene Maria Paula Franceschini is in charge.

What kind of a bishop is this who would rather share with the poor their suffering and their hope, and celebrate the liturgy in a stable, rather than round out with his presence the banquets of the landowners? What took hold of this bishop?

The Spirit of God! And this is exactly what the large landholders and their allies do not like, as we can deduce from the following report:

> On December 16, 1971, Luis Barreira de Souza, a tenant farmer from Serra Nova, was arrested because he had let the bishop and his companions stay overnight in his house. His arrest followed upon instructions from the governor of the State of Mato Grosso.
>
> At the conclusion of a long period full of conflicts between the Codeara Company and the tenant farmers from Santa Terazinha, a village in the prelature, the inhabitants of the area were subjected to pressure tactics from the military: the school and the medical clinic were destroyed. The repression reached its apex with the opening of legal proceedings against one of

the priests of the prelature, French-born François-Jacques Jentel. Condemned to six years imprisonment by the military court in Campo Grande, he was incarcerated for sixteen months before the highest military court set him free.

On June 7, 1973, a detachment, consisting of servicemen from the army, the air force, and the military police, under the command of Colonel Euro Barbosa de Barros, forced its way into the bishop's residence. Members of the pastoral team of the prelature were tortured with electrical shocks, then were not seen for several days, and finally were taken to Brasilia, the capital of Brazil. There they were all forced to confess that Bishop Casaldáliga was an agitator and that he wanted to incite the people to armed struggle. A number of them were told that they would have to undergo interrogation by the military police; they had to submit to questioning in São Félix and Goiânia.

Bishop Casaldáliga's response was prophetic: "This is a time of trial and endurance, my brothers and sisters, but it is also a time of faith, of unity, of strength. And it is the hour for decision: either with the people and Christ, or against Christ and the people. No one can serve two masters, Christ said" [DIAL, No. 249].

When Dom Pedro would not let himself be intimidated, efforts were expended to expel him from Brazil, because he was Spanish-born. To justify this measure he was attacked on the radio, on television, and in the press. But statements of support came from all parts of the country.

The São Paulo Justice and Peace Commission, together with other organizations, published on September 18, 1977, a document with the following assertions:

When certain missionaries are threatened with expulsion, and when many others have already been expelled, it is really the people who are in fact and primarily expelled—and this has been going on a long time. These are the simplest persons, the ones who are chased away from their plot of land or massacred in their villages; condemned to a beggar's life or obliged to work for starvation wages; relegated to vegetate on the margins of the big cities, always subject to suppression by the police or to outrages by their employers; the ones who are threatened and intimidated if they dare to claim their most elementary rights.

Despite the persecution, the priests stood up for their bishop:

Dom Pedro is still our bishop, and he will continue to exercise his office among us. Even if one day he is expelled, he will still be the bishop of São Félix. No power in the world can revoke the appointment of Dom Pedro to be our bishop, which the Holy Spirit entrusted to him on the day of his episcopal ordination, October 23, 1971, and which all of us, deeply moved, experienced with him. The Lord is our strength, we sing in the psalms. He will always be among us when we gather in his name (Matt. 18:20). We commit to him today, with emphasis, his church of the prelature of São Félix.

On August 17, 1975, Cardinal Aloísio Lorscheider, president of the Brazilian Bishops' Conference, went to the church of São Félix in support of Dom Pedro Casaldáliga. Other bishops sent a letter to Cardinal Arns, archbishop of São Paulo, in which they expressed their unreserved solidarity with Dom Pedro.

The Jesuit publication *Orientierung* reported the following:

The Spanish newspaper *Vida Nueva* [New Life] printed on July 25 a detailed, on-site report on the accusations against Bishop Casaldáliga: the role of the military academy and what Archbishop Sigaud had done. Earlier, on June 11, it had stated that a "decision was expected from Rome." But meanwhile Cardinal Lorscheider, president of the Bishops' Conference, had intervened, and Cardinal Arns of São Paulo could inform Bishop Casaldáliga of the words spoken by Pope Paul VI himself: "Whoever touches the bishop of São Félix touches the pope" [No. 15–16/77].

Bishop Casaldáliga on Authentic Voluntary Poverty

I was asked to write two pages on the subject of voluntary poverty and I should like to keep my contribution within the confines of that ideal.

We have all been taught, to a greater or lesser degree, the meaning or meanings that poverty has in the Bible. And we know that, in the final analysis and to the extent that we approach the fullness of time—when the Son of God will come as judge—the poor in the Bible are the downtrodden, the oppressed. They live on the other side of the divide from the rich, the mighty, and the exploiters.

The poor, as poor, open themselves to God. The rich, as rich, close themselves off from God. God, for his part, can communicate himself only to the poor, those who are ready for him.

Mary, mother of Jesus, expressed it in her Magnificat:

Tell out, my soul, the greatness of the Lord,
rejoice, rejoice, my spirit, in God my saviour;
So tenderly has he looked upon his servant,
humble as she is.
For, from this day forth,
all generations will count me blessed,
so wonderfully has he dealt with me,
the Lord, the Mighty One.
His name is Holy;
his mercy sure from generation to generation
toward those who fear him;
the deeds his own right arm has done
disclose his might:
the arrogant of heart and mind he has put to rout,
he has brought down monarchs from their thrones,
but the humble have been lifted high.
The hungry he has satisfied with good things,
the rich sent empty away [Luke 1:46–53].

She thereby framed the best theology of poverty, uniting the legacy of the Old Testament with the new theology of poverty that Jesus would live—in his words, his deeds, his family and work conditions, his messianic struggles with the established powers, his final, magnanimous surrender in his death on the cross.

In practice, all of us "educated" Christians talk about pov-

erty of spirit. And we are, to a greater or lesser degree, roman-
tically enthusiastic about it. Bethlehem, Nazareth, Francis of
Assisi, Charles Foucauld—they all figure easily in our spiritual
conversations, in our dreams.

But can poverty be only a dream? How great an abyss is
there between our spiritual poverty and the objective poverty
of "the others"? How could the religious orders and congregations, looking back over the centuries, and without pangs of
conscience, reconcile the individual poverty(!) of their members with the collective wealth that cries to heaven? How can
we, well fed and well established, keep our peace of conscience
vis-à-vis the two-thirds of humankind that are not well off and
suffer hunger?

In view of the poverty of the majority of humankind, the
children of God, our brothers and sisters, is spiritual poverty
anything else but social sarcasm? Is it anything other than anti-
evangelical blasphemy?

All must answer for themselves, before God and in the light
of the objective circumstances of their life. I cannot in this
context give any universally valid advice. But I believe that, in
any event, we can discourse on poverty only if we also discourse on justice and liberation, if we discourse on all aspects
of life.

It has been said that "love that is not political is not love."
Obviously, this is also applicable to Christian love. The poverty
of the gospel is necessarily political. Because it shows how the
two-edged sword of the Word of God penetrates to the core of
the structures of exploitation, dominance, avarice, luxury, and
consumerism that dehumanize the lives of millions of human
beings, the life of entire peoples and continents: those who ter-
rorize as oppressors, living in superfluity, and those who are
enslaved as the oppressed, living in hunger.

Voluntary poverty, therefore, necessarily includes a political
option, a decision, a true class-option. My putting it this way
must not be more scandalous than the tragic reality that we
have around us, that of a people in fact divided into classes.

The gospel is, to be sure, for all classes. But differently. For
the oppressor and rich classes it is a condemnation and an insis-
tent cry for a radical change of life. For the oppressed poor

class it is a liberation to encouragement and hope.

The Spirit of Jesus, of course, goes behind and beyond all theologies. And the poverty of the gospel is something more than political and social protest and solidarity.

Certainly it is in no way conformism.

It can no longer be a "good excuse" for those who retreat before the conflict, thereby leaving their brothers and sisters alone in the conflict.

Nor can voluntary poverty—the poverty of the gospel—be reduced to the performance of acts of self-denial.

Nor does it consist in simply giving away what is superfluous, being generous in a "charitable" way. . . .

It is more, much more. As with Jesus, who, "was rich, yet for your sake became poor, so that through his poverty you might become rich" (2 Cor. 8:9) with the life of God, so true evangelical poverty must be a true incarnation in the life and struggle of the poor.

It means to lose oneself, to lose one's class, to lose respect and security; with one's own life as the scandal of the cross, to give an answer to idolatrous and enslaving greed and the consumer mentality, to exploitive and colonialistic economy and politics. It means to accept the risk that corresponds to the daily risk of the life of the poor. It means to strip one's own family or one's own institution of privileges—especially when it is a matter of something that boastfully calls itself religious and evangelical.

It means simply to live from the work and with the insufficient wherewithal that the poor must be content with. To eat, dress, travel as the poor eat, dress, travel. To struggle with them in society and in the church (it too is divided into classes) in their political and trade-union struggles and for the other needs of the poor as a class.

It is not a question of letting misery alone, much less of harmonizing it for the others.

What it is a question of is to search for an ever-growing equality of opportunity, in fellowship, always with the participation of the poor and together with them.

If it is not so, then our poverty has nothing to do with the gospel of the poor of our Lord Jesus Christ, the Son of God, who became a poor and marginalized human being, before the Sanhedrin and the Pretorium, but who is the only true liberator of humankind [from a letter of Bishop Casaldáliga to Martin Lange].

Ecuador's *Campesinos* Voice Their Accusations

Ecuador is a Latin American nation that lost a great part of its territory in a war with Peru and has had to contend with enormous economic problems for centuries. Although today it is listed among the countries that export oil, it is still an economically dependent state, and the new riches have not brought any improvement in living standards to the majority of its citizens, namely the tenant and landless farmers.

We will take one diocese as an example: Riobamba.

Bishop Leonidas Proaño, who took part in the Puebla Conference, polled the communites of his diocese beforehand as to their opinions. In their answers the *campesinos* themselves described their situation:

In our country, 19,000 persons earn more than 30,000 sucres (approximately $1,290] per month, while over 1.2 million workers earn only 350 sucre [$15] per month. The continued impoverishment of the mass of the population leads—as the Bishops' Conference of Medellín emphasized—to despair before an inflexible structure that is the result of institutional power and injustices that cry to heaven.

Social change in Ecuador reminds one of the change from a feudal to a capitalistically oriented society in which social life is stratified into a pyramid of exploitation and repression: those at the top owe it to the exploitation of people by other people, and, in order to maintain their position, repress and trample on those at the bottom.

On the political plane enfeeblement and repression of the people are the inevitable consequence. Disillusioned by the unending succession of politicians and embittered by all that transpires in the name of politics, the masses are distrustful and suspicious of all "liberation" projects. The march toward liberation has become a Good Friday procession that goes on forever.

But what does the Bible say to these *campesinos* and to us?

Christians, as true followers of Christ, are called to put themselves on the side of the poor and to struggle with them so that they pattern the course of history. When the poor become aware of their salvific and redemptive mission, they become church. They become the people of God, and their march to full freedom becomes irreversible.

The episcopal conferences in these lands where lay persons and priests are victimized if they stand up for justice should investigate each case. When there is sufficient evidence, they should speak out for an official and public recognition of the new martyrs of the faith, whose love of neighbor did not take fright even at death.

The *campesinos* wrote (March 15, 1978) in a letter to the bishops assembled in Puebla:

We, the Quechua-speaking landworkers of the diocese of Riobamba, where Leonidas Proaño is bishop, want to describe to you our problems. Perhaps you did not know that we live a life that for the majority is meaningless? Persecution, illiteracy, no food, no medicine. Worse: we are dying like flies! When we think about it, we come to the conclusion that everything opposes what justice and equality demand. That is why we hope you will discuss and support us, as the commandment of Jesus demands.

We ask of you no more than the following:

• That you meet every five years, if not more often. The problems are urgent and we need orientation. Ten years is as if a person is neglecting his own kind.

• That you get together and talk among yourselves. Some of you say one thing, and others say the opposite. How are we supposed to know what is what?

• That you undertake a far-ranging evangelization of

Latin America. And denounce injustice and what is going on in each country.

• In Ecuador only two of the bishops are working with the poor. The same is true of priests: only a very few are working with the poor, the landworkers. The others, instead of helping the poor to become aware of their situation, foster instead the repression and misery.

• Preach the gospel to your priests, so that they will no longer have only their own good in mind, but work with the people at the grassroots and not with the high and mighty. Do something with the priests who oppose the process of conscientization. They are a danger for our communities and our countries. There should not be any priests who repress other persons and take money from the pockets of the poor who have nothing to eat.

• We are having problems with the sects of a foreign nation, the U.S.A. There is disunity and dissension. These persons get money, lots of money. They outwit the people. You, honored bishops, should say something about this and denounce the sects.

• You should speak out about the injustices under which we suffer, the hunger and illiteracy. We are being put to death. This is something you should discuss, for this is the task that our Lord has given and it has nothing to do with communism.

• You should talk with the lowly, with the little people who know what hunger is. The ones at the bottom count for nothing. But were we not born in this country? Those of us who are Indians have an even worse time of it! We ask the question: why is there no peace, no equality, no justice for us, but only for the mighty? Whoever the president of Ecuador happens to be, the land belongs only to the rich.

• You should know that we need land, fertilizers, and machinery, so that we could plant something. By our own resources we will not get far. The banks demand money when we borrow some. We are powerless, and when a drought comes, it's even worse.

• We landworkers in the villages and hamlets do not know about one another, we are not united, we do not protest. We are hungry and sick, and there is no water. We are not allowed to organize; we are thrown out, thrown into prison, and walked all over. We ask you, brother bishops, would it not be marvelous for you to give backing to our poor people, the Latin American landworkers? Justice, peace, equality—this is what we want. Everyone wants this. But we do not get it. The whites make problems for us Indians; they dominate us.

• You should also let the North American people know what their government is doing to us, and what the sects are doing. It would be better if they would stay where they came from. Why don't they just stay there and do something for their fellow citizens?

• We plead with you also to denounce how the rich countries of Europe and the U.S.A. steal from us the products that we, the poor and small countries, produce. Prayer alone is not enough.

• Brother bishops, forgive the poor writing and the mistakes. The persons who wrote it are representatives of the Quechua-speaking pastoral regions, of the Christian communities of Cicalpa, Columbo, Flores, and Cebadas [DIAL, No. 487].

Leonidas Proaño:
Bishop of the *Campesinos* and Indians of Ecuador

A woman who has long been active in the conscientization program and worked together with Bishop Leonidas Proaño of Riobamba has written the following of him:

"He respects these persons, takes an interest in their history, and knows how to keep silence in order to let them speak for themselves. But he lifts his voice, loud and long, when the mighty try to take away the word or even the life from the poorest of his brothers or sisters," a Jesuit said of him.

For this reason he has been slandered and persecuted. For this reason too he received the visit of a delegate of the Holy See, who was to gather information on the state of affairs in the diocese of Riobamba. This "honor" is accorded only to those bishops who stand on the side of the people and represent their interests. We can expect that Bishop Enrique Angelelli, who also defends the cause of the poor, will receive a similar visit.

What did Bishop Proaño do to earn this investigation?

In its edition of April 10, 1973, *El Comercio* of Quito published an open statement followed by the signatures of several hundred signers: Bishop Leonidas Proaño was the first to implement the law on agrarian reform by disposing of the possessions of his diocese. He founded the radio schools for the people, which have so far given lessons to over 13,000 adult illiterates in fifteen provinces. He was the founder of an agrarian institute in which the conscientization of thirty-three indigenous communities was being worked on and which was preparing new leadership potential. With the help of the CEAS [Center for Social Studies and Work], he founded twenty-five work associations. His diocese was the first to have fifty grassroots communities in it. As head of the Pastoral Department of CELAM, the Latin American Bishops' Conference, he founded IPLA, the Latin American Pastoral Institute, in Quito; in eight successive courses, already 420 priests, religious, and lay preachers have received training.

Four days later, on April 14, 1973, *El Tiempo* of Quito published, under the heading "Short Notices," a detailed report on Bishop Proaño: "According to the latest, fairly complete figures, in the year 1962 the province of Chimborazo had 276,668 inhabitants, of whom 107,779 over the age of ten were illiterate; 78 percent of the population lives from the land, but only 7 percent owns land of its own.

"In view of these social and economic conditions in Ecuador, the person who entrusted this diocese to Bishop Proaño could have said 'Here is your diocese!' in a tone of voice similar to that of someone assigning a missionary to the most unpromising and heroic of tasks.

"What was needed? Some more 'associations for a happy death'?—the premature death that nearly 180,000 Indians are condemned to? Bishop Proaño shouldered his task unstintingly, and therein lies the merit that is indisputably his."

These and other unbelievable difficulties not mentioned in the newspaper article had to be resolved. There were not only the natural difficulties resulting from three centuries of neglect and fear, but also the contrived barriers thrown up by vested interests that the bishop of Riobamba would have most liked to break through.

And there was no means they [his enemies] recoiled from using!

For example, they dealt him a severe and painful blow by driving away his most dependable and faithful co-workers. And others had to go away, leaving behind an atmosphere of uncertainty and mistrust.

A number of priests from diverse dioceses in Ecuador drafted a declaration in which they stated: "It is the duty of the church in Riobamba to stand trial for Christ and his work, that is, the liberation of humankind. In silence, astonished and anxious, we ask ourselves the question: what will be the judgment from Rome? In these hours of doubt and reversal, official support of Bishop Proaño by the church would reawaken, in many wavering hearts, confidence in the church and would favor the position of the church in Ecuador" [NADOC, April 18, 1973].

The priests of Riobamba "reject most forcefully all the accusations and slanders that have been circulated recently against their bishop by sources unqualified to pass such judgments, and which were intended to influence public opinion, confuse the people, and impress the delegate of the Holy See as easily as possible."

Members of religious congregations added, in another joint statement: "In the case of the church of Riobamba, two directions have crystalized and they cause conflicts of a special type. The defective or false understanding of the bishop's intentions led to the formation of an opposition for which any means, any weapon, even the basest, is judged appropriate. In our opinion this attack campaign crested in the Holy See's dispatching of an apostolic observer to a 'diocese in collapse,' when other dioceses, passive and inactive, were left in peace."

A group of priests in Quito brought out the background of the apostolic visitation even more clearly:

"1. This investigation was not initiated by either the bishops' conference or Bishop Proaño himself.

"2. This investigation was the initiative of a very small group of traditionalists and oligarchs who saw their interests threatened by the pastoral work of Bishop Proaño."

In this context it is worth mentioning that the apostolic delegate also made a "courtesy visit" to the diocese of Ibarra. From a religious point of view, this is one of the least active and most reactionary dioceses. Its bishop, Silvio Luis Haro, is a well-known archeologist and he dedicates a great part of his time and work to this avocation. Was the visit really meant to be investigative, or was it intended only to play down the undisguised mistrust aimed at the diocese of Riobamba?

The thorough investigation by the apostolic observer, Fr. Jorge Casanova, and his secretary, Fr. Carlos Longo, lasted two weeks. In order to become as familiar as possible with the situation of the Riobamba church, the papal investigator took a room in a countryside inn. His secretary stayed in the bishop's house. Together they toured the diocese, visited the indigenous settlements: "We questioned more than two thousand individuals, only thirty-five of whom spoke against the bishop."

Many incidents that deeply impressed the papal observer showed that the inhabitants of Chimborazo were stoutly on the side of their bishop. At the end of a liturgical celebration for the rural population, a woman said to all those present: "Only since Bishop Proaño came here have our eyes begun to see, our mouth to talk, and our legs to run."

At his departure the papal observer stated that he "had gained a very good impression of the leadership of the diocese" and of the "open atmosphere in which the visit had taken place."

In the following months, the word went around that the storm had quieted down; the Holy See approved of and sanctioned the pastoral work of Bishop Proaño. And then many remembered what he had said to them: "I am confident; the light will dissipate the shadows" [*Noticias Aliadas*, May 10, 1973].

The positive impressions of the apostolic visitor did not, however, mean the end of Bishop Proaño's way of the cross. The following year, 1974, a massive campaign was waged against him. He was accused of being a "rebellious cleric," a "Communist disguised as a prelate," who "concerns himself with his peasant brethren" and tells them that "it is the task of the people to fight against the monster of capitalism." What brought on this attack was the Mass that he held for the victims of the coup d'état in Chile. But even this witch-hunt propagranda campaign was not to be the last (see pp. 128ff.).

We should like to note here that it is not always only the military regimes or atheists hiding behind the cloak of a fictitious Christianity who inflict painful wounds on the church. Often they are persons who are acting with good intentions, churchgoers, and even members of the hierarchy. Despite everything, we remain confident that God is powerful enough to turn evil into good.

Chapter 4

The Indians:
Condemned to Extermination

In Latin America there are, according to various estimates, more than 20 million Indians. Two major groupings must be distinguished:

1. Nearly 20 million, constituting major ethnic strains, compose the population majorities in at least Bolivia, Ecuador, Guatemala, and Peru. Even before the arrival of the Spanish, they were hierarchically patterned and were rather easily integrated into a colonial regime: the tribute that they had previously paid to Indian overlords was then paid to the Spanish conquerors. Their fate is sketched in the first three chapters of this book: the Indian movements in the highlands represent a conscious search for the right to work on a parity with the *campesinos*.

2. By contrast, the "unacculturated" ethnic societies (numbering perhaps 1.5 million Indians) in the Amazon and Orinoco basins, the upper reaches of the Río de la Plata, in southern Chile, and in Central America have preserved their independent selfhood with an amazing persistence. The present chapter is devoted to them.

The Brazilian Indians: An Obstacle to "Progress"

In an interview with the German Catholic Press Agency KNA *(Katholische Nachrichten-Agentur)*, Egýdio Schwade, then secretary of the Brazilian Indigenous Missionary Council, CIMI *(Con-*

selho Indigenista Missionário), had the following to say on the situation of Indians in Brazil:

> *Schwade:* Without any thought about the Indians who live there, roads are built through their territories. Owners of landed estates who are interested in acquiring a certain tract of land receive documents certifying that no Indians live there. They then avail themselves of their opportunity with reckless abandon. This is true of private owners and of multinational corporations.
>
> *KNA:* Does it apply to any German corporations?
>
> *Schwade:* If, for example, Volkswagen or Mercedes-Brazil wants land, they get it. Official investigative commissions certify that no Indians live there: they do not live there *any longer*—that is true!—because they have been forced to leave their land. The FUNAI [*Fundação Nacional Indianista,* National Indian Foundation] has its own methods.
>
> *KNA:* The FUNAI, the governmental organization for the protection of Indians?
>
> *Schwade:* It disregards its own regulations; its functionaries are corrupt. Money means more to them than do the Indians. They are often the very ones who produce the documents that camouflage land thefts. They see to it that Indians no longer live in certain areas. The FUNAI maintains the fundamental position that the Indians must either be integrated—into the basically European-oriented social order—or disappear. We have come upon tribes in which no more babies are being born. They are on the verge of extinction [KNA, December 22, 1977].

The Brazilian Bishops: Voice of the Indians, Part I

A document of the Indigenous Missionary Council, CIMI—drawn up in preparation for the bishops' assembly in Puebla—treats of the situation of the Indians in Brazil. Some extracts follow:

> The history of the Indian peoples of this continent, from the end of the fifteenth and the beginning of the sixteenth century,

is the history of a protracted massacre. In the nearly five centuries of colonization and exploitation, millions of human beings fell victim to the Spanish and Portuguese conquerors; they destroyed whole cultures and enslaved whole nations.

In Mexico and Guatemala, the Spanish plundered the Aztec and Maya kingdoms in their entirety and eradicated their culture. Tenochtitlán, the Aztec capital, counted some 300,000 inhabitants, according to historians of the conquest. Cuzco, the Inca capital, situated in the Cordillera range of the Andes (in what is now Peru), was at the time of its conquest the fourth or fifth largest city in the world, in population. Today only fragments remain to give some idea of its size.

These peoples numbered between 70 and 90 million. One and a half centuries later the number had dwindled to 3.5 million.

The Indian Peoples of Brazil. Around the year 1500, the Portuguese estimated that there were about 7 million Indian inhabitants in Brazil. Today this population has shrunk to 180,000 or maybe 200,000, which is 35 times less than before and only 2 percent of the total population that today owns the land that really is theirs. For the Indian survivors, it is as if an overwhelmingly stronger nation had penetrated their territory, slaughtered their children, robbed their riches, and after total victory had built up a new kingdom at the expense of the labor of the enslaved, the true lords of the land. Unfortunately, this process of extermination continues today.

The Role of the Church in This History. The church played a decisive role in the history of the conquest of Latin America. The sign of the cross was engraved on the swords of the conquerors. In other words, there was agreement between church and conqueror in the undertaking of colonization, under the motto: "to extend the faith and the empire."

In the eyes of the Indians, the white missionary and the white invader—sons of the same mother, arriving on the same boat, proclaiming the same faith—represented the same interests and were both guilty of the enslavement of their children. And so some missionaries fell victim to Indian resistance.

There were instances of valiant defense of the Indian rights, as in the case of Bartolomé de Las Casas, who denounced encroachments of Indian rights. But they were exceptions to the rule.

Conscientization of the Church. In the past, the missionary died at the hand of the Indians who were defending their land and their freedom. Today the missionary dies on the side of the Indian as a victim of the new colonial lord. Fr. Rudolfo Lunkenbein was one of them; he died in Merúri, Mato Grosso, on the side of the Indian Simão Cristino.

This fact has a deep significance. The dead missionary lies dead on the side of the Indian, on the side of the oppressed. He is victimized by the same power that the Indian was subject to for these five hundred years. The death at Merúri is like the death of a prophet that opens vistas allowing a glimpse of the future to which the history of humankind is headed. The death at Merúri is the sign of a new mission.

Fr. Rudolfo Lunkenbein and the Indian Simão Cristino (Brazil)

In the "Pastoral Letter to the People of God" dated October 25, 1976, the representative commission of the Brazilian Bishops' Conference published the facts about the Merúri murders:

The events in Merúri, in the State of Mato Grosso, were, at bottom, closely connected with the land survey that had been promised to the Indians. Two days after the surveying had begun, on July 15, 1976, more than sixty persons—landowners, their bodyguards, and settlers—barged into the Salesian mission station at Merúri. They were looking for Fr. Rudolfo Lunkenbein, to take the law into their own hands.

Fr. Gonçalo Ochoa was seized by them and maltreated. Shortly thereafter Fr. Rudolfo appeared, accompanied by some Boróros Indians. He did not react negatively to the provocation but tried to persuade the intruders to settle the matter in accordance with the law. Some of the Indians wanted to do something to protect Fr. Rudolfo from the aggression they sensed was threatening.

Lourenço Rondon, the Boróros chief, was shot. Three more

shots rang out; Fr. Rudolfo was hit and died ten minutes later. The shooting continued. Other Indians were shot; five of them and one intruder were wounded. One of the intruders, Aloisío, was killed by a bullet in the face and by knife wounds. The Indian Simão Cristino was wounded. When his mother, Tereza Cristino, went to his aid, she too was severely wounded. The intruders fled not long after that, leaving Aloisío's corpse and one of their cars behind. The wounded were brought to Barra do Garça. Simão died on the way. He was buried the next day, and Fr. Rudolfo two days later. The police handed over Aloisío's corpse to his family [Press Service of the Secretariat of the German Bishops' Conference, December 28, 1976].

Who was Simão Cristino? His sister Genoveva talked about him in the following terms:

Of Tereza's eight children, only Simão and I, Genoveva Boro-botoudo, were still alive. Simão liked children. It was his great pleasure to be with them. Children would crowd around him and he would tell them stories. He was always ready to help them, with money or feathers for decoration. He gathered the feathers himself. He knew a lot about medicinal herbs from the forest. He made a tincture from arnica blossoms, administered it to others, and explained everything. Just before his death, he was collecting arnica for an old man. We were becoming anxious because he seemed to have disappeared. But then he came back with the medicine for the old man. He was very patient and never became angry [*Boletím do CIMI,* July 1976].

Rudolfo Lunkenbein was born April 1, 1939, in Doringstadt, near Bamberg, West Germany. Even as a young boy he wanted to become a missionary. He came to Brazil in 1958. After further training, he *lived* with the Boróros Indians in Merúri, from then until his death.

Fr. Lunkenbein, or "Lunke," as his friends called him, was very gifted, very industrious, always ready to help others, outgoing and happy. Why then was he murdered? Because his murderers considered him the most influential person standing in their way when they wanted to take the land of the Boróros.

In 1973 he was elected to CIMI *(Counselho Indigenista Missionário)*, the Indigenous Missionary Council. The council had seven members, one of whom was Fr. Burnier (see pp. 109ff.); its president was Bishop Tomás Balduino (pp. 37ff.); his deputy was Bishop Pedro Casaldáliga (pp. 46ff.).

In August 1974 the first assembly of the council took place in the mission station of Merúri, where Fr. Rudolfo had meanwhile become the superior. In September 1975 some Indian chiefs held a meeting there. One of them said: "The whites do not understand that we are all brothers."

Small wonder that the Indians of Merúri had been on the brink of despair when Fr. Rudolfo arrived there in the mid-60s. They were not building new homes, were not following the ways of their own culture, and had lost their self-esteem. The women drank a birth-control juice made from wild flowers. The tribe wanted to die out. No baby had been born among them for six years.

Fr. Rudolfo reflected on his activities and tasks as a missionary. He wrote:

> The first thing is to help this people to find their own way; to bring them to self-consciousness; to make clear to them what lies within them, what powers they are neglecting, what responsibility they are shirking, what a glorious tradition they are simply allowing to disappear. I set myself the task of defending their rights. They are waging a constant struggle for their land rights against the whites—for the land that had been given to them [H. G. Röhrig, *Lasst uns leben*, Bamberg, 1978, p. 14].

After Fr. Lunkenbein's death, the German consul general wrote to his parents: "The success of his work is most evident in the fact that in this Indian settlement that was giving up its will to live, there are now seventy children."

The Indian chief, Lourenço Rondon, who himself was shot in the courtyard of the mission station, wrote the following in a letter he addressed to "the civilized world":

> We now have a new hope, and we are prepared to change the ways of our recent history. And how will we change the

ways of our history? Will we reach for weapons? Should we take on the whites the way they take us on? No! True Christians do not act like that. Weapons do not solve problems. Weapons are the sign of cowardly persons. We want to draw together and unite. Maybe we will die out, but we do not want to let others assume control over us. We demand that others treat us like human beings! [*Lasst uns leben,* p. 55].

The Boróros went into mourning for thirty days for Fr. Rudolfo and Simão Cristino. On Fr. Rudolfo's chest—he who had become their brother—they placed the magnificent headgear of their chiefs.

The Brazilian Bishops: Voice of the Indians, Part II

Incarnation. All means conceivable are used to prevent missionaries from taking upon themselves, fully, the life of the Indian village.

The missionaries believe in the active presence of the Word, and try to interpret its signs. They encounter them in the outstandingly human values—numerous and eloquent—that ethnic life still retains and fosters, as also in the myths of their origins and their heroes, in which the veins of the Old Testament promises shine through. To the eyes of faith, these values are seen as clarified by the light of the gospel: community of goods, authority by service, respect for humanity, respect for nature, a religious atmosphere.

In order to preach the gospel to others, missionaries must first take it upon themselves. To the extent that missionaries really take part in the life of the Indians, they take upon themselves the fate of these human communities, make their concerns their own, and incorporate their culture, in order later to be able to translate the Word and preach to them the Savior as the one who fulfills their deepest hopes and strivings.

Proclamation of Salvation. For the Indian peoples, God's promises go beyond the Exodus and will be fulfilled only in the struggle for liberation and the recovery of what they have lost. Missionaries see themselves bound to this struggle: the regaining of their self-consciousness as a people, of their culture, their dignity, their land, their hope.

There is verified here the statement of the Second Vatican Council that God wills to save persons not as individuals but as a whole people (*Lumen Gentium,* 9). It is peoples and nations that, by divine mandate, are to be protected from extinction.

The Capitalistic System. After the abolition of slavery, capitalism developed a much more effective and subtle form of exploitation: hired labor—indispensable for the establishment and progress of industry. The manpower for industry came from agriculture. The capitalistic system reached out to the fields, uprooted the landworkers from the land, erected for itself a monopoly, and then developed for itself extensive land and livestock enterprises in which there is room only for animals and machines. We are right now living through precisely this stage of development in Brazil.

The Brazilian Indians, hunted down since the first days of colonization, retreated to the wilderness and today are fighting for the last patches of land that they can still use. Because the Indian population is relatively very small, its contribution in terms of workers for agrarian production has no great importance. But the same does not apply to their remaining lands, the borders of which are forever being changed and reset anew, with the intention of constantly tightening the "noose" around the Indians and making it impossible for them to live outside the lines of demarcation determined by the prevailing system.

This is the first and the greatest difficulty for the missionaries who work for the protection of the Indian: struggle against a system that needs a monopoly of the land and therefore cannot tolerate "unproductive land," that is, land not being used for the pursuit of profit, such as the Indian territories.

The Image of the Oppressor. The second major difficulty is that the Indians associate the church with their white oppressors. This association goes so far that missionaries who share their lives and devote themselves to their protection can still be told by them: "You are very concerned about us, but you are killing us internally." Another missionary explains: "They call the basic missionary principle into doubt. By what right can we offer a people something that will deeply influence their view of the world and even change for them the meaning of life?"

Government Guardianship. The introduction of a guardianship law by the Brazilian government, without listening to the Indians or those who struggle with them, has set up a great obstacle for missionary work. This law gives to the agencies that implement official Indian policy a police power for handling Indian affairs. It thereby allows for repressive handling of any attempt on the part of Indians to hold meetings or seek any form of internal organization for the protection of their rights.

The Radical Contradiction. The life of Indian society is an extremely severe criticism of the bankrupt capitalistic system. Indian society proves that it is possible to attach more value to human nature than to capital; that it is possible, healthy, and "worthy of the human condition" to keep the means of production in common ownership; that it is possible to give social order a social footing; that it is possible to live from nature without destroying it; that the human being can work in order to live, instead of living in order to work; that freedom, festivity, and joy are possible. The Indians are living proof against the false values that our civilization holds. That is the reason why the Indians are unbearable to our civilization.

For the Renewal of the Church. The Indian mission offers the church an outstanding opportunity to test itself in the purity of faith and the light of the gospel. Some missionaries who maintain a deep and spirited contact with the life of an Indian group ask themselves whether they do not encounter in them "the life of the gospel that they have the duty to preach." At the same time, these missionaries can test with greater exactitude the alleged values of so-called Christian civilization, as also the imperfections and failings of their own ecclesiastical structures that allowed such values to pass into and help shape a world of inequality and domination, judged and condemned by the Spirit.

At least one theologian has said that the world of the Indian incorporates the ideal conditions for a true and completely unfalsified renewal of the church [*Boletím do CIMI*, March/April 1978].

Chapter 5

The Hellhole of the City Slums

Industrialization is taking hold of Latin America too. The *campesinos* who cannot any longer bear their misery and deprivation on the land hope they can improve their lot in the cities. The flight from the land (see the section on Bishop Adriano Hypólito, pp. 116ff.) has dire consequences:

1. It eases the way for the purchase of large tracts of land by the multinationals, and, by the same token, applies the brakes to the urgently needed agrarian reforms.

2. *Campesinos* are uprooted, torn from their accustomed natural and cultural milieu. They are easy prey for the *magical cults*, especially prevalent in Brazil, which cater to escape from the world. Those who take part in these cults should not be condemned out of hand; Christians should instead make earnest efforts to make these poor unfortunates feel at home in the church, for "anything you did for one of my brothers here, however humble, you did for me" (Matt. 25:40). In the past this was often made more difficult by the prevailing European image of a Christendom bent upon the happiness of the *individual*. In Chapter 4 it was pointed out that, for example, the Christian value of community is lived in a more convincing way by the Indians than by many Christians. The supreme problem area of Christianity in contemporary culture can be characterized as that of a lack of inculturation.

3. The cities are mushrooming. For example, of the 26 million Argentinians, 10 million live in Buenos Aires. In 1950 approximately a fourth of the Latin American population lived in cities

counting over 20,000 inhabitants; by 1975 that fraction had increased to a half.

4. The slumdwellers live in "shelters" that the large landowners would not keep their horses in; after all, they have a market value. Someone who lives in one of these urban slums is asked where he lives; he answers: "In the daytime I work; at night I hide myself."

In the Hellhole of the Slums

In Lima (Peru) the slums are called *pueblos jovenes* [new cities]. In 1977 there were 417 of them, in which 1,100,000 persons were "living." They had too little for life, but too much for death.

In Quito (Ecuador) 38 percent of the families (out of a total population of 700,000) have only one room to live in. In Guayaquil (Ecuador) at least 40 percent of the 800,000 inhabitants live in slum areas.

In San Salvador, the capital of El Salvador, 150,000 of the total population of 700,000 inhabitants have no indoor plumbing; 100,000 have "taken possession" of unused land and have built huts for themselves out of sheet metal, cardboard, and other scrap.

In the city of Bacabal in northeast Brazil only 3,000 of the 45,000 inhabitants have anything better than part-time, short-term employment.

Buenos Aires (Argentina)

In Buenos Aires in 1977, according to an estimate made by the newspaper *Cronista comercial* (Commercial Chronicler), there were more than 200,000 vacant apartments and rooms that could have been rented out; half a million persons could have been housed in them. Nevertheless, on Holy Thursday that year the inhabitants of one of the slum quarters, *villas miserias*, were driven from their dwellings. Their "goods" were loaded onto trucks and dumped in open fields [*Noticias Aliadas,* September 15, 1977].

Priests from the slum areas of Buenos Aires protested on July 9, 1978, against the expulsion of their people by the military regime of General Videla:

At least as regards the *villa de colegiales* quarter, it can be proved that the civil authorities for resettlement carried loaded weapons, that many inhabitants were punched, reviled, and yelled at, that women were propositioned and promised better housing if they would cooperate, that city officials demanded money for the same consideration, etc. It is not just a question of normal human weaknesses, such as can be found everywhere, but of serious abuses in the exercise of public functions [*Noticias Aliadas*, August 17, 1978].

Bogotá (Colombia)

From 1958 to 1974 the population of Bogotá rose from 2.5 to 3.5 million. At least 40 percent live in misery. But the rich live very well, and without a bad conscience.

On October 27, 1974, five Jesuits and twenty inhabitants of the El Dorado slum quarter were arrested because they had "taken over" some unused land. The Jesuits explained:

We believe that it became clear to us, once and for all, what it means to "be Christian." Does it mean to perform certain religious exercises? To go to church on Sunday? To give alms to the poor? Or, to act in a true spirit of fellowship and make our own the situation of injustice and oppression experienced by many of our fellow humans, and therefore to strive to help justice break through, to be able to love one another as equals, inasmuch as we truly commit ourselves? [*Noticias Aliadas*, November 14, 1974].

Subversion: To Become Poor with the Poorest

Fr. Juan Alsina (Chile)

On September 20, 1973, under the Bulnes Bridge over the Mapocho River, the corpse of Fr. Juan Alsina was found. He had been shot ten times—in the back.

Spanish-born, he was just thirty-one years old. He had worked as vicar in Puerto San Antonio. In May he had moved to Santiago and had lived since then in a slum area, *población*, on the south side of the city. During the day he worked in a hospital in San Juan de Dios. As a priest in the active ministry he celebrated the liturgy on Sundays in his *población* and he ministered to Christian groups.

Since the military putsch under General Pinochet his life was in danger. *Any* priest who lived in a slum area, earned his living as a worker, and spoke at Mass like a prophet was under suspicion.

On the vigil of his death, unable to sleep, he wrote the following:

> We wanted to put new wine in old wine skins, but we had neither wine nor skins, at the moment. We were at the end of our tether; we had found a path, but now once again we are surrounded by boulders. Those who are still on hand are going ahead. But how much longer? Maybe we will find some trees, to protect us from bullets.
>
> For two days now, there is nothing left. And we cannot speak; we just chew on something. We were so hungry for that dry bread! Each of us cut off a slice with a kind of smile. We are wandering, like sheep led to slaughter. "Into your hands I commend my spirit."
>
> We count on your solidarity. Do you understand what the body of Christ means? When we drown, a bit of your hope drowns too. When our ashes come to life again, new life will awaken in you as well.
>
> *He* accompanies us, wherever we go ["Chile," CEP (Centro de Estudios y Publicaciones), Lima, 1974, pp. 110–13].

Fr. Carlos Mugica (Argentina)

On May 11, 1974, when he had just finished celebrating the liturgy with the San Francisco Solano community, Fr. Carlos Mugica was shot down, riddled with bullets. He was quickly taken to a hospital, where he died a few hours later, scarcely forty-four years old. Dying, he said to a priest friend: "Now, more than before, we must stand united on the side of the people."

A friend of his wrote of him:

> He was one of the best-loved representatives of a renewed church for the people in Argentina. Many saw him as the leader of the Movement of Priests for the Third World [*Mov-*

imiento de sacerdotes para el Tercer Mundo].

Although he came from a wealthy family, he succeeded in beginning a new life on the side of the masses. Without hiding his background . . . he placed his life and all his means in the service of liberation.

He was the best defender the people had. He devoted his whole time to it, no matter what risks or exertions it required. It should be noted that he served as a bridge between his own class, the upper stratum of central Buenos Aires, and the masses of urban poor. In this way persons from diverse vocational sectors came to see what their Christian duty was when faced with the reality that he made known to them, and they helped him in his many undertakings.

Fr. Carlos was always faithful to his obligations as a priest, as he, in his childlike blamelessness, conceived them. Nor did he let himself become embittered by the annoyances and restrictions that the ecclesiastical hierarchy used on occasion to try to isolate him. At public meetings he always stoutly defended the hierarchy and the church; again and again he asserted his "unshakable membership" in the church, after the example of his slum quarter, which "never left" the church even though it had experienced total desertion by it.

His political option, which is as open to questioning as is anyone else's, came clearly to light in a document of the Movement of Priests for the Third World, which he helped draft: "Our solidarity with the people obliges us to state in clear terms our affiliation with the National Peronist Movement [*Movimiento Nacional Peronista*]. Today we are still convinced that it continues to take part with renewed fidelity in this process, and so we emphasize anew our intention to remain on its side and to offer it the moral support that springs from the gospel and the grace of Christ."

In his book *Peronismo y cristianismo* (Peronism and Christianity) Mugica wrote:

We Christians cannot today pray the Our Father without also doing something effective to reduce the mortality rate, which rises daily. The same is true of torture: if I do not do what lies within my possibilities to get it to stop, then I am a co-torturer of my own brothers and sisters.

We Christians are called on to be witnesses to the truth and to fight against injustice with all our means, even if it leads to arrest, torture, imprisonment, or indeed death itself.

Of his priesthood Mugica said:

The priesthood that we have received from the church and that we exercise in communion with the bishops obliges us to exert ourselves to sow the seed of faith in the heart of humankind, and never stop doing so. We know that this gift of God sets and anchors the root of whatsoever type of true liberation.

To take away from the people the basis of their life and hope constitutes an enervation of their power of renewal. The respect and special standing that the faith of our people accords to the priest we want to accept only to the extent that it serves the wishes and the interests of the people themselves [*Noticias Aliadas*, May 23, 1974].

Moreover, in the slums of Buenos Aires, any priest who works for the good of his people is tauntingly called "Father Mugica."

Daniel Esquivel, Workingman (Argentina)

He was thirty-one years old. His shoes were covered with dust from his walks through the slum quarters. In winter he wore a threadbare sweater. He did construction work, as an electrician. At a very early age he had been a member of the Young Catholic Workers, a catechist in the diocese of Lomas de Zamora, and until recently a member of the pastoral team for Paraguayans in Argentina. He had been born in Paraguay, the son of a farmer, and had lived as an immigrant in Buenos Aires for seven years.

A fellow worker said of him:

He was a good person. Or, as we say, he was never satisfied with halfway measures. He was open-minded, obliging, always ready to help.

A housemaid:

> He never complained about his situation. Of course he became
> tired, hungry, sick; at times he was laid off from work. But he
> was the type to encourage others with a laugh, a good word,
> and full trust in God, or perhaps in human beings, inasmuch as
> he saw him in them. It was easy for him to win the affection of
> others, because he was very natural, goodhearted, and open. It
> could be said that his work, his life, was not the most orderly,
> but I think that he was and lived the person he was. He often
> pointed out that in a group not all are the same, but the impor-
> tant thing is to help one another, stick together, always respect
> the other person [key word, "Charism"; see 1 Cor. 12; Rom.
> 12].

A priest:

> He had a deep faith, which he would let come to the surface
> without thinking about it, and he dedicated his life to God
> without setting any limits to it. For us priests he was a good
> example for our pastoral ministry. We knew that Daniel had at
> one time wanted to become a priest, but, because he had had
> only a few years of elementary schooling, no diocese would
> accept him. We tried all we could to do something about it, but
> to no avail. He would have had to have completed elementary
> school, then high school, and finally the years of philosophy
> and theology. "I'd like to become a priest, but without giving
> up my construction work," he said. Years would have to go by
> before we could live as worker-priests, and we haven't yet
> reached the stage where he as a worker could have become a
> priest.

Another workingman:

> Daniel lived in continual union with Christ. That's why his life
> was a unique apostolate. He never wanted or intended a change
> of his life, from being always prepared for service to his fel-
> lows. No one can say that Daniel was a hypocritical Christian.
> To live always in the presence of the poor was really the content

of his life. He was fully convinced that the only way to peace, to justice, and especially to what we need for a new society, consisted in living according to God's plan, now, among and with the poor.

Daniel was taken from his home early in the morning of February 1, 1977. Some cars had driven into the slum quarter where he lived. Armed men got out, beat him and two companions, put them into wooden boxes, and disappeared. After days of torture, the two other men were released, but Daniel was retained. No further word has been heard about him since that time.

Twenty days later Bishop Desiderio Collino of Lomas de Zamora wrote in a Lenten pastoral letter:

We can in all certitude state that Daniel was never involved in political questions, nor even once in questions concerning his homeland (Paraguay), much less was he involved with guerrilla groups. All our personal efforts to date to find out from various authorities where he is have been fruitless.

I say with emphasis that even in self-defense against subversive activity it is not right to strike down someone who is unarmed; torture is still a serious sin; the taking of someone else's property is theft. The use of force is allowable only to the extent necessary. A weapon does not entitle its user to infringe on the personal rights of another person, or their right of ownership. Authorized officials can and must in given cases suspend "constitutional rights" for a time, which in no way means that all rights for all citizens can be suspended, much less that citizens can be handed over to the whims of armed individuals or groups (whose crimes are allowed or even approved of by the government). So far as it is also understandable that within given limits a mistake is possible, to the same extent care is demanded that such measures are not taken without provision for subsequent revision. But we, on the contrary, are at the point of copying the ways of the most merciless form of totalitarianism—Marxism. Without justice, peace is not possible. Without Christian love of neighbor, the following of Christ is pious fraud. "Who wants peace must defend life."

Daniel, wherever he may be, is an example for us Christians.

If he is in "his Father's house," he is there to pray for us for the grace we need for the pastoral ministry. If he is still in detention somewhere, in the suffering that is allotted to "the children of God in his image and likeness," we believe that Daniel will show that he is there for the sake of Christ; he will encourage the weak, he will pray with them—yes, he will sing songs with them in the Guarani tongue, in the devout and lively songs that narrate the history of the Paraguayan people, a history filled with fearful ill treatment but sustained by courage and hope.

"If they take me prisoner, I will serve Christ as a prisoner; in my cell I will write his name with the blood of my heart."

Good Shepherds (Peru, Bolivia, Mexico)

In May 1976 Bishop Luis Bamberen, as president of the Commission for Social Work of the Peruvian Bishops' Conference, demanded of the government of General Morales Bermudez an investigation into the disappearance and assumed murder of various unionized workers, and the allegations made against those responsible for the torturing of political prisoners:

> The Christian spirit in a social undertaking shows itself in the way that the poor and oppressed are treated; in them the presence of the Lord is encountered, his struggle is taken on and his mandate for a more just society.
>
> The present situation must be changed and improved: we are opposed to the disturbances that disrupt peaceful working conditions, and the dismissals that result from them. We are opposed to the violent suppression of conflicts that could have been resolved by dialogue. We are opposed to the legislation that tolerates the defamation of leaders nominated by worker groups to become their lawful representatives.

This message was published only by the newspaper *La Prensa*. The six other daily newspapers in Lima, four of which had been nationalized two years earlier, kept silence [*Noticias Aliadas*, May 13, 1976].

On June 4, 1976, the entire slum quarter of Vitarte, in the environs of Lima, gathered in support of the 840 workers of the Nylon factory, all of whom lived in Vitarte; they had been on strike for six weeks. The main road was blocked for five hours with whatever the people could find to erect a blockade, to give themselves some protection against physical attack by the police.

The striking workers were making three demands: (1) a wage increase of 70 soles (approximately 31 cents) justified by the rise in the cost of living; (2) the rehiring of six co-workers; and (3) prevention of the sale of a part of the factory to another entrepreneur, which would result in the loss of wages sought by the workers.

On July 11, Cardinal-Archbishop Landázuri Ricketts of Lima visited the strikers. He went there because he knew about the troubled situation. He spoke for an hour with the workers on strike and agreed to accept the role suggested to him: as a mediator; in order to have previous guarantees observed and to prevent a break-off of dialogue with factory officials. Some days later the cardinal learned that the workers had been seized by the minister of labor. As on similar occasions, the official press kept silence on these events [*Noticias Aliadas*, October 28, 1976].

On July 1, 1976, the standing council of the bishops of Bolivia sent a document to the government in defense of workers on strike. The document spoke of the complaints of the workers about the arrests of their union leaders and co-workers, about the accusations made against dismissed workers, about the mistreatment of those arrested, and the house-searches accompanied by plundering.

The bishops met with some success on certain points, on behalf of the workers, but some of them were doubtful that the government would keep all its promises. Their doubt was founded on their experience in similar cases in the past, and their doubt proved correct.

There are further examples of the church's taking the side of workers in Latin America. It has had to pay the price for it—in blood. Its struggle in fellowship for equal opportunity for workers cost two Mexican priests their lives.

Fr. Rodolfo Aguilar (Mexico)

At approximately 7 A.M. on March 21, 1977, two persons came to Fr. Rodolfo Aguilar and asked for his assistance as a priest. He went with them immediately. At 9:30 A.M. a shot was heard in the house of Sergio Durán, a friend of Fr. Aguilar's. When Sergio arrived home at 10 o'clock that morning, he found there the corpse of the priest, with a bullet in it. Sergio and his wife had just come back from Monterrey, where they had spent their honeymoon. They were both arrested by the police, together with another of Fr. Aguilar's friends, David Noé Zamorran. Officials of the Suterm labor union, who entered the house as the police were taking away the corpse, could confirm that there were no weapons there.

Rodolfo Aguilar was born in Mexico City on November 28, 1948. He entered the seminary in 1961 and was ordained to the priesthood on September 16, 1974, by Archbishop Adalberto Almeida y Merino of Chihuahua. Some days later he was named pastor of Holy Name of God parish.

He began his work with a survey of the parish, which included thirteen city divisions with a population of more than 15,000 persons: on the one end, the industrial zone with its factories, on the other end the holiday resort area for the wealthy, and between them the shantytown of the disenfranchised, without water, without postal delivery, without public services.

His bishop said of his death: "In fact, the death of Fr. Rodolfo . . . has given the people new motivation. From then on they have worked with the awareness of a new reality; groups meet, have discussions, and search out ways to go ahead."

Fr. Rodolfo Escamilla (Mexico)

On April 27, 1977, at about 4:30 P.M., Fr. Rodolfo Escamilla was shot from behind by a tall young man in his mid-twenties.

Rodolfo Escamilla was born in the tiny village of Moravatio in the Mexican state of Michoacán on August 24, 1920. He was ordained to the priesthood on September 23, 1944, after having studied at the seminary in Montezuma, New Mexico (U.S.A.).

Appointed vicar in Zacapa, Michoacán, the site of one of the largest wood pulp factories in Mexico, he founded a school for vocational and union training. The beginning of persecution dated from the same time. The union leaders of the "good and faithful" political party in power never forgave him for helping to found an *independent* labor union. They threatened him, killed several workers, and used political pressure to induce his bishop to make him leave his community. He was sent elsewhere, but the workers never forgot him; they continued to go to him, wherever he was, to ask him advice and support.

He was forbidden to enter the state of Michoacán because of alleged danger to his life. And so he joined the bishops' Mexican Social Secretariat *(Secretariado Social Mexicano)* in Mexico City.

The spirit that filled men like these two priests becomes clear in paragraphs from a letter that Fr. Rodolfo Aguilar wrote to his bishop on the day of his ordination:

Dear Father and Bishop!

I should like to spell out my reply to the invitation to be a collaborator in the work of salvation, before my Lord Jesus, who appears in the sacrament of bread and who takes form in my fellow human who is poor and oppressed. Today and always in the history of humankind, salvation is liberation, Easter, renunciation of all infidelity, oppression, and injustice.

With my own life I want to fashion a prophetic and priestly response to the call of God, my Father, and to the call of humankind, my brothers and sisters.

Full of enthusiasm, I freely agree to live the life of proclaiming the gospel that Jesus lived. I am duty-bound to my oppressed brothers and sisters, and I willingly offer my life for their and my liberation.

I renounce forever any human privilege or personal desire, any private possession, in order to be able to dedicate myself freely and utterly to the creation of a new human community. Because of this choice, I see myself barred from entering into an exclusive commitment to one person, and so I renounce marriage, a family, in order to fulfill the history-making task that Jesus commits to me, a call and mission that I have discovered in the silence of prayer [DIAL, No. 389].

Chapter 6

The Educated Join with the Oppressed

The Ideology of National Security

The following contribution was written by Horst Goldstein, a student of Dom Adriano Hypólito, the bishop of Nova Iguaçu, in the state of Rio de Janeiro, Brazil:

Since the end of World War II, certain political circles in the U.S.A. and elsewhere have taken as an underlying principle that the world is divided into two great camps: the one Western, democratic, free, and Christian; the other Eastern, communist, unfree, and atheistic. And this worldwide confrontation between the two blocs was anything but static. Let only certain "crisis areas" be mentioned here: Korea, Vietnam, the Dominican Republic, the Arabian peninsula, Africa. And so, in the U.S.A. the National Security Council came into existence as early as 1947, with its infamous CIA [Central Intelligence Agency]. As an organ of the federal government, this council was to strengthen, by lawful and unlawful (Watergate) means, the administrative branch of the government vis-à-vis the American Congress, in order to facilitate movement into focal points around the world, of which Latin America was one.

Among university students, the urban proletariat, and rural populations in Third World countries, the awareness grew that they were not really *underdeveloped*: they were being *kept* underdeveloped. By the same token, the Catholic Church, since Vatican Council II and the Bishops' Conference of Medellín, changed from a stabilizing to a threatening factor vis-à-vis those who profit from injustice. The deplorable condition in Latin American nations was and is maintained by military dictatorships.

In the 1967 version of the Brazilian national constitution, the armed forces were assigned the responsibility of "defending the Fatherland and guaranteeing the three constitutional bases of power, law, and order." Since the constitutional changes of 1969, it is also incumbent on the armed forces—in view of the alleged failure of the three constitutional bases and the alleged political immaturity of the people—to reorientate anew the whole destiny of the nation. The goals of the armed forces now are "essentially for the implementation of the *policies* of national security" (Art. 91). In direct subordination to the president of the republic, the Council for National Security has become the highest consultative body to the president and, in the U.S.A. pattern, is entrenched beyond all parliamentary control. It is incumbent on the Council of National Security to "determine the permanent goals of the nation and the radical principles of national policy." In view of these new constitutional realities—we are told—many democratic practices must undergo a change. Every power shift to the presidency weakens the parliament. What the federal courts can do has been restricted. Labor unions and the universities have been further weakened by becoming agencies of public opinion formation and discussion. In all schools a new department has been introduced: "moral and civil training."

On the basis of the understanding that the world is divided into two blocs, and the free, democratic, Christian West is constantly threatened by the atheistic and communist East, the government asserts that Western and Christian civilization must be defended against every enemy from without, and even more from those within. Because the church has shown itself to be a "soft spot" in the fabric of the free world—a nursery of subversion, a Trojan horse of communism—it must be watched with distrustful skepticism. There is no choice—so we hear—but to have appropriate military and police officials question lay persons, religious sisters, priests, and even bishops about their theological and pastoral ideas.

In a declaration of the War College in 1970, the following were singled out as manifestations of subversion: corruption, student unrest, strikes, rural organizations, demonstrations of the people, intellectual and esthetic movements, political gatherings, conflicts in political parties, reforms in the Catholic Church, terror in the cities, armed conflict in the countryside, sabotage, assassinations, disappearances (of persons).

The aim of these forceful activities is alleged to be the destruction of the highest values of the human person, a destruction that attacks society and the nation, and draws the very essence of the state into sympathy, so that weaknesses can be converted into the introduction of a new "social order."

The church's understanding of itself as the people of God demands an outright rejection of the ideology of national security. How this is to be done will depend upon the circumstances. In the "Pastoral Letter to the People of God" issued by the representative commission of the Brazilian Bishops' Conference, CNBB, in October 1976, these dauntless words are to be found: "The ideology of national security elevates itself above the needs of personal security. It spreads out over the entire Latin American continent, reminiscent of what happened in the countries under Soviet domination. Latin American regimes that adopt this ideology declare anti-subversive war on all countries that do not agree with the authoritarian organization of society. This doctrine has led the regimes to adopt the same characteristics and practices that are prevalent in communist countries: abuse of state power, arbitrary arrests, torture, and the suspension of freedom of thought."

In February 1977, the plenary assembly of the Brazilian Bishops' Conference expressed itself in more subdued terms: "The church does not question that the modern state has the right to implement a policy of national security. A proviso, of course, is that this security leads to genuine *peace*, understood as the positive result of cooperation with the people, that the aims of this security are co-determined by the people, and that it corresponds fully with the demands of the political and moral order.

"Inasmuch as security is closely linked with the common good, it is by its very nature an unconditional demand that has the survival of the nation as a goal, and which for its part demands the conscious cooperation of the entire citizenry. But if the state, in the name of this demand, arbitrarily diminishes the basic rights of the person, it upsets the foundation of the entire moral and juridical order.

"Security dare not be a privilege for particular systems, *classes*, or political parties. On the contrary, it establishes a responsibility for the state in the service of the entire nation. Therefore it dare not sacrifice any fundamental rights in order to safeguard special interests.

"Security as a good of a nation is irreconcilable with a constant insecurity in which the people is forced to live. This comes especially to light in the use of arbitrary *means of oppression*, from which people cannot defend themselves: arrests, inexplicable disappearances of persons, degrading trials and hearings, acts of violence that unscrupulous terrorists without further ado perpetrate in secret, and taking into consideration the fact that this type of crime often goes almost completely unpunished."

Living for Justice:
The Brazilian Lawyers Eugênio and Lúcia Lyra

If Christians from the professional ranks take an interest in the importance of fellow humans from the "lower" classes, they incur the suspicion of the military, which controls the government in almost all of Latin America, and the propertied class in league with them. The professional persons will be accused of wanting to overthrow the prevailing system by force, even when their intention is simply to prevent *camponeses* from being driven off the land where they live. Bishop José Rodrigues de Souza of Juazeiro wrote in a letter to Martin Lange about the case of Dr. Eugênio and Dr. Lúcia Lyra:

Dr. Eugênio Alberto Lyra was born on January 8, 1947, in Bonfim, which is a diocese neighboring Juazeiro, both in the state of Bahia. In 1970 he obtained his law degree from the Law School of the Federal University of Bahia. On September 22,

1977, at the instigation of land thieves, he was murdered in Santa Maria da Vitória by a hired killer.

The region of Santa Maria de Vitória, on the far side of the São Francisco River, together with some other regions, was considered by the government ripe for land reform. Because instances of land theft were a commonplace there, the Federation of Agricultural Workers—Bahia Division (FETAG-BA) turned to Dr. Lyra for legal assistance for the agricultural worker unions in Santa Maria da Vitória, Coribe, and Bom Jesus da Lapa. Although he was aware of the dangers he would be subjecting himself to, he went there and dedicated his young life to the defense of the landworkers, homesteaders, and owners of small farms. He thereby made out of his profession a priesthood against arbitrariness, violence, and lawlessness. With all his energy, he fought against domination and injustice, and offered up his life as a sacrifice in the defense of equality, freedom, and human dignity.

On September 28, 1977, by invitation of the legislative assembly of the state of Bahia, he was to speak before a parliamentary investigative commission on the problem of land thievery. He had ample documentation on the matter of property rights and abuses in the area. Because this material would have exposed many prominent persons, it was decided to put him to death. And thus the voice of a brave and resourceful lawyer was stilled. With tears in his eyes, a worker said: "The death of Dr. Eugênio has shortened our lives."

Dr. Lúcia Maria Athaide Lyra, thirty-seven years old (in 1978), the wife of Dr. Eugênio, was herself a lawyer. Three months after his death, her first child was born, a girl, who was baptized with the name Mariana.

Lúcia Lyra was the inseparable companion of her husband and lived through the same struggle in the defense of the homesteaders and small farmers. She always, especially on the death of her husband, showed herself as the "valiant woman" of whom the Bible speaks. In 1978 the FETAG-BA hired her to handle its legal matters: she would carry on the struggle of her husband in defense of the landworkers. She is a cheerful and socially outgoing woman, always ready to give public addresses on the subject of land problems in our region.

Víspera (Uruguay)

A group of intellectuals in Uruguay founded the magazine *Víspera* (Vespers), which earned international recognition for itself.

On April 30, 1975, the government of Uruguay ordered the discontinuation of the magazine, after its founder and director, the attorney Dr. Héctor Borrát, had been arrested. He was released some time later, but kept under house arrest. Exile was the final step.

On May 6, 1975, those responsible for *Víspera* published an explanation, from which the following extracts are taken:

The accusations can all be boiled down to the first objection against its publication, as soon as it was realized that it would be a journal that would address itself to international currents at work in Latin America in the religious, social, and political arena, whether among university students (International Movement of Catholic Students) or scholars (International Movement of Catholic Intellectuals).

The costs of publication were covered by foreign funds; Pax Romana was the first to help, and then the German episcopal funding agencies Adveniat (headquartered in Essen) and Misereor.

The accusations made by the government were aimed not only at *Víspera* but also at the German agencies Adveniat and Misereor. Because *Víspera* could not be published without their financial help, they, according to the accusations, had a share in the responsibility for the extreme danger that the journal represented. Adveniat and Misereor were not allowed to make further financial contributions because they had been financing nothing less than a publication that, according to the five major criticisms of the government, showed "strong support of and constant agreement with subversive movements operating in Latin America and other parts of the world, to bring down the lawful and constitutional social order, and install governments that oppose human rights and democracy."

The German and other funding agencies not named in the accusations were thus accused of supporting revolution in Uruguay, Latin America, and on the international level. Because these agencies were dependent on the bishops, the accusations redounded to the bishops. And because Misereor worked together with the West German government in Bonn, supervising help to developing countries [see *Materialien*, No. 30, published by the Federal Ministry for Economic Cooperation, Bonn, April 1973], very serious responsibility redounded to West Germany.

The Radio Station of the Archdiocese of São Paulo (Brazil)

Many dioceses in Brazil have their own radio stations, which have been a great help in educational undertakings: alphabetization, evangelization, and conscientization programs. They have made their contribution towards helping the disadvantaged to become aware of their rights.

Because of this last-named result of radio work, the radio station Radio Nove de Julho (Radio 9th of July) of the archdiocese of São Paulo was closed down by order of the government. Cardinal Paulo Evaristo Arns spoke of "a feeling of extreme disappointment" and stated in a sermon on November 1, 1973: "Precisely today, on the 30th anniversary of my ordination to the priesthood, we heard the bad news that the government has revoked its approval of Radio 9th of July."

The Shutdown of Radio Pio XII (Bolivia)

On January 13, 1975, troops of the Bolivian army occupied the miner settlements of Siglo XX, Llallagua, and Catavi, and dismantled the Catholic radio station Radio Pio XII. Six Oblate priests and a theology student gave the Bolivian Bishops' Conference a detailed account of the takeover:

Froilán Gonzalez, a student of theology, was staying overnight on a tour through the parish (Siglo XX). At 4:20 in the morning he was rudely awakened by seven agents who had their guns pointed at him. The command was given for everyone there to line up against the wall, with their faces turned towards the wall and their hands raised above their heads. Shortly afterwards Fr. Gustavo Pelletier, the pastor of Siglo XX, was also brought there. He had got up when he heard the uproar and confronted five agents rummaging through the desk in his office; he was forced at gunpoint to join the others.

Somewhat later . . . Fr. Gustavo and Froilán were taken to the military barracks at Uncia, where they were put with some miners who had also been seized. It was then that they learned that the radio station had been closed down, because many groups of miners regularly listened to its programs. In addition personal items—pocket radios and other things—belonging to the priests were confiscated [NADOC, No. 388].

Professor and Workingman: Fr. Maurice Le Febvre (Bolivia)

Maurice Le Febvre was born on August 6, 1922, in Montreal, Canada. He entered the Oblates in 1942, earning his licentiate in philosophy three years later and his licentiate in theology in 1949. In 1953 he went to Bolivia. For five years he served as pastor in Llallagua, in the Catavi mining district, and worked closely with the most active labor union in the country.

In 1958 he was transferred to Espíritu Santo (Holy Spirit) parish in the slums of the Bolivian capital, La Paz:

Come with me to the slums, to celebrate the Easter Vigil. After you have crossed the railroad tracks, and the sidewalk ends, you will stumble over stones and sink into mud. You can smell the stench of fish but you can't see anything, because there's no street lighting here. You come to a wide, open space with a hut in the middle of it. That is the church. Six yards wide, nine yards deep, nine feet high, a roof and three walls of bamboo, the uncovered earth for floor. About a hundred persons have gathered here to light their candles from the light of Christ.

This does not live up to the customary picture of worship. If someone wants to bring the proclamation of the *Lord* to Latin Americans, they should not speak in the church, because "the church of service" [of service to lay persons by priests] is a confirmed invalid here, consisting only of old women, very young children, and middle-aged men who most often are very reserved and outspokenly immovable. No, you must look to another public: to the people in misery, undernourished, out of work, uneducated, homeless. How could they be interested in even the best possible lesson in religion if they are not given help to escape from their misery?

I spent the whole of November building up a discussion circle. We talked about the reforms that Latin America needs: agrarian, financial, legislative, social assistance, and the teaching of the church on social conditions and development [from three letters written by Maurice Le Febvre in 1963].

Fr. Le Febvre went to Europe in 1963 to study sociology in Italy, France, and Switzerland, because he thought that it would help him to better serve the poor. He earned his degree of sociology in 1967.

From Rome he wrote:

One of the most important duties of a priest is to be available to everyone. He must especially get to know and understand everyone very well. He must pose the same questions, with the same words, as do the poor; he must live as they do. Then we will truly proclaim the *Lord*!

After his return to La Paz, in 1966, he wrote:

On workdays I'm in the office from 8 A.M. to noon, and from 2 to 6 P.M. —but often we go on as late as midnight. I celebrate Mass and read my breviary at night. On Saturdays and Sundays I generally take part in community gatherings.

My house, like my neighbor's, has no running water and no toilet. There is only one room, but the floor is wooden and the walls are plastered. I pay $10 a month rent and have the same problems as my neighbors whom I run into day after day on our muddy street. It is not easy to be poor when you know it could be avoided.

There are two ways to escape misery: with force or without force. I believe in the latter alternative, if it succeeds. But if it turns out to be unsuccessful, then obviously we must fall back on the first alternative—and without waiting one or two centuries.

In June 1968 he gave his first lecture in the National School for Sociology in La Paz; in 1969 he was named dean of the faculty. A friend related of him: "He was very gifted. Even more than his research and books, his studies of life and of the people were outstanding. He had friends everywhere. He was a very quiet person. He was at once very capable and very simple."

In 1970 he, together with three other priests and a Methodist, was exiled because he had tried to force the army, by a hunger strike, to hand over the corpses of freedom fighters to their parents.

A month later he could return, after a change in government. His students carried him on their shoulders to the university.

Shortly before his death he left the university because he had finally tired of the pretenses of the elite. He went to work as a miner in a cooperative that was living from a small tin mine: he wanted again to live fully with and like the poor.

On August 17, 1971, General Banzer led his coup d'état. Fr. Le Febvre was studying when the Red Cross called on him to help with the wounded. At the Red Cross headquarters he was given a Red Cross flag for his car. Together with another priest, one or two American nurses, and one other person, he drove to the battlefield. There he was cut down by gunfire. His companions hid themselves at the end of a street and tried to go to his aid. Although they carried a white flag, they were shot at every time they tried to get near him. Only after two hours were they able to reach him. But by that time he had bled to death.

The Student Alexandre Vannuchi (Brazil)

On March 17, 1973, Alexandre Vannuchi, a student at the Catholic University of São Paulo, died. His death was *officially* attributed to a "traffic accident." In fact, Vannuchi had found himself in the hands of Commissioner Fleury, the head of the infamous "death squadron" that, without respect for any law, hunts down everything that it considers communistic.

Dom José Melhando Campos, the bishop of Sorocaba, near São Paulo, who was "bound in Christian friendship with Alexandre," wrote in a declaration:

In view of the facts of the case, we must ask ourselves the following questions:

- Why was his family not notified about the "accident"?
- Why was the young man's corpse not handed over to his family?
- Which member of his family was allowed to identify the corpse before burial?
- Why did his family first learn about his death from the newspapers on March 23, when, according to the police, Alexandre died on Saturday, March 17?

The police had his personal identification papers: they included his photo and details about his family. And there was another way he could have been identified: by the Catholic University, where he was in the fourth year of geology and was very well known.

If we take seriously the insistence of the gospel on the love of truth and justice, we cannot keep silent. This senseless act of violence deserves, like all the other similarly disguised cases, our deepest abhorrence. This is in accord with what the Brazilian Bishops' Conference recently stated, that every attack on human rights in this country must be protested, regardless of who is involved.

It is not for us to refute the accusations that the police have brought against this student: God alone knows; *God* is his judge. But it is obvious and beyond all doubt that he was done away with in an inhuman way, and that in a normal procedure he could have explained and defended himself, and, if necessary, could have admitted his deeds and assumed his responsibility for them [DIAL, No. 7].

Chapter 7

Valiant Women

Bishop José Rodrigues de Souza (Juazeiro, Brazil) called Dr. Lúcia Lyra one of the valiant women of whom the Bible speaks (see pp. 85ff.). Because of the hardships she underwent after the death of her husband, her daughter was born with a permanent defect; nevertheless, Lúcia struggled on valiantly like a prophetess for justice, and by so doing she brings Christian hope to the *camponeses*.

In the Old Testament, the ancestresses of Israel (Sarah, Rebecca, Leah, Rachel), the prophetesses (Miriam, Huldah), and those who rescued the people from disaster (Deborah, Judith, Esther) are held up for commendation as valiant women.

The Apostle Paul could not deny in his epistles that he was a learned rabbi, and he gave thanks to women for their "help," a word that often refers to efforts on behalf of the Christian mission (see John 4:39; Acts 20:35; 1 Cor. 16:16) and in the Christian community (1 Thess. 5:12). Paul refers to Phoebe as a deaconess and administrator; she deserved help "for she herself has been a good friend to many, including myself" (Rom. 16:1-2).

Some of the fathers of the church knew how the earlier church had been served by women. Thus Theophylact: the Samaritan woman "became an apostle, given a priestly blessing by the faith that took hold of her heart; she taught the whole city." And Augustine: "The Holy Spirit made Magdalen an apostle to the Apostles."

How, on the contrary, women at the time of Jesus were thought of in Palestine can be gleaned from the Rabbi Jehudah: "God be praised, who created me not as a heathen, not as a woman, not as an ignoramus!" In a court of law, the testimony of a woman was not considered to be conclusive. Women were not allowed even to wait on table if male company was present. To try to teach women religion was considered patently hopeless. In view of these and similar ideas of his contemporaries, Jesus acted in a nearly unbelievable way vis-à-vis women: he talked with them, which amazed even his disciples (John 4:27). Especially Luke had much to relate about the women in Jesus' milieu, such as those "who had been set free from evil spirits and infirmities, . . . who were providing for them out of their resources" (Luke 8:1–3).

Valiant women can also be found in Latin America: *religious sisters*, who, in the past, saw their role as that of imparting a solid education to the daughters of "the elite," have since turned over their schools to lay staffs and given up the security of the cloister in order to share the destitution in slum quarters: suffering shared is suffering halved! They take care of prisoners and help with the formation of cooperatives. The work of a Franciscan sister was praised in these terms: "No *man* could have done it!"

Wives stand by their husbands when they go on strike or fight for their land, to make possible a life of human dignity for their children.

Mothers, despite deprivations, raise their children to become free Christian persons.

These women do not seek attention for their efforts for the kingdom of God, because, as Christians, they consider their contribution to be the most taken-for-granted thing in the world. Without them the church would collapse.

A Countrywoman Demands Equality (Honduras)

In September 1978, Moncha de Sosa, who lives and works in a rural area of Honduras, wrote a letter to the Latin American bishops:

I wish to say to the bishops . . . that it is very important for them to speak about the situation of women, because it is a subject that has been left untouched. Women are talked of as inanimate objects, although we all know that God created man and woman with equal dignity and with equal rights, and that woman is every bit as capable as man, and thinks as he does, and works for a new world. There are many who think that we were put on the earth to bake cakes. It is my wish that our rights be proclaimed, because we are Christians [DIAL, No. 488].

Doña Tingó: Victim of Injustice (Dominican Republic)

Impoverished landworkers in the Dominican Republic recite this prayer: "Doña Tingó, we will follow you, to sow justice in the furrow that you have plowed." Doña Tingó was murdered on November 1, 1974, at the age of 58. Why was a pious widow with seven children shot to death?

More than fifty years earlier, Don Polo had come to the region of Hato Viejo near Yamasá. Wild hogs were the only living creatures in the area. Don Polo and his comrades built animal traps and together put up the first house for miles around. By their hard labor they made the land fruitful.

One of Don Polo's sons, Felipe, fell in love with Florinda, a dark-skinned maiden from Villa Mella. The capable young woman "bewitched" him with her bubbling gaiety and her thirst for life. They were married in Hato Viejo; Don Polo gave them land for their use.

Florinda and Felipe grew cassava; they planted banana and orange groves. They had ten children, three of whom died in early life.

Florinda was well liked because she boosted the spirits of her fellow humans. Her neighbors and friends gave her the nickname Tingó.

When her husband died, she managed the small farm by herself, and no man could have done a better job of it.

When the women were working in the fields, Doña Tingó sang songs she made up herself, songs that gave praise to the Creator. The women worked very hard because they wanted to give their children a better future.

Meanwhile, in the capital, Santo Domingo, the territory of Hato Viejo was sold, and the *campesinos* who had worked the land for over fifty years knew nothing about it. Doña Tingó, when she learned of it, joined the Christian agrarian leagues. She was a respected leader in them.

At the beginning of this chapter, one group of "valiant women" was not mentioned: the *widows*.

Widows and orphans are often referred to in the Bible as being particularly deserving of help. Moses cried: "A curse upon him who withholds justice from the alien, the orphan, and the widow!" (Deut. 27:19). Jesus warned: "Alas for you lawyers and Pharisees, hypocrites. You eat up the property of widows, while you say long prayers for appearance sake. You will receive the severest sentence" (Matt. 23:14). David sang of God: "Father of the fatherless, the widow's champion" (Ps. 68:6).

Widows took upon themselves important tasks in the early church: women had to be over sixty to be *formally* inscribed as widows on the rolls of the church (1 Tim. 5:9). They had to be pious (5:5) and have accomplished good works (5:10). These widows dedicated themselves to good deeds and service in the community (5:10), and were therefore provided for by the community (5:16). It can be concluded that they were recognized ecclesiastical office-holders.

In early 1974 a ruffian named Pablo Diáz came to Hato Viejo, with the intention of seizing the land. To underscore his claim of ownership, he had a fence put up around the lands of the *campesinos*. He had their huts blockaded, and had tractors run over the harvest already gathered by the *campesinos*. He wanted to force them to "sign away" the land and leave it. Note well that these were the families who had wrested the land from the forest and had been the ones to make it arable.

Doña Tingó would not give in; her neighbors followed her lead.

Policemen and some sleazy types whom Pablo Diaz had hired skulked around Doña Tingó's hut night after night, screaming and shooting guns and calling out: "Go away, Witch Tingó, you troublemaker!" She answered: "God and Don Polo gave me this land. If someone is going to take it away from me, they are going to have to take away my life!"

Pablo Diáz tried to get the *campesinos*, including Doña Tingó, arrested—he who claimed the land, wrongly, and they who had cultivated it! The police were not ashamed to let an unarmed woman be harassed. Pablo Diáz's hirelings showed her a rope and acted out how they intended to hang her with it. They shoved a thorn-branch into her stomach. But Doña Tingó remained harder than granite. "I will not sign [the form giving up her claim to the land]. This land belongs to us!"

On November 1, 1974, the court case against the *campesinos* of Hato Viejo was opened in Monte Plata. Doña Tingó submitted a petition against Pablo Diáz. But he was not there; he had some other "business" to attend to.

When Doña Tingó returned home that evening, her children crowded around her and told her that Turin, one of Pablo Diáz's hired thugs, had untied the pigs in the yard. Doña Tingó left her family eating supper and went outside to tie up her animals again. Turin, in ambush, brought her down with two shots from an old musket. Her children streamed out of the house when they heard the shots, but the assassin escaped. Old Don Polo appeared and saw his daughter-in-law "stretched out on the ground like a wounded dove of peace."

Doña Tingó was mourned by all her neighbors. Everyone prayed for her. A man from the group lamented: "The mother of us all, the mother of Hato Viejo, is dead." Another man corrected him: "No, don't believe it, my friend. Tingó's blood will bear fruit. It cries out like the blood of Abel—against Cain. This blood will be the best seed that Tingó ever sowed in Hato Viejo."

In the Sermon on the Mount, Jesus had promised Doña Tingó and the friends for whom she gave her life: "How blest are they who hunger and thirst to see right prevail: they shall be satisfied. . . . How blest are those who have suffered persecution for the cause of right, the kingdom of heaven is theirs" (Matt. 5:6,10).

Alicia Domon: Mission to the Most Abandoned (Argentina)

The cardinal-archbishop of Paris, the archbishop of Toulouse, the president of France, and many other French citizens have asked the Argentinian government over and over again about the French nun Alicia Domon, who "disappeared" on December 8, 1977.

Representatives of the Argentinian Bishops' Conference have

stated: "We do not know whom we can ask; we do not know to whom an inquiry should be directed." But Argentinian journalists investigated and wrote reports, knowing they were risking their lives for doing so.

Alicia Domon came from a French worker family. Three daughters became nuns. Alicia received one or two letters a week from her family.

She went to Argentina like so many other foreign religious—full of good will but lacking the necessary orientation. But she soon perceived the extreme need of those "who had no one" (cf. John 5:7).

In 1967 she began to bring the gospel to children and prepare them for their first communion. For years afterward, she visited them and their families, at regular intervals, in their homes. Her first pupils were soon able to themselves take over the work of evangelizing other children.

She turned to the people in the slums, who had not received any notice from the church. In 1969 she was the first religious woman to move into a slum area, Lugano, one of the grimmest in Buenos Aires.

She stayed there for five years, living exactly like her neighbors. She went to work in the morning as a housekeeper, like many other women in that slum quarter, in order with her underpaid half-day wages to meet her extremely modest needs.

From midday until well into the night, she devoted herself to her neighbors, whom no one had ever cared for before. She accompanied them to the hospital, looked after their children, taught them, and conducted religious services.

When once she was questioned about her work in the slums she answered with a smile: "I didn't come here in order to tell people what they had to do, but in order that we could help each other and share life's joys and sorrows, here where we take each other for what we are. I have probably received more than I have given."

A woman friend of Alicia said: "When she listened to someone, she did it with a kind of wonder, as if she found in everyone something new. And so we felt good when we talked about our needs with her. We all liked her."

Alicia listened with the patience of an angel to those who waited for the crumbs to fall from the tables of the affluent and wolfed down ravenously whatever was more or less palatable. Whoever was slow or considerate of others had to go hungry. Because Alicia listened to them, slowly but surely they began to express their inner thoughts, to distinguish between right and wrong, good and evil.

Through Sister Alicia's work, the slumdwellers experienced *freedom* for the first time in generations: "The Lord . . . is the Spirit, and where the Spirit of the Lord is, there is liberty" (2 Cor. 3:17).

Alicia told the downtrodden about him who the night before his death on the cross expressed the wish that his followers *share* his memory. Her friends understood quickly. Of their own accord, they went to help the sick and the unemployed. They talked over their common lot together; they shared in fellowship the little that they possessed and held celebrations in honor of God their Savior. They began to organize themselves, to demand, nonviolently, their rights as human beings.

After five years, Alicia came to realize that the rural population needed her more than did the inhabitants of the city slums. And so one day she quietly took leave of the people in her slum quarter who had become her friends. They gave her their blessing.

She went to the small village of Perugorría in the province of Corrientes, to a poor family with a houseful of children. For room and board she worked hard in the fields. She thus experienced in her own body the exploitation of the *campesinos*. In a region encompassing 193 square miles of arable land, the *campesinos* owned not one square foot. And so they sharecropped for the large landowners, pledging half of their harvest to the owners—who were also the ones who set prices on harvested products. The owners in turn sold the goods at much higher prices, because they could eliminate all competition. The *campesinos* had to buy the necessities of life on credit against the following harvest. They sank deeper and deeper under the millstone of debt. They became easier and easier to exploit.

Alicia took part in the *campesinos'* strikes, to get a higher price for tobacco. She worked wtih the Christian agrarian organizations. She learned about the imprisonment, abduction, and torture of young landworkers who had run the risk of forming Christian agrarian associations.

In 1977 she went to Buenos Aires again, to help a young country girl who had twice been abducted, tortured, and detained in prison. At last the opportunity came to leave the country. Alicia was there to help with the emigration formalities.

The military chose that time to conduct house-searches in Perugorría. A policeman was puzzled to find no clothing in the house that Alicia lived in. In fact, she had nothing more than the clothes she was wearing—like the *campesinos*, whose dire need she willingly shared.

She stayed in Buenos Aires and did hourly work as a housekeeper. She began research on a study, "The Prostitution of Immigrant Girls from Paraguay and Bolivia, and the International Centers that Control This Manipulation of the Innocent."

Screams from the torture chamber gave Alicia no rest. Out of concern for others who have been tortured, we cite only the case of Teresa Sosa, who went through hell in the Villa Devoto prison:

> They began to torture me early in the morning. Naked and with my skin wetted down, I was tied to the *parilla* ["perch"—a wooden beam suspended horizontally between supports at each end, suggestive of the perch or roost in a bird cage]. They tortured me with electrical shocks on the most sensitive parts of my body.
>
> After a while I lost consciousness. When I came to, I was lying on the floor, on a small mattress, and I was bleeding profusely. I was three months pregnant at the time.
>
> A doctor treated me; I was given injections to stop the bleeding. Then they came for me again, to torture me.
>
> Because the bleeding would not stop, they gave me blood and serum injections.
>
> They started again to torture me with electrical shocks; this time I was seated on a chair.
>
> Questions that give me endless pain: Why did the bishops not speak out when my baby was aborted? Are my relatives and friends also being tortured? How are they? Or has my family already been exterminated? Are my children being taken

care of? Does anyone believe the lies that are being told about me? Does anyone still pray for me?

Jesus is with me in prison. *He* is tortured with me. *He* is my last hope! [CIMADE, Comité d'intermouvement auprès des évacués, Paris, February 16, 1978].

These outrages brought Alicia, at the end of 1976, to the Ecumenical Movement for Human Rights *(Movimiento ecuménico por los derechos humanos)*, sponsored by Protestant churches; it was not officially recognized by the Catholic Church. It had been founded in February 1976, one month after the armed revolution under General Videla. Alicia worked with the families that had been the object of persecution for their Christian principles; she encouraged them and demanded that their human rights be honored.

She especially concerned herself with the mothers of the thousands of political prisoners. She collected material for use in their defense, gave Christian encouragement, helped with locating court records and writing announcements for the newspapers.

Because of a demonstration of mothers before the national congress, Alicia was held for twenty-four hours. She stayed with the mothers whose hearts were broken by the sufferings of their children.

On October 15, 1977, the close relatives of political prisoners submitted a petition to the national congress. Eleven women and thirteen men were arrested; Alicia was not among them. When they were released, the relatives went right on with their activities. They undertook a collection of signatures in solidarity with the prisoners on the occasion of Christmas.

For that Christmas Alicia prepared religious exercises for the mothers of those who had "disappeared"; her intention was to dissipate some of the darkness of their desolation by the light of the gospel.

An unbeliever said to Alicia at that time: "Dear Sister, thank you for being with us!" He discovered little by little something "new and good" in Alicia's person, and because of her became a Christian. The same thing happened to many others.

Alicia wrote in a letter to the archbishop of Toulouse: "I beg you not to do anything in order to save me that could be disadvantageous to others. I am ready to sacrifice my life."

On December 6, 1977, she visited a family she was friendly with and told them that her task was heavy. And so she asked the blessing of the grandmother who was held in high esteem in the family. The old lady countered: "I am the little sister who asks *you* for a blessing." But Alicia insisted: "No, please bless me."

Two days later, December 8, there was a regular meeting in the parish church of Santa Cruz (Holy Cross) for the mothers of those who had "disappeared." Money was to be turned in for a protest petition at Christmas.

At 8 o'clock that night, as the women were leaving in small groups, automobiles drove up, with policemen out of uniform. They arrested sixteen persons, including Alicia; the others were able to get away. The money they had collected "disappeared."

Two days later Sister Leonie Duquet, who had been living with Alicia, was abducted. According to the testimony of reliable witnesses, the two religious were put to death in the Buenos Aires naval school at the end of December that year (KNA, September 26, 1979).

Of the sixteen women, five were later set free. None of them knew anything—or did fear seal their lips? Despite the sensation, the Argentinian Bishops' Conference made no public statement on the whole episode. This intensified the fear.

An Argentinian priest who knew Alicia personally was of the opinion that, because of the success of her cooperative work, she knew she had to die.

She kept to the words of Jesus: "When I was hungry you gave me food; when thirsty you gave me drink, when I was a stranger you took me into your home; when naked you clothed me; . . . when in prison you came to visit me. Anything you did for one of my brothers here, however humble, you did for me" (Matt. 25:35,36,40).

Sheila Cassidy: A Doctor Not Allowed to Help (Chile)

Sheila Cassidy was born in 1937 in England, the daughter of a vice admiral in the air force. Her family migrated to Australia and she went to school there, beginning the study of medicine in 1956 at the University of Sydney. From 1958 she continued her studies in England, where she passed the state examinations in medicine in 1963. During her internship in Oxford, she decided to specialize in emergency and plastic surgery.

It was at that time that she came to know Consuelo Silva, a young Chilean woman who was studying medicine on a British scholarship. Sheila met her again in Leicester where she was working in the emergency ward of a hospital. The two young women became good friends and it was not by chance that she chose Chile when she decided not to accept the constraints of the British national health system. In December 1971 she embarked for Chile.

The next years were not easy for Sheila Cassidy: she had to learn Spanish and she had to adapt herself slowly to the Chilean social, cultural, and economic context. Salvador Allende was then president. With Consuelo she learned the country from the roots upward. She worked in several hospitals in Santiago. There she could order prescriptions for her patients that they could not afford.

Up to that point, Sheila Cassidy had not concerned herself with politics. That changed when, on September 11, 1973, in the bloody coup d'état, Allende was killed and a military government under General Augusto Pinochet took power. The Englishwoman came to know a system that strove to crush out every reminder of the socialist Allende and considered all means to that end good.

In 1974 her friend Consuelo died. Sheila became friends with foreign priests and sisters who were living and working in the slum sections of Santiago. She found herself getting deeper and deeper into that kind of work and finally took over the medical directorship of a clinic for the poor in El Salto, one of the most miserable slums in the city. How could the gospel be brought to the suffering when they could not afford the medical help needed to free them from their suffering?

Dr. Cassidy's collaboration with ecclesiastical circles brought persecution in its wake. In January 1976 she spoke out before a commission of the United Nations in Geneva on her arrest and imprisonment:

On October 21, [1975], a Chilean priest telephoned me and said that he had a request to make of me. He then came to our house and told me that a wounded leftist revolutionary needed medical attention: he had two gunshot wounds in his leg. He asked me if I was prepared to help that man, and I agreed. I was fully aware of the danger of being discovered, arrested, interrogated, and sent into exile.

She was then taken to a sisters' convent where she saw Nelson Gutiérrez. The bullet in his leg could not be removed and she made it clear to him that he could not stay underground much longer: he would be endangering the lives of those helping him. In addition delirium could be expected, which would make him a further danger to his friends. She suggested therefore that he seek asylum in the residence of the papal delegate. Gutiérrez agreed and he found asylum there.

The evening of October 31, 1975, Sheila went to the house of a missionary society where she was attending to an American nun who because of overwork had suffered a nervous breakdown. The house was surrounded and shots rang out. Sheila Cassidy was arrested and taken to one of the centers of the secret police, DINA [*Dirección de Inteligencia Nacional*, National Intelligence Administration]. There she was subjected to electrical shock torture three times; her strength finally gave out and her torturers got the confession they wanted.

At a later date she reported on the second of the three electrical shock tortures:

> I was ordered to undress and then I was again tied down on the tabletop. This time they put an electrode in my vagina and electrified me with a movable electrode. The pains were much more severe this time. Although they had said that I should move my fingers when I was ready to talk, they gave me any number of shocks before they removed the gag from my mouth so that I could talk. After about twenty minutes of repeated shock applications, I confessed that I had treated Gutiérrez in a sisters' cloister. They found the thought fantastic and did not believe me; I had lied to them before. They interrogated me further and tortured me with electrical shocks. After about an hour they believed me. I was untied, dressed, and we drove in a car to the cloister. After I pointed out the building to them, they brought me back to the prison.

I'd like to add that my guards—during the two trips through Santiago—said to me more than once: "It would be a lot simpler for us just to kill you and be done with it." It was said casually, but I had no reason not to believe them [*Index on Censorship*, Writers and Scholars International, London, Vol. 5, No. 2].

Sheila Cassidy was afterwards locked up with three other women and, the following days, had to write out a "confession" that was dictated to her. Then she was kept for nearly three weeks in strict isolation in the Cuatro Alamos prison of the secret police. From there she was taken to the Tres Alamos station for political prisoners, where she was kept until December 1975. Diplomatic efforts then proved successful and she was set free but had to leave the country immediately. In England she made public disclosure of what she had gone through.

She became a novice in a convent of English Benedictine nuns:

I remember the time when I was lying naked on the bed, with my arms and legs stretched out, and I was tortured mercilessly. I had the impression that I was present at the passion of Jesus more as a participant than as an onlooker. It was not the feeling one has when meditating on the sufferings of Christ, when one is a bystander, seeing someone else suffering and having deep sympathy for that person. Mine was a very clear impression that *I* was *there*, suffering with Christ and no longer merely as an onlooker [B. Cooper, *Meeting Famous Christians*].

Sheila took to herself the words of Jesus: "When I was ill you came to my help. I tell you this: anything you did for one of my brothers here, however humble, you did for me" (Matt. 25: 36,40).

Cardinal Raúl Silva Henríquez, the archbishop of Santiago de Chile, stated on November 5, 1975, regarding the imprisonment of Dr. Sheila Cassidy and other Christians:

The ecclesiastical authorities condemn the treatment of priests, sisters, or lay persons that is an obvious expression of agreement with the principles of hate and violence: it flatly contradicts the spirit of Christ.

It is totally different in the case of those who, inspired by the dictates that the gospel contains, believe that they are acting according to their conscience when they want only to save the life of those to whose aid they have been called, regardless of the political options they may have taken. It must be remembered that Christian love is different from other kinds of love precisely in the fact that it rests on mercy without limitations. Those who act with this motivation have the right to be heard, understood, and respected by a public official brought up in the Christian spirit. The church trusts that those responsible for national security are also capable of treating matters of this sort in this light [DIAL, No. 259].

Chapter 8

Be Patriotic: Kill a Priest!

In 1977 many walls of houses in the cities and towns of El Salvador (see pp. 24ff.) had painted on them the slogan: "Be Patriotic: Kill a Priest."

Why did the military regime tolerate this incitement to murder—a regime that postures as the guardian of "national security"? (see pp. 82ff.). Because a priest who goes to those in destitution, lives with them, takes them seriously, defends and encourages them, and stands up for their rights becomes a threat to the privileges of the military and the rich, whose well-being is dependent on the poverty of the masses. This is verified in all the nations in Latin America with military governments.

The Martyrdom of Fr. Henrique Neto and Edval Nunes da Silva in Recife (Brazil)

In the decade from the Latin American bishops' conference in Medellín (1968) to 1978, the number of progressive priests imprisoned, abducted, murdered, or exiled reached 850 [*Veja,* São Paulo, April 19, 1978]. One of the first was Fr. Neto.

On May 27, 1969, parts of a human body were found in a tree on the grounds of the University of Recife. They were what remained of the unbelievably mutilated corpse of a priest who had been arrested and battered to death on the same day: he had been dragged along through the streets by a car. Before that he had been horribly tortured. Thus ended the life, at the age of twenty-eight, of one of the closest co-workers of Archbishop Helder Câmara.

Fr. Antônio Henrique Pereira Neto taught sociology at the university and was entrusted with youth and student ministries by Archbishop Câmara. He was butchered as a warning to Câmara in his struggle for the poor, for a society in fellowship. The government put a ban on reports of Neto's death. Nonetheless, seven thousand believers attended his burial.

Fr. Henrique's work had been nonviolent. His bishop said on a trip through Canada:

> I respect and I will always respect those who, after conscientious and mature reflection, choose the way of violence. I myself have always been and I remain of the opinion that I should rather be killed a thousand times than kill another person. I believe in the power of nonviolent moral pressure—the power of the peaceable. But we must reflect very carefully before condemning the oppressed and the violence that springs from despair.

On March 26 and 27, 1975, Archbishop Câmara was called on once again to state his mind on the murder of his co-worker when the court case was reopened. He wrote in a letter (April 16, 1975): "I was told by telephone that I should choose my words very carefully if I did not want to lose another of my priests."

On November 20, 1978, Archbishop Câmara lost another co-worker, Edval Nunes da Silva. Edval had left the seminary in order to work with the oppressed; in effect, he was Fr. Neto's successor. He was arrested and tortured. Released, he reported on the torturing. He was arrested again, tortured again, and this time he died, from damage done to his kidneys. At his death, like Fr. Neto, he was just twenty-eight years old.

On May 27, 1978, Archbishop Câmara held an anniversary memorial service for Fr. Neto. During the service he walked to the grief-stricken mother of the priest and embraced her.

The next day the president of Brazil, General Ernesto Geisel, visited Recife. Helder Câmara was not on hand to greet him, for, as he said: "Today is Sunday and I must celebrate Mass five times, and the evening Mass in Planeta dos Macacos [Planet of the Apes], one of the newest slum areas in Recife. That's where all the people live who have come here from the interior, after their land has been taken away from them."

Fr. João Bosco Burnier: Martyr for Justice (Brazil)

João Bosco Burnier was born on July 11, 1917, in Juiz de Fora in the state of Minas Gerais, into a family with an illustrious background. His father, the engineer Henrique Burnier, was the son of the famous Brazilian Central Railroad builder, the engineer Miguel Noel Nascentes, and grandson of the lawyer Dr. Michel Noel Burnier, who, for political reasons, had been banished from France. His mother, Maria Cândida Penido, was the daughter of Dr. João Nogueira Penido, from a well-known, well-established family.

João Bosco entered the archepiscopal seminary in Rio de Janeiro, where he spent his high-school years. In 1933 Cardinal Sebastião Leme sent him to Rome, where he studied philosophy at the Pontifical Gregorian University and was one of the first students in the Pio Brasileiro College. While in Rome he decided to enter the Jesuits; with the approval and blessing of Dom Leme, he returned to Brazil and, on October 2, 1936, entered the Jesuit novitiate in Nova Friburgo, in the state of Rio de Janeiro.

On July 27, 1946, he was ordained a priest in Rome and received his degree in theology a year later. In mid-1948 the general superior of the Jesuits, Johann Baptist Janssens, brought him back to Rome and named him secretary of the Latin American assistancy. He returned to Brazil in early 1954 as vice provincial for the region of Minas Gerais, Goiás, and Espírito Santo.

In early 1958 he became novice master in the Jesuit novitiate in Itaici in the state of São Paulo. He held this office until 1966. He devoted himself to the training of young Jesuits and he did pastoral work in neighboring parishes.

At his own request he entered the Jesuit mission in the prelature of Diamantino in the state of Mato Grosso. The ten years that he spent as a missionary were lived in great intensity, and with the enthusiasm of a much younger man. At first he worked mainly with the newly founded parishes scattered throughout the vast hinterland of the prelature. At a later stage he turned to direct ministry to the Bakairi and Xavante Indians, taking pains to learn their language.

The CIMI (*Conselho Indigenista Missionário*, Indigenous Missionary Council) commissioned him to formulate the six ground principles that have been used ever since in the pastoral ministry to the Indians throughout Brazil. At the February 1976 CIMI meeting in Diamantino, on the regionalization of the ministry, he was elected the CIMI coordinator for the northern part of the State of Minas Gerais [*Boletím do CIMI*, November 1976].

In the "Pastoral Letter to the People of God" (see pp. 64ff.) the death of Fr. Burnier was narrated:

On October 11, 1976, Fr. João Bosco Burnier . . . accompanied Bishop Pedro Casaldáliga [see pp. 46ff.] on the return trip from a meeting of priests in which the problems of the Indians were treated.

When they got as far as the little town of Ribeirão Bonito in the commune of Barra do Garças the bishop and the priest went to the police station to protest the arrest and torture of two local women. Eight days earlier the police chief Félix, a member of the military police of the state of Minas Gerais, had been killed. This happened at the same time as the police were arresting, with brutality, the children of Jovino Barbosa. The death of the police chief resulted in the sending of a large contingent of police from Barra do Garça to Ribeirão Bonito. Fear and dread reigned among the populace. Many were arrested, beaten, and tortured.

Margarida Barbosa, the sister of Jovino Barbosa, was detained from October 4 to October 11 and tortured by the police. She was forced to kneel with outstretched arms on broken bottletops; needles were thrust under her fingernails and into her breasts; she was beaten. For the entire time there she was given nothing to eat or drink. On October 11, at 5 P.M., screams were heard on the street: "Don't beat me!"

Santana Barbosa, the daughter-in-law of Jovino Barbosa, was seized at the same time, two weeks after her baby was born, and was raped by several soldiers. Her husband's fields under cultivation, their house, and all the rice in storage were burned to ashes.

The suffering of these two women moved Bishop Casaldá-liga and Fr. Burnier to speak with them in the Ribeirão Bonito jail. They both tried, unsuccessfully, to substitute themselves for the two women. The police reacted with insults and the threat that if they continued trying they would be publicly accused of violence. Fr. Burnier was punched and gun-butted in the face; then he was shot in the head with a dum-dum bullet.

He remained conscious another three hours. He received the last sacraments and consecrated his suffering to God for the people and the Indians. Dying, he was taken to Goiânia where, at 5 P.M. on October 12 (1976), he died of his wounds.

One week later a liturgical service was held for Fr. Burnier. *Alvorada* (Dawn), the newspaper of the bishop of São Félix, reported on October 21, 1976, on the events that followed the Mass:

After the Mass the women who had been tortured invited the people to pray the rosary for Fr. João. As is the Christian custom, one week after death a huge wooden cross was carried to the place where he had been murdered. Full of faith, praying and grieving, a procession formed; everyone carried a lighted candle. When they arrived at the spot where the murder had been committed, the cross was put in place.

The people said: "They want to take the cross away, but we will never forget; we will put up another one. The only purpose this jail serves is to lock up the poor, the small farmers and shepherds, and torture them. Never has a rich person been seen in this jail."

With these thoughts, the people decided to break down the doors of the jail, so that no innocent person would ever again be held and mistreated there. All took part, driven by zeal and the thirst for justice.

"Is it violence, what we are doing? Violence is killing our priest and burning down our houses!"

The people of Ribeirão Bonito celebrated the liturgy, erected the cross, and tore down the jail—all in one continuous motion [Amnesty International, Bonn, *Kirche in Opposition—Brasilien* (Church in Opposition—Brazil)].

Carlos Murias and Gabriel Longueville (Argentina)

The Franciscan Carlos Murias was born on October 10, 1945, in Córdoba (Argentina) and was ordained to the priesthood at the age of twenty-seven. Gabriel Longueville was born on March 18, 1931, in Estables (France) and was ordained to the priesthood at the age of twenty-six.

The two met in the parish of Chamical in the Argentinean province of La Rioja. It is famous for its vineyards and also for the outrageously unjust way that its surface area is legally parcelled out. This has at times been defended by physical force. Enrique Angelelli, the bishop of La Rioja (see pp. 114ff.), Bishop Vincente Zaspe, the bishop of Santa Fé, and a papal legate had stones thrown at them.

The little town of Chamical is the site of a guided missile base maintained by the air force. The military chaplains went hand in hand with the wealthy landowners and the military figures in league with them. Thus there were, so to say, two churches in that tiny locality: one for the little people and one for the mighty.

On July 18, 1976, Carlos Murias and Gabriel Longueville were forcefully led away from the church. A search was carried on for them for two days, but in vain. On July 21 their wake was begun. The next day their corpses were finally found—two and a half miles distant from the church. Bishop Angelelli, the papal nuncio to Argentina [Pio Lagli], the archbishop of Santa Fé, and forty-three priests celebrated the Mass of the Dead.

Bishop Angelelli said: "We sense that the priests Carlos and Gabriel are two symbols." The community erected at the place of their death a great wooden cross with a cement base. The murderers took shots at it at night. Eventually, when they could not bring it down that way, they exploded it with dynamite.

Bishop Angelelli himself took over the orphaned parish of Chamical, to encourage the community. During the nine-day period of mourning he prayed for the great gift of forgiveness, to win pardon for the guilty ones.

Less than three weeks after the death of the two priests, Bishop Angelelli, on August 4, 1976, died in a mysterious traffic accident.

Chapter 9

The Bishops Too

Archbishop Oscar Romero:
Martyr for the People of God in El Salvador

Fifty-three bishops of the Latin American Episcopal Conference meeting in Puebla signed a letter, dated February 10, 1979, to the archbishop of San Salvador, Oscar Romero. They encouraged him to "continue on the narrow and thorny path" that leads to the building up of the kingdom of God.

After the military coup d'état of October 15, 1979, the situation in El Salvador worsened. Archbishop Romero therefore turned directly to the military in his last Sunday sermon, on March 23, 1980:

> Soldiers, you are not obliged to obey a command that contradicts God's commandments! No one can be obligated to carry out an immoral law. Think how late it is for you to be recovering a good conscience!
>
> In the name of God and in the name of a suffering people, whose laments reach to heaven, I ask you, I beg you, I implore you: stop the oppression!

In El Salvador itself, this sermon could be heard only on a Costa Rican radio station: the archdiocesan radio station in San Salvador had been destroyed five weeks earlier in a bombing [*Orientierung, 7/80*].

Was the archbishop's appeal the reason why, the next day, while he was offering Mass in the chapel of the Carmelite Nuns' hospital, he was shot to death?

Strike the Flock in Order to Get at the Shepherd (Brazil)

When the sixty-page document on the Amazon region, signed by five bishops, was published in 1973, it was regarded by the Brazilian government as highly subversive; the printers were arrested because the government did not dare do anything to the bishops.

The archbishop of Goiânia, Fernando Gomes dos Santos, then issued a pastoral letter to be read in all the churches. In it he said:

> It is not right that those primarily responsible remain unscathed by the penalties prescribed by law while the owner of the printing office and his co-workers are arrested and incur material disadvantages, and their families must bear the consequences. In our unique capacity as the ones who signed that document, we assume full responsibility for what we published and we hereby surrender ourselves to the police. Freely and consciously, we accept whatever consequences may come to us for what we did in the pursuit of justice and the struggle against injustice.

The Death of Bishop Enrique Angelelli: An Accident?

Enrique Angelelli was born in 1923. He entered the seminary at the age of fourteen. In 1949 he was ordained to the priesthood in Rome, where he had studied. He obtained the licentiate in canon law and then did pastoral work in Córdoba, Argentina. In 1968 Pope Paul VI appointed him bishop of La Rioja.

Bishop Angelelli became a symbol in Argentina of the segment of the church that opted for the poor—an option that showed itself in the lifestyle of those who adhered to it. He was also a magnet, attracting vocations: his diocese, with 160,000 inhabitants, was soon the one in Argentina best supplied with pastoral help.

Many followed him, many hated him. In Antillaco he was

stoned. In the capital of the province he was forbidden to proclaim the gospel on the radio. Why? Because to those obsessed with wealth and power the gospel—which reveals God's predilection for the poor, the weak, the oppressed, the exploited—seems very subversive. But the bishop did not lose hope:

> My friends, even if the local radio station silences the voice of God—the voice of liberation, which must nonetheless come to the people—because it is afraid to take a stand against the government, we do not forget that the power and the life of the gospel grow from their own inner content. The Spirit that blows when and where it chooses will certainly find other ways to bring the living word of God to every locality and every living heart.

Later the voice of the church in the local newspaper of La Rioja, *El Independiente,* was reduced to silence.

Bishop Pedro Casaldáliga (see pp. 46ff.) has said: "the gospel has nothing to do with diplomacy." Bishop Angelelli practiced that dictum when the visit to La Rioja by the president of Brazil, an army general, was approaching. Another general submitted the program for the impending visit to the bishop, who smiled and posed the question: "Will you allow me, General, to add a small detail? Namely, that the bishop of La Rioja will not be paying his respects to the president. A bishop cannot shake hands with someone who oppresses his people."

Fr. Arturo Paoli, Latin American superior of the Brothers of Charles de Foucauld, gave this moving testimony on Bishop Angelelli:

> His objection was not doctrinaire; it came rather from his unshakable solidarity with his people. The day he defied a general could end with a peaceful, simple meal at the table of simple people, and his lightheartedness would be contagious. I was always struck by the way he found such moments of joy in the midst of a very unpleasant situation.
>
> Identification with the people also explains the composition of his programs for the pastoral ministry. There was resistance to them, even from those whom he wanted to rescue from the

centuries-long oppression and their own inertia that led them
to believe there could not be political or economic progress for
them.

Bishops described by St. Ambrose as "themselves made of
gold, they transformed wine in wooden chalices" have not disappeared from the church.

It has been related that shortly after the murder of Fr. Murias
and Fr. Longueville (see p. 112), whose parish in Chamical
Bishop Angelelli himself took over, a wealthy landowner from La
Rioja said: "Why were those priests put to death? The 'big shot'
we have here is the one who ought to be put to death."

The "big shot" he meant was Bishop Enrique Angelelli, who
died in an automobile accident on August 4, 1976. An accident?

To Learn from the Poor: Bishop Adriano Hypólito (Brazil)

Adriano Hypólito was born in 1918, a Brazilian of Italian ex-
traction. In 1937 he entered the Franciscans. From 1938 to 1943
he studied philosophy and theology in Olinda and Salvador. He
was ordained to the priesthood in 1942. He was then named director of a student residence; he did language studies and research in
church history. In 1962 he became director of studies in the Franciscan theological seminary in Salvador. The following year he
was named auxiliary bishop of the archdiocese of São Salvador da
Bahia, and was put in charge of the training of priests.

In 1966 he became the bishop of Nova Iguaçu, on the outskirts
of Rio de Janeiro. There he campaigned for improvements in the
public health and social assistance systems. He took great pains in
planning the pastoral ministry, the founding of women's clubs
(the church can reach men only with great difficulty because they
must work the whole day in order to provide for their families as
best they can), and the founding of grassroots communities. "Lay
persons are my best co-workers"; recall the royal priesthood of *all*
the faithful (1 Peter 2:9).

His work with the poor was so successful that those obsessed
with wealth and power felt the need to give him a serious warning.
At dusk on September 22, 1976, Dom Adriano Hypólito was abducted in Nova Iguaçu by six armed men.

He found himself in the car of his nephew, Fernando, who also was there. Fernando's fiancée, who had been with him in the car, managed to escape. The bishop and his nephew were separated; they were both blindfolded with hoods, beaten repeatedly, and finally pushed out of the car on a remote country road. The bishop was discovered two hours later, naked, tied up, and smeared with red paint. His torturers had threatened to kill him, "like all the other Communist priests." The AAB (*Aliança Anticomunista Brasileira,* Brazilian Anti-Communist Alliance) took credit for what had been done to him.

Bishop Hypólito, without rancor, reported on the abduction and maltreatment. He had the attitude of the Jew who, before his death in a gas chamber, had written on a piece of cardboard: "Lord, when you come in your glory, be mindful not only of those of good will. Be mindful too of those of bad will. But do not think about the horrible things they have done, their misdeeds and acts of violence. Think about the good that we accomplished on the basis of what they did to us. Think about the patience that some have shown, the courage of others, the camaraderie, the gentleness, magnanimity, and loyalty that they have kindled in us. And one day, Lord, let the fruits that we have brought forth be their redemption."

The "lesson" that the enemies of the church gave to Dom Adriano because they feared the loss of their privileges occasioned the Brazilian Bishops' Conference to make a public statement the following day:

The directorate of the Brazilian Bishops' Conference considers it its duty to speak out on what happened:

1. It states its full solidarity with its confrère in the episcopacy, Dom Adriano Hypólito, who gives an astonishing example of Christian witness for the good of the poor in the church of Nova Iguaçu. His nephew Fernando is included in the same solidarity.

2. We say again, and emphatically, that it is an honor to the church of Brazil when its sons are attacked by those who, because of their upbringing, are unable to grasp in its full depth the Christian import of the church's commitment to the oppressed. They confuse Christian motivation with an ideologi-

cal influence that we utterly reject. The Church knows well the baseness of the tactics used against it. Such a violent misdeed, which fits into a whole chain of similar violent misdeeds, does not cause it fear. On the contrary, its joy is great because this means that it has been found worthy of the 2,000-year tradition of those whose Christian lives have been sealed with blood [DIAL, No. 330].

In 1977 Bishop Hypólito was given an honorary doctorate in theology by the University of Tubingen, and he had taken part in Vatican Council II. In 1978 the Brazilian Bishops' Conference named him a participant in the third CELAM (*Conferencia Episcopal Latinoamericana*, Latin American Episcopal Conference) general assembly to be held in Puebla de los Angeles ("City of the Angels") in Mexico. Despite these lofty honors in recognition of his work, Dom Adriano is still the object of threats. The Justice and Peace Commission of Nova Iguaçu stated on April 2, 1978:

> On Holy Thursday of this year we learned that new threats have been made against the bishop of our diocese, Dom Adriano Hypólito. "The bishop of Nova Iguaçu has not learned his lesson." And so plans for more "punishment" have been laid, more violent this time, so that "this bishop who cannot keep his mouth shut will have to spend some months in a hospital."
>
> Accordingly, for some time now, Dom Adriano, when he is on trips or visits to various communities for pastoral purposes, is followed by a helicopter. A date was set for his "punishment," but something went wrong and it had to be postponed.

The bishop is not the only one who suffers violence, as the following extracts from a letter dated March 27, 1978, by the Nova Iguaçu Justice and Peace Commission to the Brazilian minister of justice make clear:

> The diocesan Justice and Peace Commission, an office of the diocese of Nova Iguaçu, sees itself urgently called on to bring to Your Excellency's notice certain events that unsettle, more and more severely, the population of the *Baixada Fluminense*

[literally, "lowlands in the state of Rio de Janeiro," i.e., the outskirts of the capital]—and this at a time when the entire nation has been called on to work together in defense of human rights.

The diocesan Justice and Peace Commission, on this occasion, wants to point out the increase in crime in this important, pain-wracked region of Brazil. In view of the widespread uncertainty, the climate of violence fostered by the arbitrariness of the police, an atmosphere of tension, fear, and anxiety has gradually enveloped a great part of the population. They want to live and work here within the law. And so they want to be reassured that public officials will bring about the atmosphere of security in which community life can develop, under the rule of peace and justice.

We ask Your Excellency to unite with those who show themselves most concerned today that the pockets of violence be banished from our midst. They result, naturally enough, from the continual worsening of the living conditions of the thousands and thousands of Brazilians who live on the circumferences of the major urban centers, including Rio de Janeiro. The particular events in question: from January until today (March 27, 1978), not fewer than ninety-five corpses have been found in Rio de Janeiro's slum areas; in Queimados, a section of Nova Iguaçu, a 96-year-old man was dragged off and cannot be found.

As to the dead, besides other horrors, from castration to mutilation of other bodily organs, there are indications that they were first handcuffed. We realize that the slum areas of Rio de Janeiro have become the refuge for Brazil's impoverished marginal citizens. For physical survival they are forced to leave their rural homes; they flock to the centers of the big cities, and from there spread out to surrounding areas. On the outskirts of Rio de Janeiro, to a certain degree not yet plundered by real estate speculation, the poor from other Brazilian states settle in. They build a hut, send for their families, and begin the Way of the Cross every day: commute and sleep. Their wages hardly suffice to pay for public transportation and the rent of a hut or lease of a tiny plot of land where they fancy they will one day build a brick house. The overwhelming majority of these houses never go beyond some initial stage of construction; they are almost never completed. In these hovels live persons who breathe, and so they must eat. The dwelling place is incomplete and the diet is inadequate. This sets off the whiplash-reaction: the hopes of the new city dwellers turn to their opposite—despair, despondency, revolt.

Should not thoughtful and concerned persons have what it takes to search for a solution for Rio de Janeiro's slum problems? And this problem [the ninety-five dead] results precisely from the amassing of suspicion and disdain leveled at the hordes of migrant pariahs. One cheerful statistic estimates that there are at least 2 million of them in the unofficial but real concentration camps that surround Rio de Janeiro.

While the family breadwinners are out, their children are sleeping and growing up in unfinished houses. And the seeds of despair, helplessness, and rebellion are planted in them; crime is the harvest. When bridges, pedestrian viaducts at street crossings, and magnificent halls for displaying fashion models and the latest triumphs of technology are under construction, the marginal creatures know about them, willy-nilly, and they try to get at least some crumbs for themselves, legally or otherwise. Hence the mushrooming criminality, lawlessness, violence. "Installing a light in a dark street is enough to reduce the crime committed there."

Bishop Hypólito on the Theology of Liberation

Bishop Hypólito, who speaks German very well, gave a lecture on November 29, 1978, in Munich on "The Hope of the Poor." Major extracts follow:

I have been bishop of Nova Iguaçu since 1966. The city and the diocese lie within the outskirts of Rio de Janeiro. It is small in area, about 700 square miles, but has a high population density, with more than 2 million inhabitants. . . . The population of the diocese grew for the past ten to twelve years at the rate of 12 percent per year—and not because of a high birthrate . . . but because of immigration from rural areas. For the most part, they are young, eager persons who have no future on the land; full of hope they come to Rio de Janeiro or São Paulo.

Most of those who live in Nova Iguaçu work in Rio de Janeiro. They leave here at 3 o'clock in the morning and do not return until 9 or 10 o'clock at night. So you can imagine how difficult it is for us to come into contact with them, "catch hold" of them. We have a chance only on Saturday afternoons or Sundays.

How can we free these persons from their slavery? Most of them earn a minimum income—1,560 cruzeiros—equaling about $76 per month. In May of this year, that minimum income was closer to $97 in buying power, but by November inflation brought it down to $76. By May of next year it will probably be down to about $59. For years now we have been living with an inflation rate of 40 to 45 percent which means that a 100-cruzeiro banknote loses nearly half its value every twelve months.

If I speak in critical and harsh tones, I do so out of love. I love my homeland ardently, and precisely because I love it, I want to speak the truth.

Our topic today is the theology of liberation. This theology is still very young. It came into existence within the past fifteen years. Its theologians, formed by the Latin American social context and schooled in Europe, are also young. Not one of its important representatives is more than 50 years old.

The theology of liberation is still searching for its way, its own individuality, its own formulation and systemization. It is not really a new theological system or a new school of theology. Perhaps it will be one some day. For the time being, it is a new way of doing theology. The theology of liberation was born from practical life in Latin America. . . . It is first of all a lived and experienced theology. The church in Latin America experiences liberation from within its own reality before it comes to write a scholarly theology of liberation. It is more a life-theology than a book-theology.

From the social sciences it learns to discern clearly the signs of the times and to envisage the problems of humankind at a deeper level. My generation, during the years spent studying philosophy and theology, also studied the social sciences, but only as a help to a better understanding of our general upbringing and culture.

Although there was a subject called "pastoral theology," it

concerned itself chiefly with formulas, for example, how the priest should distribute communion or hear the confessions of women.

To be sure, the theology of liberation does run the risk of evaporating into practice or of being infected by some Marxist "theology" to become a sham theology that would provide a platform for terror or the use of violence, and could be a means or instrument for seizing political power.

But one thing we dare not forget: all those who are working out the theology of liberation base themselves on both practical life and revelation. To clarify somewhat the difference between traditional theology and the theology of liberation, one of these theologians cites the episode of the burning bush in the book of Exodus. Moses was tending his father-in-law's flock. The angel of the Lord appeared to him in fire flaming out from a thornbush. Moses saw that the bush was on fire but was not being consumed. He became curious and moved closer to the bush. Then came the dialogue with the Lord and the great revelation: "I am the God of your forefathers, the God of Abraham, the God of Isaac, the God of Jacob." Moses hid his face for fear. Then God gave the great mission to Moses. "I have indeed seen the misery of my people in Egypt, I have heard their outcry against their slave-masters, I have taken heed of their sufferings, and have come down to rescue them from the power of the Egyptians and to bring them up out of that country into a fine broad land; it is a land flowing with milk and honey. . . . The outcry of the Israelites has now reached me, yes, I have seen the brutality of the Egyptians toward them. Come now; I will send you to Pharaoh and you shall bring my people Israel out of Egypt" (Exod. 3:7–10).

Traditional theology, even today, is of course interested in the wondrous appearance of God, the miracle, the revelation. It stops here and meditates. The theology of liberation begins where traditional theology stops. It begins with the divine utterance: "I have seen the misery of my people in Egypt. I have heard their outcry . . . and have come down to rescue them from the power of the Egyptians." The theology of liberation begins and continues with God's mandate to Moses: "Come now! I will send you to Pharoah and you shall bring my people

Israel out of Egypt." The fact of liberation means much more to the theology of liberation than does the wondrous appearance of God. But without that appearance, liberation would not have been possible.

When I, as bishop of Nova Iguaçu, reflect on the situation of our population—a situation that I live with them—I must ask myself again and again: Is this misery God's will? What is the divine plan of love for these impoverished, outcast human beings? What are the immediate and ultimate causes of these abuses? What means must I, as a Catholic bishop, as a Christian, use to liberate my brothers and sisters? How can I help these persons to protect themselves from exploitation and abuse? How can we, as alerted Christians, organize the diocese and the pastoral ministry so that the redemption won by Jesus Christ will really take place through the church, so that the kingdom of God—a kingdom of truth and love, of justice and fellowship—can begin here and now, be visible here and now?

Jesus Christ is, for us and for the pastoral ministry, the point of departure. In the work of the church for humankind, the kingdom of God is the highest goal—a goal that must become visible but cannot become fully realized on earth.

In that lecture, Dom Adriano stated that he had been *converted* only when he became bishop of Nova Iguaçu. Very late in life, someone might observe! But *from what* was he converted?

> Yesterday I saw an animal
> In the filth of the barnyard
> Looking for something to devour
> In the garbage.
>
> When it found something,
> It didn't taste it,
> Didn't even sniff it.
> It wolfed it down ravenously.
>
> The animal was not a dog,
> Nor a cat,
> Nor a rat.

> The animal—my God!—
> Was a human being.
>   Manuel Bandeira

"Anything you did for one of my brothers here, however humble, you did for me" (Matt. 25:40) [from Conrad Contzen and Hermann Schulz, *Ein neuer Himmel, Eine neue Erde*, Wuppertal: Jugenddienst-Verlag, 1978].

What is meant by conversion? Adriano had always been conscientious, but it was not until he was a bishop that he became acutely conscious that it is not right for a priest to be—or to train a priest to be—someone who works *for* the poor and the weak, teaches them how they should leave their destitution behind them, for example, by founding an association with a priest at its head. This only brings the disadvantaged ones into a new dependency— on priests, alms, professional persons. Instead, pastoral workers *together with* those of divine predilection—the poor, weak, downtrodden, exploited—must collaborate in the building up of the kingdom of God. In this the poor are equal partners: "Lay persons are my best co-workers" (Adriano Hypólito).

But how does one begin with persons who feel themselves of less importance than the saddle horse of a landowner because it is better fed? The first step must be to make it clear to these poor creatures that each one of them is the living image of God, and that therefore they have a worth that no one dare deny them.

How can the priest help them in this, stand by their side? He can live and work *with* them, and *treat* them as the offspring of God. Most important of all: look for and bring out the good that is in them!

Dom Adriano continued:

What does the pastoral ministry of the diocese of Nova Iguaçu undertake in the line of liberation of our enslaved, subjugated fellow humans? . . . The grassroots communities of various types, the biblical circles, the diocesan works of charity, the women's clubs, resident associations for adults, counseling agencies, etc. The women's clubs, for example, are groups of women, young and older, who meet once a week and receive instruction on housekeeping, sewing, cooking, bringing up children, and the like. But they also learn about—how to put it?—"small things," like how to make something out of tin cans or plastic bags that can be sold, and thus help their husbands or fathers financially. The resident associations are groups of adults, mostly men, who meet once a week, on Saturday, and talk over the problems of their particular neighborhood and how the situation could be improved. Maybe they should approach the mayor, or a certain city office, or themselves do something. These associations have a considerable influence on changes in local politics. Then we have the *Comissão de Justiça e Paz* [Justice and Peace Commission], a pastoral program for industrial workers, another for agrarian workers, for youth.

A weekly publication on the liturgy plays a very important role. We distribute 28,000 copies every week, which is a significant number for our circumstances. Then there are the training centers; to date [November 1978], more than 15,000 persons have taken instructions in these centers. And we have a house of prayer, the Brother Jordan House. Since last June—in just half a year—two thousand persons have been in this house. Our catechetical institute holds all kinds of meetings, days of recollection, retreats, and the like.

Today a German woman asked me: "Is the practice of religion forbidden in Brazil?" In reply I must say that our military regime has never forbidden the exercise of religious duties. . . . But if the practice of religion leads to an impulse on life in the world, for the liberation of human beings, then conflicts arise. A religion divorced from life will never cause a conflict. But a religion that comes alive, exercises an influence on practical life, including politics, will lead to conflicts.

What is the goal of the pastoral work of our diocese? We start from the faith and we pursue the goal of conscientization—raising the level of the people's awareness of themselves and the world around them. This is a salient point. They are trained to acquire a critical sensitivity so that they cannot be manipulated as they were before. They are trained to make an analysis of social processes; they are helped to see the necessity of co-responsibility and commitment. They are trained to the values of unity and harmony, and resistance to exploitation. And all this from the viewpoint of the faith, according to the biblical model: "Come now, bring my people out of Egypt!" Hence the tension between church and state, between church officials and some priests and lay persons.

What are the principal values communicated by this conscientization? From the gospel we receive inspiration, over and over again, for the pastoral ministry as a joint undertaking of our church. The following principles of our faith are, among others, the ones that tend to predominate: God's plan for the world and humankind is a plan inspired by love; God is a father; we are the offspring of God, and we are brothers and sisters to each other; Jesus Christ is our brother, our savior and liberator; the salvation and liberation that Jesus Christ brought us by his teaching, his life, his death, and his resurrection encompass the whole person and all persons, take hold of them as individuals and as society; the social abuses in our society are not the will of God but either a collective sin that cries to heaven or an un-Christian subjugation that cries out for dissolution and liberation. God needs us and realizes his plan of love through us. We bear responsibility. The prophetic mission of Jesus Christ and the church has been entrusted to us. And that prophetic mission, sealed by the mystery of the cross, imposes on us the obligation to maintain a critical stance and to be a sign of hope, that is, bravely to denounce social abuses in both church and state.

I believe that the church is worthy of belief only if the prophetic office is also exercised within the walls of the church; that we must ask ourselves repeatedly what is not what it should be in our church, our structures, the work that we are doing. This aspect of the prophetic mission could find expression in such judgments as: that is not right! That is not God's will! The other aspect is that of the hope-filled pointing toward the objectives of hope: the possibilities for a better social order through commitment to the poor and the masses, the persecuted and oppressed, and in defense of human rights. Things can be better! There *must* be another way!

As to methodology, we must state that we do not resort to

physical force; we apply moral force, for example, strikes and protests. As Christians, we cannot defend violence that entails bloodshed. We must make use of all the opportunities available for the defense of human rights, the defense of the poor, the persecuted, the suffering. That is lived and experienced theology of liberation. That is pastoral ministry in service to our unredeemed, enslaved, exploited brothers and sisters. That is salvation. That is the good news of the gospel. At least for us Latin Americans, that is the church.

Dom Adriano was so exuberant and open in conversation that Martin Lange said to him without hesitation: "In the early church there was a saying: 'Don't let martyrs become bishops; they are so fanatical!' " Dom Hypólito, who is surely a martyr in the early church's understanding, was very amused by the remark. Like a proud father, he showed photographs of persons from his diocese. On the photograph of a house he commented: "That's only a house of prayer, but from prayer we draw our strength."

Bishop Enrique Alvear Urrutía:
Is Mercy Subversion? (Chile)

In June 1976, an auxiliary bishop of Santiago de Chile, Enrique Alvear Urrutía, had an encounter with the police. The bishop reported on it in an open letter:

On May 1, I brought medicine to someone kept under house arrest; the private residence was under the control of two DINA agents [*Dirección de Intelligencia Nacional*, National Intelligence Administration, the infamous Chilean secret police; because of protests, it was officially "disbanded," but it continues under a different name]. When I was leaving the house, one of them said to me: "You are under arrest." When I asked to see his DINA identification, he showed it to me. When he learned that I was a bishop, he telephoned for instructions. I was asked the name of the person who had given me the medicine, but I refused to answer.

About two hours later another official came; he told me he would not identify himself and would not disclose the name of

the agency he represented. I answered that his DINA affiliation had been clear to me for a long time. He asked me for
personal identification details. Beyond that, I would not
answer his questions. When I said that I wanted to see the arrest warrant, he said: "You have not yet been arrested, but you
will be." Then: "Because you will not cooperate in the struggle
against communism, which is harming Chile, you can go."

When I left, a photographer followed me and tried to take
some photos. The people of the neighborhood, who witnessed
the scene, kept a serious look on their faces and did not glance
at me when I passed by them.

A DINA functionary followed me for some blocks. He was
very upset when I turned around and asked him if he was following me.

1. The commandment of love obliges us to forgive, and I
forgive with all my heart those who cause me unpleasantness.
Still I believe that, over and above the strictly personal level, we
must express our regret and protest over the lack of respect for
persons who have been deprived of their freedom, contrary to
right and law.

2. Furthermore, the incident leads us to the conclusion that
it is useless to point out where persons are being detained and
to demand arrest warrants when there are functionaries who
pay attention to neither the one nor the other.

3. I have personally informed the president of the supreme
court and the minister of justice about the incident, and I
turned over to them the necessary written documentation so
that they, for their part, could inform the minister of the interior [*Noticias Aliadas*, June 3, 1976].

Violation of the Right of Hospitality:
The Arrest of Seventeen Bishops in Ecuador

A meeting of bishops, priests, religious sisters, and lay persons
from diverse Latin American and other countries opened in
Santa Cruz, near Riobamba, Ecuador, on August 9, 1976. Our
intentions were: (1) to share our experiences in the pastoral
ministry; (2) to become better informed of the present situation of the peoples of Latin America; and (3) to discuss what

we as bishops could do for the people.

At 5 P.M. on August 12, fourteen policemen out of uniform forced their way into the building in Santa Cruz where the meeting was being held. They were armed with machineguns, rifles, and pistols, and they had tear gas canisters in their hands. Brutally, and without any explanation, they led us to a police bus that took us to the barracks of the Second Regiment in Quito. Before we came to Tambillo, they let me out, because, as a policeman explained to me, they had received new orders.

They took me to the ministry of the interior. After they had me wait for three hours, they took me, at 1:30 in the morning, to the office of the minister. For a conversation? No, to make accusations against me. Without offering me a chair, the minister of the interior bombarded me with accusations. He said that the meeting was "subversive." We were accused of being agitators; he said we were planning how to get the people to rise up against the government. I was shown documents—not from the meeting [see No. 10 in "The Government's Plan against the Bolivian Church," p. 15]—as proof that the meeting was an exercise in subversion. I answered that the documents were not part of the working papers of the meeting, but my explanations were not accepted. The police took me to the barracks of the Second Regiment in Quito, where the sixteen other bishops were being held. They kept me apart from the others; later on, they allowed me to speak with two others being held.

On August 13, at 2 o'clock in the morning, armed policemen again forced their way into the same building in Santa Cruz. The few persons still there were told to pack the luggage of all those who had come from abroad to attend the meeting. They were to be sent back as "undesirables" and "dangerous aliens."

The cardinal, the papal nuncio, and the bishops who belonged to the standing committee of the Ecuadorian Bishops' Conference presented a petition to the minister of the interior for our release. They said to him in his office: "We will not leave this room until they are released." The minister realized that he would have to withdraw the "mandate" ordering the foreigners to leave the territory of Ecuador. But the police had ordered six of them to leave immediately. They had been driven in a small bus to the Colombian border and there deported without papers.

Thanks to the efforts of the cardinal, the papal nuncio, and the other bishops, we were set free the evening of August 13, after having been held for twenty-four hours in the barracks of the Second Regiment in Quito [DIAL, No. 331].

This was the report of the bishop of Riobamba, Leonidas Proaño, which he gave on August 27, 1976, on the radio program "Hoy y mañana." The following bishops took part in the meeting:

Argentina: Vincente Zaspe, archbishop of Santa Fe

Brazil: Antônio Fragoso, bishop of Crateus; Cândido Padin, bishop of Bauru

Chile: Enrique Alvear Urrutía, auxiliary bishop of Santiago (see the immediately preceding section in this chapter); Fernando Ariztía, bishop of Copiapó; Carlos González, bishop of Talca (on all the bishops of Chile, see the last section in this chapter)

Ecuador: Leonidas Proaño (see Chap. 3)

Mexico: Sergio Méndez Arceo, bishop of Cuernavaca; Samuel Ruiz García, bishop of San Cristobal de las Casas; José Pablo Rovalo, former bishop of Zacatecas

Paraguay: Ramón Bogarín, bishop of San Juan de las Misiones

Spain: Victor Garaygordóbil, prelate of Los Rios in Ecuador

U.S.A.: Robert Sánchez, bishop of Santa Fe (New Mexico); Patricio Flores, auxiliary bishop of San Antonio (Texas); Juan Arzube, auxiliary bishop of Los Angeles (California); Gilberto Chávez, auxiliary bishop of San Diego (California)

Venezuela: Mariano Parra, bishop of Cumaná

After the accusations were made public, Bishop Proaño refuted them:

The following points in the declaration of the ministry of the interior I emphatically deny:

• "Secret entry into Ecuador." The foreign bishops entered the country at the airports of Quito and Guayaquil with valid travel documents and they went through all the customary entry formalities. Was their entry "secret" because they were not wearing solemn liturgical vestments?

• According to the statement of the deputy minister, the "theme of the meeting had to be found out." One or two officers would have sufficed for that purpose. The armed break-in at the Santa Cruz building and the rough handling of the bishops, priests, and lay persons certainly had more the appearance of a presumption of guilt.

• The most serious accusation is that the meeting had to do with subversion. But the documents produced to substantiate this charge were not part of the working papers of the meeting.

• It was a serious slander against the foreign participants to be accused of interfering with the internal affairs of Ecuador. Those of us who are Ecuadorians have the right to know what is going on in Ecuador. Ecuadorians have described the present situation; their work can be used to throw light on the pastoral experience in Riobamba. Again, as Latin Americans we have the right to know what is going on in Latin America. In the exercise of this right, the bishops met in Medellín in 1968 [second general assembly of the Latin American Bishops' Conference] and gave their evaluation of the Latin American situation. Or is it thought that the gospel and the faith have nothing to do with the visible reality of human life?

• It was stated in the ministry of the interior that numerous Latin American prelates "are having difficulties with their respective governments." This mode of expression seems to suggest that between the government of Ecuador and that of other countries there is an agreement to the effect that certain bishops who campaign for justice are to be hindered in the exercise of their Christian duties [DIAL, No. 326].

The arrested bishops wrote in a letter to Pope Paul VI:

Our fraternal meeting had exclusively pastoral purposes, namely joint reflection on the difficulties of evangelizing our respective dioceses in today's historical context.

Because we are concerned that slander or false accusations could be made against Bishop Proaño, against us, or against other participants, we hereby give Your Holiness our episcopal

word that during those study days no actions, talks, or reflections took place that were themes beyond our mission as
shepherds.

   We close this letter in peace and confidence because we know
that "the disciple is not over the master," and we share with the
Apostles the joy of suffering for the Lord [DIAL, No. 326].

An Argument of Force (Chile)

The three Chilean bishops at the meeting in Santa Cruz,
Ecuador, after their release, had to undergo further provocations
upon their arrival at the airport in Pudahuel, Chile. Bishop Ariztía gave the following commentary on the incident:

> I am not the only one who thinks that the demonstration
> against us was not spontaneous. It was planned, and first of all
> by the press. It is common knowledge here that newspapers like
> *Clarín* or *Puro Chile* aim at destroying persons, condemning
> and obliterating them in public opinion, without allowing for
> any measure of self-defense. These publications disappeared—
> fortunately—for a while, but—unfortunately—have appeared
> again, with different names. I can name *El Cronista* and *La
> Segunda* and attest that these newspapers are new versions of
> *Puro Chile* and *Clarín*. They are responsible, in their own way,
> for evoking the climate necessary for the demonstration at the
> airport. The banners that some persons were carrying were
> also not spontaneous. Anyone who witnessed what happened
> at Puadahuel could tell that it was a police operation, or-
> ganized and directed by officials out of uniform [DIAL, No.
> 65].

The Catholic Church in Chile excommunicated the persons responsible for the attack on the bishops.

   At a press conference held later, a reporter asked Bishop González whether, on that occasion, he had been threatened with
death. His answer:

> At the airport exit . . . one of the attackers and the driver of his
> car swore at me. He said that we would be "taken care of"

later. "Remember me well," he said. "Take a good look at my face, so you'll remember me later." I have identified that man in a photograph that was printed in the newspapers. It would be a good idea for the authorities—if they really intend to investigate the incident—to make an effort to find out who that individual is, what organization he belongs to, what he did that day, and who sent him to do it. . . . That man showed me his identification card, a DINA [secret police] card. But just at that moment policemen came between us and prevented his giving the order for our arrest and seizure. There were three of us in the car.

Carlos Camus, now bishop of Linares, closed the press conference with the words: "It was not the force of an argument [that they used against these bishops] but the argument of force" [DIAL, No. 65].

Chapter 10

In the Hellhole of Torture

Condemnation of Torture by Pope Paul VI

In the general audience he held on October 21, 1970, Pope Paul VI said:

> It is for us a painful duty to summon persons of good will to reflect on certain occurrences that are taking place in the world. They are occurrences that, because of their nature, their particular significance, and their frequency, assail the sensitivity of all human beings. They are much more than mere occasional exceptions to the rule; they appear to be indications of a sudden moral decline.
>
> What occurrences are these? Torture, for example. It is spoken of as a contagious disease that is spreading out over many parts of the world. Instances of torture—namely, those horrible and inhuman police methods by which confessions are torn from human lips—are to be condemned unconditionally. They are outlawed today, both in the exercise of justice and the defense of public order. They are intolerable even when performed by subordinates without orders or permission of higher authorities. The latter incur the responsibility for these criminal and outrageous acts of violence. They must be condemned and eliminated. They are not only an attack on bodily integrity, but much more an attack on the dignity of the human person. They denature the essence of and lower the esteem owed to juridical authority. They stir up hatred and vengeance

134

that are long-lived and have a contagious effect [*Unité des chrétiens*, (Lyons) No. 25].

Letter from a Brazilian Torture Victim

On February 19, 1972, sixteen months after the pope's appeal, a Brazilian prisoner wrote the following letter from prison:

We spend 160 hours each week in a cell that measures 18 by 7.5 feet. There is absolutely nothing positive in this prison life. Permeating everything is the element of uncertainty: at any given moment we can be summoned by an investigator and turned over to those who apply physical force. The customary method of interrogation is torture, which in no way takes second place to the methods of General Massu in Algeria or Himmler. The worst about it is that now it is carried out with scientific procedures. Doctors assist at the torturing, to prevent the death of the victims: it is important that they remain alive—only up to a certain point, of course. After that, the prisoner can die. In the last three months, there were thirty deaths because of torture. The official report is that they died in a brawl or because they resisted arrest. It seems to me of the greatest importance that the presence of doctors at torture sessions be referred to the International Association of Doctors, or the French Association of Doctors, or the International Red Cross.

The practice of torture is not coming to an end. On the contrary! With every passing day it becomes more brutal and more scientific. Until around the end of 1970, only a few prisoners died by torture, because they resisted to the very end; most victims could be returned to prison. Since 1971 death because of torture has become much more common.

Cases of psychological trauma are no longer a rarity. There have been instances of induced madness. Not long ago a priest from Rio de Janeiro, Gerson Conceição de Almeida, and the sociologist Lucio de Brito Castelo Branceo, were arrested. One month later the forty-year-old sociologist was reduced to the mental state of an eight-year-old child.

In the majority of countries governed by a dictatorship, torture is one method used to stifle the voice of opposition. Terror is the means they use to bring the people to silence.

What strikes me is the similarity with the course of events in Germany in 1932 and 1933. How afraid the bishops were to oppose oppression and injustice! How many concessions were granted! Here too there are bishops who say that men and women are incarcerated because they "went too far," and priests because they "were involved with subversion." In general, it can be said that they put the blame on the imprisoned rather than on the government; that they would rather show themselves conciliatory to the government than commit themselves to and suffer with the people!

And still we have faith, we have hope. The Holy Spirit breathes where he wills. It is important for the church to go ahead; otherwise it will become more and more difficult for it to witness that Jesus Christ is God, and that to be a Christian means love, service, and duty on the side of the poor [DIAL, *Lettre à un ami*, 1972].

On the Altar of "National Security"

Torture has not come to an end, as Pope Paul VI pleaded. In a radio address on July 15, 1978, Bishop Román Arrieta of Tilarán, Costa Rica, said:

Respect for human life, for example, is said to be one of the imperatives that derive from the Christian faith. But what happens at the moment of decision? Who but Christians murder their own brothers and sisters in Latin America? They are murdered in the jails after they have been subjected again and again to horrible torturings. Or they are murdered in an open field and then listed as "missing." And all of this on the altar of "national security!"

All those who commit these crimes that cry to heaven claim that they are baptized and they call themselves Christians!

As many examples in this book show, those whose faith inspires them to give up their lives for their brothers and sisters suffer as did Jesus Christ. They undergo inhuman torture, inflicted on them as if by wild animals, not human beings. Torture to the point of death. Torture by men who call themselves Christians and defenders of a "Western and Christian" social order.

Hence, in the last chapter of this book, something must be said about torture. But not too much, out of concern for our brothers and sisters who have had to suffer so much. And these horrible deeds must not in any way be treated as "sensational" by the mass media.

It is hard for the tortured to talk about what they had to undergo. It is a humiliation that darkens in them the image of God. And so we will cite only one concrete case of torture that one of our brothers had to endure.

The Martyrdom of Tito de Alencar Lima, (Brazil)

The latter day martyr of the church is named Tito de Alencar Lima, a member of the Dominican Order. In a letter he wrote, he recorded the boast of his torturer Captain Albernat: "If Tito does not talk, he will be broken interiorly. Because we know how to do our work without leaving any visible signs. And if he survives, he will never forget the price he had to pay for his tenacity."

The torturer wants to destroy the very personhood of his victim!

Tito, together with several of his confrères in the Dominican Order in São Paulo—Betto, Ivo, Fernando, Giorgio, and others— was arrested and, like them and thousands of other prisoners, he went through a long and indescribable torture process under Commissioner Fleury, the head of the infamous DOPS [*Departmento da Ordem Política e Social*, Department of Political and Social Order] and the "death squadron."

Tito was born on September 14, 1945, the fifteenth child in a family in the impoverished northeast of Brazil. He resolved to enter the Dominican Order and made his vows on February 10, 1967. The political radicalization after the coup d'état in Brazil in 1964 and the Institutional Decree No. 5, which brought the new government far-reaching powers, had the effect of impelling leftist interests to organize themselves, in order to give a response. In November, Carlos Marighela, leader of the ALN [*Aliança de Libertação Nacional*, National Liberation Alliance], was murdered by the state police; from then on, they began to arrest members of the Dominican Order on the grounds that they were accomplices of Marighela. A publicity campaign against the Order was launched at the same time. The newspaper *O Globo* reported: "They have betrayed their faith and have converted to communism. Then they betrayed Marighela. They are the new Judases."

In the legal proceedings held in October 1970, the Dominicans were accused of guilt on two counts: against the church, which they had become faithless to, inasmuch as they had joined the Communists, and against the Brazilian law of national security, inasmuch as they had supported the ALN.

Tito, already weakened psychologically, was subjected to a frightful brain-washing that induced in his heart a series of guilt feelings. He was afraid that he had admitted too much under the agonies of torture. He wrote at that time the lines that Dom Helder Câmara later made public:

> The police put liturgical vestments on me and forced me to open my mouth, as if to receive the Eucharist. They inserted an electrical wire at that moment, and my whole mouth turned into a single blister. I felt drained of all strength, unable to bear my pain any longer. There was only one solution: to give myself over to death.

On the day after his suicide attempt, the psychological torture was intensified:

> They said to me: "Your situation from now on will become worse because you are a priest who attempted suicide and you are a priest-terrorist. The church will excommunicate you." They were trying to make me go mad.

Some days later a band of guerrillas took an ambassador as hostage and effected the release of fifty political prisoners. Tito was one of them. He was set free and immediately sent out of Brazil.

He went first to Chile and then to Europe. Until June 1973 he lived in the Dominican priory of St. Jacques in Paris, where he took up his studies again. But the condition of his health demanded psychological treatment. He began psychoanalysis, but stopped after a while. He lived full of anguish and thought that he was constantly under observation, under accusation.

In June 1973 he decided to go to Lyons, where he thought he would find a more peaceful locale for his studies. In September, after the military putsch in Chile, he seemed to be distant, absent, impenetrable. He fell into a delirium of fear; he imagined that he heard at all times the voice of his torturer, Commissioner Fleury, ordering him to "confess everything" or else the members of his family would be tortured. He did not want to eat.

The Dominican community experienced severe difficulties throughout that winter because of the visit of Tito's sister Nildes, who came from Brazil to be with him for three weeks. At first he tried to pose as the self-assured young man Nildes had known before. But then he broke down completely and revealed the abyss of his suffering. Together they went to Dr. Rolland, director of the Edouard Herriot Psychiatric Hospital in Lyons, and tried to give each other support.

When his sister returned to Brazil, Tito formed the opinion that he was no longer worthy to be a Dominican, that he deserved to be expelled, as Commissioner Fleury had told him. He was living in the hellhole of anxiety, brought on by the hell of torture.

He spent the last part of his life in Villefranche-sur-Saone, where he found work with a gardener. After one week, which included a visit from his Dominican confrères, he lost his job. He had no will to work.

When a Dominican knocked on his door, on August 10, 1974, there was no reply. The door was then broken down. Tito had hanged himself.

Dr. Rolland wrote a detailed analysis of what Tito de Alencar Lima had gone through. We cite one passage by way of illustration:

He underwent psychological as well as physical and moral torture, when the symbols of his religious life were reviled. Some of his comrades had undergone very similar treatment and were able to talk about it afterwards. But Tito discovered behind the cruelty of his torturers, their blind fury and insensitivity, something that radically differentiated him from his companions, namely the unimaginably monstrous image of the human being: these torturers who were tormenting him were created after the same image that he was, composed of the same flesh, fellow Brazilians, brothers possibly. And they showed themselves so crazed, were so filled with hate when they beastially attacked their victim, in order to destroy him. This image must have gripped him often; it forcefully broke his own image of himself, in the manner of a negative exposure that allowed the difference to disappear that others could retain between the human being and the executioner. From then on, Tito despaired of human nature, others, himself [DIAL, No. 192].

The Hope of the Suffering

Christians in the torture chamber can have hope in him who came to free the imprisoned, give sight to the blind, raise up the downtrodden. Because he, two thousand years ago in Israel, proclaimed a God who loved human beings—whose predilection was for the poor, the weak, the oppressed, the exploited. He too was tortured, derided, and hanged on the cross as a criminal. He too was a victim of the "ideology of national security" of the Roman Empire and its local minions.

By the resurrection God confirmed his preaching and life. He now shares joy and suffering with those who come together in his name to become true brothers and sisters. And more: he identifies with those who suffer and he suffers with them: what someone does for any of his brothers or sisters is done for him.

He will come again one day to make everything new and to wipe away all the tears—and to judge the living and the dead.

How utterly unfortunate are those who are possessed by wealth and power, who shut out from themselves—possibly forever—the good news of the gospel.

Epilogue

God Came to El Salvador

BY SISTER PATRICIA JACOBSEN, M.M.

Carol Piette, Maryknoll Missioner

Maryknoll Sister Carol Piette's last known act was to push her friend, Sister Ita Ford, through a side window of the jeep they were riding through the River El Zapote near Chalatenango, El Salvador, when a flash flood crashed through the ravine. It was August 23, 1980, and the Sisters, working with an emergency relief team for refugees, had just taken a released prisoner home. Two seminarians accompanying the Sisters escaped; Sister Ita was dragged along the river bottom but managed to grab a root when she resurfaced. The next morning Sister Carol's body was found 13 kilometers downstream.

Through that afternoon and night, the *campesinos* came in a steady stream to the church to pray for Sister Carla (as she was known to them) and then to accompany her in procession along the winding road to their poor little cemetery. They called her "Martyr of Charity"—one who gave her life for her friends. Nothing meant more to Sister Carol than being a friend. She often spoke of herself as "a beat-up lady" who just wanted to be with the poor beat-up people of the world. At her death, her friend Sister Carolyn Lehmann characterized her:

> Pilgrim, clown, beat-up lady
> was how you saw yourself
> the rest of us, the world
> you called circus.

We love you as Carla,
woman of God, artist, poet,
sensitive, suffering.

We shared laughter and tears
a search for new dreams
a love for Chile, and God's poor.

You journeyed farther,
fearless, hopeful and happy,
and arrived home so early.

We miss you deeply.
Continue to walk with us now.

Carol Ann Piette was born on September 29, 1939, in Appleton, Wisconsin, the youngest in a family of two boys and two girls. She was graduated from St. Mary's High School in Appleton and then studied for one year in Marquette University before entering Maryknoll in 1958.

She had a deep sense of being a pilgrim and began her journey in Chile in 1964. During language school she studied Spanish more by delving into Chile's poetry than by memorizing vocabulary. Impatiently forging on, as if she did not have enough time, she left language school early and began teaching poor children in Chilean and, later, Buzeta. She looked upon those eight years with the children and their parents as solid preparation for the next stop along her pilgrim way. In 1973 she and three others, including Sister Ita, went to live in a small wooden house in La Bandera, a poor area on the outskirts of Santiago. Most of their neighbors were factory or part-time workers; many were unemployed. She came to know the people well, trying with them to find solutions to unemployment, hunger, and alcoholism, comforting the families of those who had disappeared in the protracted political oppression. She helped form and nurture basic Christian communities, operated dining rooms where children and others could get one good meal a day, fostered home industries, prepared children for the sacraments. On call day and night, Sister Carol recognized she was being evangelized by the poor, and she opened herself more and more to their insights, aspirations, and values. She came to understand the gospel from their point of view, and wrote of Chile and her reason for being there:

> If one steel beam
> joins another
> a bridge can become.
> The river below doesn't change
> but the banks aren't islands anymore.
> If I can be but a small beam
> to help in Chile's progress
> Then let me stay
> until the banks
> aren't islands anymore.

In late 1979, Sisters Carol and Ita discussed with their confreres in Chile the possibility of going to El Salvador following Archbishop Romero's appeal to religious for help. They felt that their experience in La Bandera had prepared them to go to a country suffering the agony of abject poverty and uncontrolled violence, to accompany—as friends—a people in travail. Archbishop Romero spoke often of *"el pastoral de acompanamiento,"* the pastoral task of being a companion on the way. The story of the Sisters' months in El Salvador is a story of accompanying, of frustrations, of searchings, of prayers and fasting, of study and reflection, of friendships formed, of back-breaking work, and, finally, of violent death.

Sister Carol arrived in El Salvador the day Archbishop Romero was assassinated and Ita, the day he was buried. With his death the church in El Salvador was thrust into a period of transition and confusion and Sisters Carol and Ita agonized with it. During this time, they studied Archbishop Romero's homilies and steeped themselves in his thoughts. Sister Carol wrote to a friend: "The Archbishop was a man of prayer, of terrific simplicity and beautiful humility, a gentle man who hardly raised his voice in his Sunday sermons. Father Ricardo Uriosti [vicar general] recalled that it wasn't uncommon for him to say in the middle of a conversation with a priest, 'Rest a while since I feel the need to pray just a few minutes.' Then he would return after five minutes or so and resume his conversation. He was a man who lived with a profound love of the truth and justice, a deep appreciation of the dignity of the human being, especially the poor and marginated of El Salvador."

As the Sisters searched for a place to live and work, the war intensified and communities disintegrated. Leaders were killed and refugees increased to tens of thousands. These people needed food and shelter and sometimes more immediate help. Sister Carol wrote of trying to get two "guerrillas"—ages eleven and twelve—out of the hospital after an eight-year-old had been machine-gunned in his hospital bed that day. The Vicariate of Chalatenango asked the Sisters to work on the emergency relief team and it was in this service, just a few short weeks after they began the work in Chalatenango, that they set out in a heavy rainstorm the evening of August 23 to take a freed prisoner home.

"Every day of my pilgrimage since I left Chile has been one of learning and receiving," Sister Carol wrote, "learning in the university of listening to little people, in the lecture hall of pastoral agents analyzing their realities. I won't come out with a title or degree, but a more valuable education could not be achieved anywhere."

During a stopover in Panama on her way to El Salvador, Sister Ellen McDonald asked Sister Carol to write some of her ideas about pastoral work for the young women in Panama's Ministerial Formation Program. What Sister Carol wrote is a testimonial of her own life:

> 1. An attitude of continuous learning. There is no manual other than the gospel to show how to proceed in pastoral work. Many times the Spirit teaches us through those to whom we are sent.
>
> 2. An attitude of listening. We ought to listen to the people—especially the poor, the sinners, those who live farthest from the values of the world. They may even be nonbelievers, but precisely because of this, they often speak the truth that we need to hear today, for today's challenges. We should listen to one another in reflection and shared prayer. We

should listen to others in pastoral work. We should listen to ourselves. What do we repeat? What are the concerns we speak about most frequently?

3. An attitude of "half-failure," as Dom Helder Camara expresses it. Pastoral work is not geared toward success; it is directed toward the coming of the Kingdom of God. With the social and personal sin so evident in society today, the Kingdom will not come without the paschal mystery in our life and work.

4. An attitude of questioning. Because of differences in culture, very often the people to whom we are sent are reticent. Even though we come to learn and listen, we have to invite them to share through specific questions. Jesus taught with questions. It is important to ask the right questions in order to come to know the ground we are walking on.

5. An attitude of prayer. The poet says, "Caminante, no hay camino, se hace el camino al andar"—"Hiker, there is no path; the path is made by walking." Pastoral work is a process, guided by One who is the Way, the Truth, and the Life. The Master prepares the apostles, sends them out, and receives them again to listen to them and deepen their preparation. There are many risks in pastoral work—triumphalism, fatalism, discouragement, activism, individualism. Prayer is the only security we have.

6. An attitude of being a sinner. This is to see oneself as a sinner, sent to sinners. We are human and weak and we fall.

7. An attitude of being poor. Poverty is essential for a pastoral agent. We should travel light and be confident that Pentecost will come as we need it. The paschal mystery is lived by every person; the poor of the Lord are aware that they are living it and they are the ones who build the Kingdom.

A few weeks before her death, Sister Carol told Sister Ita that if anything should happen to her, her friends should not mourn but celebrate. In one of her poems, she suggests why:

> When the friend departs
> the hurting heart grows.

Ita Ford, Maryknoll Missioner

"I never said, 'Help,' or 'Save me,' or 'I'm drowning,' " Sister
Ita told her mother on a tape she sent home describing her brush
with death in the flash flood which killed her friend, Sister Carol.
"Something was happening and I said, 'Receive me, Lord. I'm
coming.' " The Lord made her wait for three more months before
he accepted her life—and all the while her hurting heart grew.

On the flight from Managua, Nicaragua, to San Salvador, Sisters Ita and Maura Clarke, who had joined Sister Ita after Sister
Carol's death, were apprehensive. The flight on Tuesday, December 2, 1980, was an hour late, but more than that bothered them.
The next morning in El Salvador the six murdered leaders of the
Democratic Revolutionary Front were to be buried from the
cathedral. Tonight, the Sisters knew, the Security Forces would
clamp down more than usual to prevent any demonstration. But
they were buoyed by the Maryknoll Sisters' regional meeting they
had just attended in Managua at which their mission congregation's commitment to work with the poor had been renewed.
"Working with the poor," Sister Ita wrote in her journal, "calls
for restraint and modesty at all levels so as not to overpower, overcome, or take over."

Sister Ita carried the burden of mourning for Sister Carol with
her when she went to the meetings. She questioned why she had
been spared and grieved deeply for her friend and sister apostle.
The Sisters there said she seemed to undergo a profound healing
during the five days they were together and by the end, she was
participating fully and seemed exhilarated. At the closing liturgy
prepared by the four Sisters from El Salvador, both Sisters Ita and
Maura expressed their conviction that God was very strongly calling them to return to El Salvador. Sister Ita read a passage from
one of Archbishop Romero's final sermons in which he described
the poverty of the beatitudes. His words foretold what would be-
fall the two Sisters less than twenty-four hours after they prayed
them. "Christ invites us not to fear persecution, because, believe
me, brothers and sisters, he who is committed to the poor must
run the same fate as the poor. And in El Salvador we know what
the fate of the poor signifies—to disappear, be tortured, to be
captive—and to be found dead."

Born in Brooklyn, New York, April 23, 1940, Sister Ita was one of three children of Mildred and William Ford. She joined Maryknoll in 1961 after finishing college at Marymount, but was forced to leave after three years for health reasons. She went to work as a textbook editor, but her desire for mission work brought her back to Maryknoll in 1971 after her health had improved.

Sister Ita began her journey with the poor in Chile during the violent years after Salvador Allende's overthrow in 1973. Chile made a profound impact on her. It was there that her commitment to the poor grew and she learned of its demands. She wrote in 1977, "Am I willing to suffer with the people here, the powerless? Can I say to my neighbors, 'I have no solutions to this situation; I don't know the answers, but I will walk with you, search with you, be with you.' Can I let myself be evangelized by this opportunity?"

After she and Sister Carol began their work in Chalatenango, she wrote: "I don't know if it is in spite of or because of the horror, terror, evil, confusion, lawlessness—but I do know that it is right to be here. I believe that we are gifted in and for Salvador now, that the answers to the questions will come when they are needed, to walk in faith, one day at a time, with the Salvadorans along a road filled with obstacles, detours, and washouts."

The obstacles grew in increasing numbers as the two Sisters responded to the needs of the "hurting, homeless, and hungry." They were conscious of the political implications of feeding the hungry in this repressive society in a state of "undeclared civil war" with its potential for ever greater conflict.

Working with Sister Maura helped soften the tragic blow of Sister Carol's death. They worked well together; Sister Maura was the outgoing contact person, Sister Ita, the thinker and organizer.

Maura Clarke, Maryknoll Missioner

In one of her letter's home, Sister Maura asked her mother for a pair of shoes. She had given her only pair away to a woman who had none. Sister Peggy Healy, who took the new shoes to El Salvador early in November 1980, said, "I don't think Maura knew how to say no. She just didn't know how to keep people waiting."

"She was outstanding in her generosity," remembered Sister

Margarita Jamias, who served with her in Nicaragua and traveled with her in the United States giving "world awareness" workshops when Sister Maura came home in 1976 after sixteen years in Nicaragua. "She would give whatever she had to the poor. She was accustomed to living in poverty. We were laughing the other day remembering how in Nicaragua she was always drawing advances on her monthly allowance of $15 because as soon as she got it she gave it away."

Maura Clarke, born January 13, 1931, of Irish-born parents from Queens, New York, loved life and seemed always to have a sparkle in her eye. "Almost every time we got together," remembers Sister Peggy, "she did a wonderful Irish jig. She had some marvelous songs and dances and she loved to celebrate."

But at the same time, in keeping with her giving nature, she was ready, if the Lord asked, to give her life away. In her last days in El Salvador, she began to think this would be asked of her. Speaking of "unknown, uncelebrated martyrs," she wrote in a letter on November 20: "One cries out: Lord, how long? And then too what creeps into my mind is the little fear or big, that when it touches me very personally, will I be faithful? . . . I keep saying to Him, 'I want to trust, I want to believe, help me!' "

Sister Maura's journey to El Salvador began more than thirty years ago on a sunny September day when John and Mary Clarke and several carloads of friends drove Maura up the Hudson to the Maryknoll novitiate. The parents, now in their eighties, sat in their apartment in Rockaway Beach, New York, the day of their daughter's funeral and recalled the day for New York columnist Jimmy Breslin. "Maura wore a green suit and I remember telling her that if she couldn't last it out and become a nun, she shouldn't be discouraged; she should come right back to me and become a teacher."

Profession as a religious and college graduation brought Maura close to home. For five years she taught at St. Anthony of Padua school in the Bronx, New York, visiting home at every opportunity, for she was very close to her parents and younger brother and sister. Then in 1959 she was assigned to teach in Nicaragua in a Capuchin parish at Siuna, a remote gold-mining community in the rain forests of eastern Nicaragua. In her ten years at Siuna, she served as teacher, principal, and even superior.

"I was not a good superior because I didn't know how to be in charge," she once said. "My gift is not in analysis. My gift is not in deciding what we ought to do."

She could do all those things well, counters Sister Peggy. But the role she played best was that of "a person who was supportive, who always saw good in others, who was very gentle, who, though not being overwhelming with affection, could always make those whose lives she touched feel loved."

From Siuna, Sister Maura went to a barrio on the shore of Lake Managua that was flooded out when the lake overflowed, then to a parish completely destroyed when an earthquake with the force of fifty atom bombs leveled downtown Managua just before Christmas in 1972. Trapped on one of the upper floors of their house when a door jammed, the Maryknoll Sisters made a rope of sheets and escaped through a window. Then, still in her pajamas, Sister Maura and her colleagues began helping their neighbors dig out bodies and care for the injured. After that she worked with basic Christian communities in a bleak, dusty barrio on the outskirts of Managua until she came to the United States in 1976 to work in mission education and promotion.

Returning to Central America in July 1980 was painful because she wanted to be close to her elderly parents, but she was happy to be back in her beloved Nicaragua. On the first anniversary of the Sandinista insurrection, Sister Peggy photographed her "bubbling with joy" at the spirit of sharing, hope, and freedom she saw in the people after almost half a century of oppression under the Somoza dynasty. She would have liked nothing better than to remain in Nicaragua where she was known as "the angel of our land," but then came the call for service in El Salvador.

Sister Maura went to El Salvador on a trial basis, reserving the final decision for the regional assembly that concluded in Managua on the day she died. But once in El Salvador, she saw overwhelming needs that could not be ignored.

One day, she wrote to Sister Margarita, a twelve-year-old boy appeared at the door with six younger brothers and sisters. His parents had been killed and the children were "nothing but skin and bones." By early November, she had made her decision to stay. On November 22, she wrote: "What is happening here is impossible but happening. The endurance of the poor and their faith through this terrible pain is constantly pulling me to a deeper faith response. My fear of death is being challenged constantly as children, lovely young girls, and old people are being shot and some cut up with machetes and bodies thrown by the road and people prohibited from burying them. . . . I want to stay on now. I believe right now that this is right. . . . God is present in His seeming absence."

Dorothy Kazel, Ursuline Missioner

"Most of us feel we want to stay here. We wouldn't want to run out on the people," Sister Dorothy wrote to Sister Martha Owen. The two Ursuline missionaries from Ohio worked together in El Salvador for five years. "Dorothy would always go an extra mile with a person who needed help," Sister Martha said.

Born of Lithuanian-American parents, June 30, 1939, Dorothy Kazel entered the Ursuline Sisters community in 1960. After her profession she taught for nine years at Sacred Heart Academy and Beaumont School for Girls in Cleveland. She was also deeply involved in ecumenical and interracial community service programs.

Popular with the students, Sister Dorothy is remembered for her work in counseling drug addicts. "She used to stay up nights with one girl to prevent her from taking dope," Sister Martha recalled. "She even had this girl come to visit El Salvador to give her an experience of a basic Christian community."

Shortly after Pope John XXIII's call to religious orders to send Sisters to the Third World, Sister Dorothy decided in 1968 that she wanted to become a missionary. She spent that summer working with American Indians in Tucson, Arizona, and became convinced that working with the poor was her mission. In 1974, the short, blond-haired religious "who reached out to so many people with her heart" accepted an invitation to join the nine-member Cleveland mission team which serves three parishes in El Salvador.

Sister Dorothy loved the Salvadoran people, but as she became more aware of the injustices in the country, she began to feel frustrated and once said she wished she "could have done more to change the structure of society there," a friend recalled. She was

to have returned to the United States in the spring of 1980 after six
years of service with the team. But Archbishop Romero's assassination in March affected her so much that she decided to stay
on. Her uncle, Robert Chapon, said he often urged her to return
to Ohio and pursue her work locally. "Her response," he recalls,
"was always the same—'maybe next year.' "

She was aware of the growing dangers in El Salvador but wrote
to her confidante Sister Martha that she wanted to stay: "If there
is a way we can help, like run a refugee center or something, we
wouldn't want to run out on the people. . . . If a day comes when
others will have to understand (if something happens to one of us)
please explain it for me."

Jean Donovan, Lay Missioner, Diocese of Cleveland

"A gut feeling" was the way Jean Donovan explained why she
chose to become a lay missioner instead of joining the Peace
Corps. Maryknoll Sister Mary Ann O'Donnell, a director of Jean
Donovan's mission formation program at Maryknoll, recalls that
the native of Westport, Connecticut, had all the marks of a good
missioner: intelligent (B average and a master's degree in business
management), loving ("I like about everyone I meet; at times I
probably get walked on because of this"), and apostolic ("It's
every Christian's job to spread the good news that God loves us").

Born April 10, 1953, Jean attributed her outgoing, vivacious
nature to her parents, Raymond and Patricia Donovan, now living in Sarasota, Florida. "My father has never been afraid to
show love," she explained to lay missioner director Gwen Vendley.
"And my mother is a get-up-and-go person who always seems to
have the energy to do something for someone else." A winning
battle against cancer by her older brother, Michael, was another
influence in her choice to give two years to the missions. "It made
me realize," she wrote at the time, "how precious life is."

The missionary spark was ignited during her junior year of college in 1973, taken abroad in Cork, Ireland. "Living in a foreign
country can expand your personality. It is really the only way to
become a citizen of the world," she said.

After getting her master's degree at Case Western Reserve University, she joined a young adult ministry program run by the

Cleveland diocese. Called "Kaleidoscope," the group became "real Christian community for Jean," recalled Sister Mary Brazytis, a diocesan youth ministry coordinator.

Although known to many of her friends as boisterous and fun-loving, Jean revealed another side in a Kaleidoscope questionnaire: "I'd like to work with people, lonely people who don't realize that God loves them." On the same form, she also noted she would be willing to commit herself to two years of mission work, preferably with the Cleveland team in El Salvador.

Her interest in El Salvador was partly the result of hearing returned team members speak about their work. She joined the team in 1978 and her spontaneity and optimistic outlook quickly endeared her to both her fellow Clevelanders and the Salvadoran people.

In El Salvador, she worked as a catechist and later with Sister Dorothy in refugee camps. Many people remember the two women most clearly "bouncing around the Salvadoran countryside in their big microbus van, transporting catechists and refugees."

God Came to El Salvador

The five-member ecumenical Canadian delegation sent to attend the funeral of the leaders of the Democratic Revolutionary Front were met at the new San Salvador International Airport on December 2, 1980, by representatives of Bishop Arturo Rivera y Damas. "Are you going with us?" a Canadian priest asked Ursuline Sister Dorothy Kazel and Jean Donovan, a lay missioner from the Diocese of Cleveland. "No," replied Sister Dorothy. "We're not from the Archbishop's office. We're here to meet two Maryknoll Sisters." "Good luck," said the Canadian, Scarborough Father Greg Chisholm. He looked at his watch. It was 6:30 P.M.

The news spread quickly. Reports out of El Salvador on December 3 claimed that the Sisters were missing. The next morning news agencies reported that their fire-gutted Toyota van had been found near the airport. That night television viewers around the world saw U.S. Ambassador Robert White, his eyes flashing with anger, arrive at a common grave in a cow pasture close to the dusty village of Santiago Nonualco. The bodies of Jean Donovan,

Dorothy Kazel, Maura Clarke, and Ita Ford were identified. The four had been shot through the head.

White had received the radio call that the bodies had been discovered while he was escorting the Canadians to the airport. They told him they had had to pass through a National Guard checkpoint on the night the missioners disappeared. Asked if the government was responsible, White replied, "Yes, indeed. We are convinced the government could do a great deal to control the violence and instill some discipline into the Security Forces."

"Maura, Ita, Dorothy, and Jean are Christ dead today," wrote Salvadoran Jesuit Jon Sobrino. "But they are also the Risen Christ, who keeps alive the hope of liberation. Their assassination has affected the entire world and moved it to indignation. But to Christians, this assassination also speaks to us of God, because these women say something to us about God.

"Christians believe that salvation comes to us from Jesus, but perhaps this might be the moment to take very seriously what in theology has been said in an excessively spiritualistic and academic way: that salvation comes also through a woman, Mary, the Virgin of the cross and of the Magnificat. Salvation comes to us through all men and women who love truth rather than falsehood, who are more disposed to give rather than to receive, whose greatest love is giving their life rather than keeping it for themselves. This is where God makes himself present.

"For this reason, even though these four bodies fill us with sadness and indignation, our last word must be: thank you. With Maura, Ita, Dorothy, and Jean, God came to El Salvador."

Index of Names

Aaken, Bishop Agustín Van, 7
Aguilar, Fr. Rodolfo, 79-81
Albernat, Captain, 137
Alencar Lima, Tito de, 137-139
Allende, President Salvador, 103, 147
Almeida, Fr. Gerson Conceição de, 135
Almeida y Merino, Archbishop Adalberto, 80
Alsina, Fr. Juan, 72
Alvear, Urrutía Bishop Enrique, 127, 130
Anastasio, Brother (Erwin Josef Kohmann), 6-8
Angelilli, Bishop Enrique, 56, 112, 114-116
Aranru, Alberto, 6
Arce, Alfredo, 14
Ariztía, Bishop Fernando, 130, 132
Arns, Cardinal Paulo Evaristo, 49, 88
Arrieta, Bishop Román, 136
Arzube, Bishop Juan, 130

Balduino, Bishop Tomás, 37, 66
Banzer, President, 12, 14, 91
Bamberen, Bishop Luis, 78
Barbosa, Jovino, 110
Barbosa, Margarida, 110
Barbosa, Santana, 110
Barros, Colonel Euro Barbosa de, 48

Bermudez, General Morales, 78
Bernal, Fr. Bruno, 30
Bogarín, Bishop Ramón, 130
Borobotouda, Genoveva, 65
Borrat, Dr. Hector, 87
Branceo, Lucio de Brito Castelo, 135
Brazytis, Sr. Mary, 152
Breslin, Jimmy, 148
Burnier, Henrique, 109
Burnier, Fr. João Bosco, 66, 109-111
Burnier, Dr. Michel Noel, 109

Caballos, Fr. Antonio, 9
Câmara, Dom Helder, 107-108; 138, 145
Campos, Dom José Melhando, 91
Camus, Bishop Carlos, 133
Carabias, Fr. José Luis, 4
Carranza, Fr. Salvador, 27, 33-34
Casaldáliga, Bishop Pedro, 46, 48, 49, 53, 66, 110-111, 115
Casanova, Fr. Jorge, 59
Casariego, Cardinal Mario, 22, 27, 33-34
Cassidy, Dr. Sheila, 102-105
Chapon, Robert, 151
Chávez, Bishop Gilberto, 130
Chávez, Bishop Luis, 28-30
Chisolm, Fr. Greg, 152
Clarke, John, 148
Clarke, Mary, 148
Clarke, Maura, 146-149, 153

Collino, Bishop Desiderio, 77-78
Contzen, Conrad, 124
Cristino, Simão, 64-65, 67
Cristino, Tereza, 65

Diaz, Pablo, 96-97
Domon, Sr. Alicia, 97-102
Donovan, Jean, 151-153
Donovan, Michael, 151
Donovan, Patricia, 151
Donovan, Raymond, 151
Duquet, Sr. Leonie, 102
Duran, Sergio, 80

Engelke, Dom Inocencio, 40
Escamilla, Fr. Rodolfo, 80
Esquivel, Daniel, 75-77

Farré, Fr. Luis, 9
Felix, Colonel José, 1
Fleury, Commissioner, 91, 137, 139
Flores, Bishop Gerardo, 22
Flores, Bishop Patricio, 130
Florinda, Doña (Tingo), 95-97
Ford, Sr. Ita, 145-147, 153
Foucauld, Charles de, 51
Fragoso, Bishop Antônio, 130
Franceschina, Sr. Irene Maria Paula, 47
Francis of Assisi, 51

Garaygordobil, Victor, 130
Geisel, President Ernesto, 108
Goldstein, Horst, 82
González, Bishop Carlos, 130-132
González, Froilán, 88
Grande, Fr. Rutilio, 25, 27-36
Gutiérrez, Nelson, 104

Haro, Silvio Luis, 59
Healy, Sr. Peggy, 147-149

Himmler, Heinrich, 135
Hypólito, Bishop Adriano, 70, 82, 116-118, 120-124, 127

Jacobsen, Sr. Patricia, 141
Jamias, Sr. Margarita, 148-149
Janssens, Johann Baptist, 109
Jentel, Fr. François Jacques, 48
John XXIII, Pope, 150

Kazel, Sr. Dorothy, 150, 152-153

Lagli, Pio, 112
Lamasa, John (John La Mazza), 15
Landázuri Ricketts, Cardinal Juan, 79
Lange, Martin, 53, 85, 127
Las Casas, Bartolomé de, 64
Le Febvre, Fr. Maurice, 89-91
Leme, Cardinal Sebastião, 109
Lemus, Nelson R., 27, 30
Longo, Fr. Carlos, 59
Longueville, Gabriel, 112, 116
López, Fr. Hermógenes, 18
Lorscheider, Cardinal Aloísio, 49
Luna, Octavio Ortiz, 24
Lunkenbein, Fr. Rudolfo, 64-67
Lyra, Dr. Eugenio Alberto, 85
Lyra, Dr. Lucia Maria Athiade, 85, 93

Maciel, Fr. Braulio, 1, 5
Manrique, Archbishop Jorge, 16
Marighela, Carlos, 137-138
Martínez, Bishop Victor, 23
Massu, General, 135
McDonald, Sr. Ellen, 144
Melia, Fr. Bartolomé, 9
Méndez Arceo, Bishop Sergio, 130
Mestre, Fr., 16
Modehn, C., xix

Molina, General Arturo, 26
Mugica, Fr. Carlos, 34, 73-75
Munarriz, Fr. José Miguel, 5, 9
Murias, Carlos, 112, 116

Nascentes, Miguel Noel, 109
Neto, Fr. Antonio Henrique Pereira, 107-108

Ochoa, Fr. Gonçalo, 64
O'Donnell, Sr. Mary Ann, 151
Oriol, Fr. José, 9
Ortega, Fr. José Luis, 9, 35
Owen, Sr. Martha, 150

Padin, Bishop Cândido, 130
Page, Fr. René, 4
Paoli, Fr. Arturo, 115
Parra, Bishop Marrano, 130
Paul VI, Pope, 16, 22, 46, 49, 114, 131, 134, 136
Paz Estenssoro, General Victor, 10
Pelletier, Fr. Gustavo, 89
Penido, Dr. João Nogueira, 109
Penido, Maria Cândida, 109
Piette, Sr. Carol, 140-147
Pilate, Pontius, 42
Pinochet, President Augusto, 73, 103
Polo, Don, 95-96
Polo, Felipe, 95
Prata, Bishop Gennaro, 16
Proaño, Bishop Leonidas, 28, 53-54, 56-59, 130-131

Queralt, Sr. Raymunda Alonso, 23

Rivera y Damas, Bishop Arturo, 152
Rodrigues de Souza, Bishop José, 85, 93

Rolland, Dr. Jean-Claude, 139
Romero, General Carlos Humberto, 24
Romero, Archbishop Oscar Arnulfo, 24, 25, 113, 146, 151
Rondon, Laurenço, 64, 67
Rovalo, Bishop José Pablo, 130
Ruiz García, Bishop Samuel, 130

Sánchez, Bishop Robert, 130
Santos, Archbishop Fernando Gomes dos, 114
Schulz, Hermann, 124
Schwade, Egydio, 61-62
Sigaud, Archbishop Geraldo de Proença, 49
Silva, Consuelo, 103
Silva, Edval Nunes da, 107-108
Silva Henríquez, Cardinal Raúl, 105
Sobrino, Fr. Jon, 153
Solorzano, Manuel, 27, 30
Sosa, Moncha de, 94
Sosa, Teresa, 101
Souza, Luis Barreira de, 47
Stetter, Fr. Carlos, 23
Stroessner, Pres. Alfredo, 2, 8, 10

Tapia, General Pérez, 12

Vacaflor, Major, 15
Vannuchi, Alexandre, 91
Vargas, Freddy, 14
Vendley, Gwen, 151
Videla, General, 71, 101

White, Robert (former U.S. Ambassador), 153

Zamorran, David Noé, 80
Zaspe, Bishop Vincente, 112, 130
Zwiefelhofer, Hans, xix, 18, 26